D0207944

Anthony Burgess Revisited

Twayne's English Authors Series

Kinley E. Roby, Editor

Northeastern University

TEAS 482

ANTHONY BURGESS.
Photograph © by Jerry Bauer.

Anthony Burgess Revisited

John J. Stinson

State University of New York College at Fredonia

Twayne Publishers
A Division of G. K. Hall & Co. • Boston

Anthony Burgess Revisited
John J. Stinson

Published by Twayne Publishers
A division of G. K. Hall & Co.
70 Lincoln Street
Boston, Massachusetts 02111

Copyediting supervised by Barbara Sutton.
Book production by Gabrielle B. McDonald.
Typeset in Garamond
by Graphic Sciences Corporation of Cedar Rapids, Iowa.

First published 1991.
10 9 8 7 6 5 4 3 2 1

The paper used in this publication meets the minimum requirements of American National Standard for Information Sciences—Permanence of Paper for Printed Library Materials, ANSI Z39.48-1984. ∞™

Printed and bound in the United States of America.

Library of Congress Cataloging-in-Publication Data

Stinson, John J.
Anthony Burgess revisited / John J. Stinson.
p. cm. — (Twayne's English authors series)
Includes bibliographical references and index.
ISBN 0-8057-7000-3
1. Burgess, Anthony, 1917- —Criticism and interpretation.
I. Title. II. Series.
PR6052.U638Z89 1991
823'.914—dc20 90-46003
CIP

Contents

Preface

Anthony Burgess got a relatively late start as a writer, not achieving publication of his first novel until he was thirty-nine. Now, some fifty books later, he can be said to have made up for that. He is currently recognized as a novelist of the first order, and as one of the very best literary journalists and essayists in the English language. He is also a film and television script writer, a translator, a constant book reviewer, a librettist, and a composer. And while it is often said that a person intimately involved with books is a writer or a reader, but seldom both, Burgess is a voracious reader of books on a broad variety of subjects. Now in his early seventies, Burgess has begun to show only the faintest signs of slowing down. If he is a bit of an eccentric genius, he is by no means off in a world of his own. He is acutely attuned to the contemporary world, all the while casting a cynical eye at it. The highbrow/lowbrow, or elitist/popular culture divisions do not mean very much to Anthony Burgess, since he rather consistently knocks down or skirts those barriers in his own work. As a novelist, he can be highly and deliberately derivative, but he can also be brilliantly original, sometimes in quick alternation.

Because of the rich plenitude of Burgess's work and the many directions it takes, any commentary on it must strain against the usual boundaries in an attempt to embrace it all. I have tried to provide in this study a cohesive and not overly technical discussion of the thirty novels Burgess has written to date. With the large and important body of work Burgess has produced, no study of this length, of even the novels alone, can pretend to approach anything like completeness. I have contented myself with an attempt to describe and define Burgess's achievement as a novelist, and have tried only to suggest, rather than develop, some lines of approach that have a greater basis in theory.

Even more than is the case with the average novelist, Burgess's fiction often proceeds in large measure from his own life experiences. And while that life experience is not so rich on the surface as that, say, of a Conrad or a Hemingway, it is definitely richer than most. This combined with the weight and fullness Burgess achieves by way of thorough literary intimacy with an astonishing range of novelists, linguists, and critics makes him one of the most protean of contemporary novelists. His work in fields other than the novel, lesser but still significant achievements, must be explored elsewhere.

In some twenty years of reading and studying Burgess's works I have familiarized myself with many, perhaps most, of the critical commentaries produced by others. I have profited from very many of these and would like to acknowledge my general indebtedness; I would especially like to thank Geoffrey Aggeler, Paul Boytinck, and A. A. DeVitis. I extend my appreciation to Professors Aggeler and Harold Bloom for reprinting my Burgess articles in critical anthologies, and I thank the editors of the *Journal of Popular Culture, Renascence,* and *Journal of Modern Literature,* and *Modern Fiction Studies* for permission to use portions of my articles previously published in those journals. I am grateful to Anthony Burgess for prompt and courteous reply to a few questions, as well as, of course, the thorough enjoyment his writing has provided me over the years. I am also grateful to his agent, Ms. Gabrielle Pantucci. My thanks go to my colleagues Robert Schweik, James Shokoff, Malcolm Nelson, George Browder, and Elizabeth Weston for various kinds of assistance, and to Joanne Foeller for her excellent word processing and secretarial skills. I thank my sons Greg and Matt for their sympathetic understanding of what has been occupying my time, and most of all, my wife, Dianne, for constant encouragement and very active assistance.

Acknowledgments

Quotations from *Little Wilson and Big God* © 1987 by Anthony Burgess. Reprinted by permission of Weidenfeld & Nicolson, New York, a Division of the Wheatland Corporation.

Slightly altered portions of my article "*Nothing Like the Sun*: The Faces in Bella Cohen's Mirror" are from the *Journal of Modern Literature*. © 1976 by Temple University. Reprinted by permission.

Altered portions of my article "Better to Be Hot or Cold: *1985* and the Dynamic of the Manichaean Duoverse" are from *Modern Fiction Studies*. © 1981 by Purdue Research Foundation, West Lafayette, Indiana. Reprinted by permission.

Portions of my article "The Manichee World of Anthony Burgess" are from *Renascence*, 1973, Marquette University, Milwaukee, Wisconsin. Reprinted by permission.

Altered portions of my article "Anthony Burgess: Novelist on the Margin" are from the *Journal of Popular Culture*, 1973, Bowling Green State University. Reprinted by permission.

Chronology

1917 John Burgess Wilson, "Anthony Burgess," born 25 February in Manchester, England.

1919 Mother and only sibling, a sister, die in "Spanish" influenza epidemic.

1940 Graduates from Manchester University with a B.A. (honors) in English literature.

1940–1946 Serves with British Army; stationed in Gibraltar, 1943–46.

1942 Marries Llewela Isherwood Jones.

1946–1954 Holds various teaching posts.

1949 Writes first novel, *A Vision of Battlements,* not published until 1965.

1954–1959 Serves as education officer in Malaya and Borneo.

1956 First published novel, *Time for a Tiger,* appears under the pen name Anthony Burgess.

1958–1959 *The Enemy in the Blanket* and *Beds in the East,* the second and third installments of *The Malayan Trilogy (The Long Day Wanes).*

1959 Invalided back to England from Borneo with suspected brain tumor.

1960 *The Doctor Is Sick,* and *The Right to an Answer.*

1961 *Devil of a State, The Worm and the Ring,* and *One Hand Clapping* (as "Joseph Kell").

1962 *The Wanting Seed* and *A Clockwork Orange.*

1963 *Honey for the Bears* and *Inside Mr. Enderby* (as "Joseph Kell").

1964 *Nothing Like the Sun* and *The Eve of St. Venus.*

1965 *A Vision of Battlements.* Malayan trilogy published in America as *The Long Day Wanes.*

1966 *Tremor of Intent.*

1968 *Enderby Outside*; published in the United States with

Enderby Inside under the title *Enderby.* Wife Llewela dies; marries Liliana Macellari.

1971 *MF*; Stanley Kubrick's film version of *A Clockwork Orange.*

1974 *Napoleon Symphony* and *The Clockwork Testament.*

1976 *Beard's Roman Women.*

1977 *Abba Abba.*

1978 *1985.*

1979 *Man of Nazareth.*

1980 *Earthly Powers.*

1982 *The End of the World News.*

1984 *Enderby's Dark Lady.*

1985 *The Kingdom of the Wicked.*

1986 *The Pianoplayers.*

1987 *Little Wilson and Big God,* the first volume of a two-part autobiography.

1989 *Any Old Iron. The Devil's Mode,* collection of short stories.

Chapter One

Biographical Sketch, the First Volume of the Memoirs, and One Highly Autobiographical Novel

A Biographical Sketch

John Burgess Wilson is Burgess's full given name; Anthony is the name he chose for himself at confirmation. He was born in Manchester, England, on 25 February 1917, a time when "the war was at its grimmest."[1] His father, Joe Wilson, was in the Royal Army Pay Corps and stationed, safely enough, for his length of service, in England. In early 1919 Joe had not yet been discharged when he came home on a regular furlough to discover that the rampaging Spanish influenza epidemic had, with grim suddenness, killed his wife and four-year-old daughter, although it had bypassed completely the two-year-old, John. "I, apparently, was chuckling in my cot while my mother and sister lay dead on a bed in the same room" (*LWBG,* 18), Burgess writes. That this event and its consequences may have played some part in fashioning Burgess into what he considers a "creature of gloom," is reasonable speculation.

The future author had been given the middle name Burgess because that was the maiden name of his mother, Elizabeth, a woman of Scottish Lowland ancestry who had converted to Catholicism upon her marriage to Joe Wilson. A singer and a dancer, she had been known in Glasgow and Manchester music halls as the Beautiful Belle Burgess. Joe Wilson's mother was Irish; his father was a member of an English Catholic family that had remained, like many in Lancashire, true to the old faith. Family legend had it that there was an Elizabethan martyr in the family, a bit of lore that obviously impressed Burgess since he allows the families of two of his characters to share this distinction: the Howarths in *The Worm and the Ring* and the Ropers in *Tremor of Intent* (although in the latter Edwin Roper discovers, to his shock and dismay, that his ancestor was a Protestant martyr, not the

Catholic one of family lore). Through several generations the Wilsons had a habit of taking Irish wives, allowing Burgess to conclude that "I end up more of a Celt than an Anglo-Saxon" (*LWBG,* 9). Like the woman he married, Joe was part of the music hall scene, playing piano in the orchestra, and later, like the fathers of the protagonists of *A Vision of Battlements* and *The Pianoplayers,* in pubs and silent-film theaters.

Burgess (I will call him that from now on, although "Anthony Burgess" did not become a pen name until 1956) acquired a stepmother in 1922. His father's new wife was a widow herself, the mother of two grown daughters of exceptional beauty. This Maggie Dwyer and her first husband, both Manchester Irish, had co-owned a large pub, the Golden Eagle, in the rowdy Miles Platting section of Manchester. The young Burgess was much impressed by this brass-gleaming "boozer of Victorian amplitude" (*LWBG,* 22) with its three singing rooms. He was not so favorably impressed with his stepmother, although she was sufficiently devoted to his father and was a good cook. The nauseatingly repulsive, sick-comic portrait of Enderby's stepmother in Burgess's novel *Enderby* is, he suggests, merely a grotesque enlargement of all the notable characteristics of Maggie Wilson. Whether justifiably or not, Burgess holds this woman accountable for a great deal. He writes, "I was brought up by an Irish stepmother and had very little love, very little affection."[2] He admits that the illiterate Maggie was, lacking the tyrannical impulse, not the wicked stepmother of fairy tales, but for her he reserves heavy blame: "I regret the emotional coldness that was established then and which, apart from other faults, has marred my work" (*LWBG,* 88). (While it is true that the meaningful emotional component in Burgess's work is small, this trait is frequently, since Burgess is primarily an ironist, of no great importance.)

Burgess was sent to a local Catholic elementary school, one fairly typical for its time, especially in its iron discipline and largely rote memorization. He remarks, as do many former students of Catholic schools in years past, on the inevitable presence of the one terror-inspiring nun who figured prominently both in school lore and nightmare—for Burgess the strap-wielding Sister Ignatius, a "sort of Lancashire fishwife got up as a nun" (*LWBG,* 59). Burgess looks back, though, on his Catholic school days with no real rancor. For him, as for his literary hero, James Joyce, they filled him with a network of thought and feeling he would not wish to be without, even if that network were there only to provide him the richly mixed emotional experience of rejecting it. Like Joyce and Dedalus, Burgess is still supersaturated with a Catholicism he allowed to lapse long ago. He prefers Roman Catholicism immeasurably over the pallid Anglicanism he so frequently decries, which is why he might hold an almost perverse fondness for a Sister Ignatius, who is decidedly not pallid.

Although inclined to be cynical by temperament, Burgess does not look back at Manchester with a sardonic eye. "I am proud to be a Mancunian," he states (*LWBG,* 15). Despite being an ugly town, "Manchester was a great city, Cottonopolis, the mother of liberalism and the cradle of the entire industrial system" (*LWBG,* 15). It had the *Manchester Guardian,* "the greatest newspaper in the world," and the justly renowned Hallé Orchestra. Manchester University, which Burgess would later attend, did not yet have a great reputation but was far stronger than people knew. In its chemistry department was the acclaimed chemist Chaim Weizmann, better known later as a president of Israel (as such, he makes a brief appearance in Burgess's *Any Old Iron*); in its history department were L. B. Namier and A. J. P. Taylor; in the English department, L. C. Knights.

Manchester was no stagnant backwater, and Burgess, despite having been lonely sometimes as a "weakly child" (*LWBG,* 32) without "enough devilment" (39) in him, was never really alienated from his environment. Although he never rode a bicycle, nor ever even wanted a ball (*LWBG,* 56), he found more than ample absorption in popular culture, as well as high culture. At the age of six, as the only reader in a circle of neighborhood acquaintances, he was called upon to read the titles in silent movie houses, one of which was right next door to where he lived. "So I began a lifetime's devotion to the cinema" (*LWBG,* 31), Burgess writes, and we learn that for one period of time he attended six nights a week. He learned, almost entirely by his own efforts, to play the piano, and soon found that music, both popular and "serious,"was becoming the love of his life. He still has a "repertory of about a thousand popular songs" (*LWBG,* 76), and "could, at a pinch, find employment as a cocktail pianist" (*LWBG,* 111). Taken to Blackpool, he sucked in the pungent, slightly raffish atmosphere of the great popular resort of the Midlands. The "popular" elements carry over to Burgess's fiction, but have generally not been sufficiently recognized. They are discussed in the next chapter, along with the more easily identifiable elements of "high" literary art. Burgess's art is almost always powered, in fact, by the forces produced from the collision of opposites, and the seemingly odd conjunctions of "pop" and "elitist" elements in his work usually result in a remarkably vital and "whole" experience. (Burgess would stake no claim to originality in the marriage of the "popular" and the serious: he would once again defer to his master, Joyce, and he is respectful of Vladimir Nabokov and Thomas Pynchon.)

Burgess's pervasive tendency to view all human experience dualistically quite possibly stems from an acute early awareness of being a Catholic in Protestant England. A bit later he became aware of a major social difference based broadly on geography: those from southern England were thought to have elegance, taste, and refinement; those from the "north" were thought to be coarse and brutish. This maddened Joe Wilson, who found that southerners spoke "lahdy dah" and "were all bloody Protestants" (*LWBG,* 13). Burgess and his father were quite dissimilar, but beneath disparities there were some strong likenesses, including their ideas about class trappings, privilege, and religion. Well after he gained fame as a writer Burgess could still say, "I tend to identify with certain minorities . . . and with all Catholics. . . . My people are the poor and the downtrodden, the drunk, the fat-bellied and the garlic-smelling, the Catholic and the sentimental."[3] Burgess's attestation may be somewhat disingenuous and sentimental in itself: he despised his stepmother for her frank ignorance, her illiteracy and poor speech, and her indelicate personal mannerisms (using tram tickets, for example, to clean food, while in the presence of others, from between her teeth). Probably (as parts of the novel *Enderby* suggest) he had unconsciously set up another opposition for himself: the idealized dead mother versus the all too physically present, very imperfect stepmother.

Burgess's young life was moderately eventful, even though he seemed to have no very close friends. When he was seven his parents sold the pub and bought a tobacconist's shop in the respectable Moss Side district of Manchester, to which they relocated. Like most children, he was victimized by a childhood injustice. He could draw quite well, but one day in art class at the Bishop Bilsborrow school, he was hit and derided by the teacher for making green leaves orange. Thus it was that Burgess discovered he was (and is) color blind. Two or three years later, when he was about eleven, his talent for drawing was good enough to win him a competition (with publication) in the *Manchester Guardian.* A while later the *Daily Express* published another of his drawings. It may be that only color blindness and nearsightedness kept Burgess from being able to add painting to writing and musicianship as professional accomplishments. A thin boy considered somewhat "delicate," Burgess was growing self-conscious about his looks: his myopia was corrected by glasses, but he chose, as both a boy and a man, never to wear them, except in the dark of the movie theater, lest he look like a "swot." (He seems heartily to enjoy the cartoon character, Mr. Magoo, with whom he identifies.)

The first strong indicator that Burgess would not be, as his relatives and antecedents had been, a member of the laboring or small trade class, came, as it did for many lower-class boys who "raised" themselves, when he was eleven. The momentousness of the "eleven-plus" examination used to be hard to overestimate. Burgess did well enough on his examinations to win two scholarships to Xaverian College, a good Catholic preparatory school in Manchester. This virtually guaranteed that the boy would be attending school until he was at least sixteen, and that then he might have a chance at a scholarship or other form of financial assistance that would allow him to attend a university. Burgess's stepmother had her nose put slightly out of joint upon learning that he would not be leaving school at fourteen as most boys did.

Burgess appears to have flourished at Xaverian College. He did well in his early studies and was soon fast friends with two of his class's most gifted students. Under the influence of the rector, Brother Martin, a southern Englishman "very keen on high-class phonemes and front vocal projection" (*LWBG,* 94), Burgess probably began to modify his Lancashire accent. Outside of school he continued to have an absorbing interest in films—the silents and the new talkies as well. At fifteen his Catholic qualms of conscience were not strong enough to keep him from sexual experimentation with a Protestant girl, and the same year he was fully sexually initiated by a fortyish widow whom he met at the central library. Burgess feels that it was not sex, though, but exposure to the thought of Martin Luther, in (surprisingly, for a Catholic school of the period) assigned class reading, that shook the pillars of his Catholicism. "The basic Christian tenets were unassailable, but the superstructure had gone wrong" (*LWBG,* 139–40), Burgess writes. Burgess laid his doubts before a parish priest who soon "told somebody that it was a sad business, a matter of 'little Wilson and big God' " (*LWBG,* 140). The two sermons on hell in Joyce's *A Portrait of the Artist as a Young Man* brought him back, very temporarily, to the bosom of the Church, but he soon dropped away, never formally to return. He was sixteen.

Artistically and intellectually, Burgess was bounding forward. He progressed from being his own remarkable pupil on the piano to teaching himself composition. He availed himself freely of the musical riches that Manchester had to offer, prominent among which were the operas of Wagner's *Ring.* Unlike his taste for the avant-garde in literature, his taste in music tended toward the works of Holst, Elgar, and Delius, the dominant English composers of a staid musical generation just past. Years later, assessing his own compositional abilities, Burgess remarked, "I found myself stuck in the British idiom of the 1930s, and I have never really become unstuck" (*LWBG,* 158). His poetic taste was advanced, as seen in his reverence for Hopkins, whose excellence was still largely unrecognized by the literary establishment. Hopkins's poetry allowed Burgess to maintain a grip on Catholic doctrine as a "mere poetic *donnée,*" and he had soon committed to memory much of the poetry of the Victorian Jesuit. He read *Ulysses* in an Odyssey Press edition smuggled in from the Continent by a liberal lay master at Xaverian, and, in discovering Eliot, was disappointed only by the small corpus. Brother Martin's reaction to Burgess's apostasy was moderate and sophisticated, and Burgess did not suffer at school. He was, for a time, editor of the school magazine.

Burgess received the higher school certificate from Xaverian and was successfully urged by Brother Martin to stay on for another year for a special series of courses that would, he hoped, well equip Burgess for the state scholarship examinations for university study. Although Burgess did well on this exam, he did not do quite well enough because the total number of scholarships totalled four for the whole city of Manchester. Thus, he began a very uneasy two-year period of being mostly at home and helping his father with his wholesale tobacconist business. He did, though, teach himself Greek and continued with musical composition. With the influential help of Brother Martin, he then prevailed on his father to pay the fees (substantial enough for the Wilsons) that would allow him to attend the mostly subsidized University of Manchester.

Burgess found, however, that he was not allowed to enroll in the university's music department because he had failed a course in physics at Xaverian and did not have the minimal qualification. (Music students were expected to know something about acoustics and the relation of tone to the expansion of metals.) Thus, in a most significant forking of the road, Burgess entered the English department instead. He had less time for music: "I still composed music, but other things got in the way—drama for the poor at the Ancoats Settlement, Joan Littlewood and her Living Newspapers, co-editorship of the university magazine, the writing of poems and short stories, beer, pub pianism (paid), rigorously sought and hardly achieved fornication."[4] Although just slightly uneven in his studies, Burgess was always intensely motivated by at least several things at any one time. He was determined to get his money's worth as a student but felt that in some ways he did not receive it: "There was too much bad lecturing—paper phonetics, the droning of Old Norse, dogmatic evaluations, the transmutation of golden poetry into prose dross."[5] Burgess's intellectual and emotional investment in his course of studies is testified to by his ability to recall vividly in *Little Wilson and Big God,* nearly fifty years after he experienced them, many particulars about course contents, professors, fellow students, and his deep involvement with numerous extracurricular activities.

B.A. honors candidates, at least in English, were required to write a thesis, and Burgess chose Christopher Marlowe's *Doctor Faustus* as his subject, the thesis being that the play was a "symbolic autobiography . . . ; Marlowe wanted to be a Renaissance man but Catholicism held him back" (*LWBG,* 228). It seems that at least one of the attractions Burgess felt for Marlowe was that he saw the supposed atheist as a man unable to really shake himself loose from the fetters that come with cradle Catholicism.

He consciously recognized the process of analogy that had been operating in his own mind, so that, as Manchester awaited the Nazi air raids of 1940, he found himself in this position: "I was a renegade Catholic who mocked at hell but was still secretly scared of it, especially as it might come any night now. I felt, despite all the biographical evidence, that Marlowe himself might be such a man, his blasphemies and beery jags the true voice of imperfect emancipation."[6] As the years passed Burgess would overcome any sharp anxiety about hellfire, but he would always be conscious of being a renegade Catholic—with the emphasis more heavily on *Catholic* than on *renegade.* Catholic theology, particularly of the Augustinian kind (discussed in chapter 2), consistently informs his view of the world and man's nature. He finds, even today, that the elaborate intellectual structure of Catholicism continues to hold its appeal for him, although the changes of the Second Vatican Council diminished the aesthetic appeal of liturgical ceremony and ritual. Taking a retrospective look at himself as a university student, Burgess writes, "I was not really anything but a renegade Catholic liberal humanist with tendencies to anarchism. . . . I do not think, nearly fifty years after, I have much changed my position" (*LWBG,* 183).

Burgess received his B.A., with honors, in English language and literature, in June 1940. He had taken his final examinations in a glass-roofed gymnasium on a day when Nazi bombers, on a daring daylight raid, had inflicted significant damage on Manchester. By October of the same year he found himself part of the Royal Army Medical Corps, posted to a field ambulance unit in Northumberland. Having demonstrated his skill as a pianist, though, Burgess was soon sent to divisional headquarters to join the entertainments section, where his chief contribution was writing special arrangements of popular songs for a dance band that traveled to various units of the division. In early 1942 Burgess applied for transfer to the Army Educational Corps, was approved, and was given his sergeant's stripes. Thus, although Burgess never achieved officer's rank (and in one part of himself probably never really wished to), he had steered a course in the army that allowed him to indulge three cherished talents: music, teaching, and writing.

In January 1942 Burgess had married Llewela Isherwood Jones; she was one of the reasons he had wished to increase his service pay. They had met at the University of Manchester, where she, four years younger than Burgess, had been an economics honors student. The Welsh Llewela (a cousin of the writer Christopher Isherwood) was fierce in intelligence and fiery of temper. Although she and her husband always loved each other deeply after their own fashion, Llewela (or Lynne, as Burgess called her) displayed, early on, unusual and unmistakable signs of trouble that was to come. She would freely have sex "without getting anything out of it" (*LWBG,* 211). But then, somewhat remarkably, she would dispense her sexual favors freely, not just to her husband, but to numerous men of her acquaintance (including Dylan Thomas). Burgess describes her attitude: "There were plenty of attractive people around and it would be a shame and a waste not to find out what they were like with their clothes off" (*LWBG,* 211). Burgess adds that "she sustained this attitude throughout a long marriage" (*LWBG,* 211). The faithless wives that appear in Burgess's fiction seem to have Lynne as their model even more than Molly Bloom. Over the years various comments have appeared in print, with varying degrees of justice, about misogynistic elements in Burgess's fiction and essays; in 1980 the association known as Women in Publishing voted him one of the sexists of the year. To postulate that some animus toward females exists in Burgess because he has unconscious anger at being abandoned, through death, by his natural mother, that he is consciously bitter about living for more than twenty years with a stepmother who did not show him any love, and that he long harbored repressed rage over the casual infidelity of a wife he loved is facile to be sure, but probably contains some partial truth.

Various brief postings in England allowed Burgess himself to partake somewhat of the free love so abundant in wartime Britain. In November 1943 he was dispatched to the British garrison of Gibraltar, where he was to remain until 1946. Although this was a safe posting, Burgess did not find it an enviable one: as he saw it, pettifogging military bureaucrats, class antagonisms, and the sheer ennui of life on the Rock made each day scarcely bearable. He was required to lecture to fractious and embittered enlisted men on the British Way and Purpose, and, against the seeming odds, succeeded. Burgess shared many of their sympathies, and once he arrived at some teaching strategies that were well suited to his natural panache, he gained his audience's attention and, sometimes, their respect. He indicates that the experience taught him valuable lessons about gaining and holding an audience's attention, lessons he was later able to carry over successfully to the craft of writing. Victor Ennis, antihero of *A Vision of Battlements,* is also stationed on the Rock, and his experiences there correspond, fairly closely, with those of his creator.

In April 1944 Burgess received word that Lynne, returning home late at night in blacked-out London from her job at the Ministry of War Transport, had been attacked. She thought that her attackers, dressed in civilian clothes, were American GI deserters. With her passionate temper, she resisted their robbery attempt and was hit, thrown down, and kicked. She was pregnant at the time and miscarried. That she was, as a consequence, ordered by physicians never to become pregnant again caused, in Burgess's view, her ever-increasing descent into alcoholism. She died of cirrhosis of the liver many years later, in March 1968, but Burgess always felt that this attack was an important cause of her death. He transmutes this wrenching real-life experience into the fatal attack on Mrs. F. Alexander by Alex and his three droogs in *A Clockwork Orange*.

Discharged in May 1946 as a sergeant-major, Burgess began a succession of jobs as a pianist, musical arranger, and teacher. He was reasonably happy as a civilian instructor at an army training college, taking pride in his teaching of a speech class, and becoming professionally interested in dialectology. When government funding for this emergency training program dried up, he found employment as a teacher in a grammar school in Banbury, Oxfordshire. He was regarded as a good teacher, but the low salary more and more cast its depressing weight on the Burgesses' spirits, causing him to leave after four years. *The Worm and the Ring,* a school novel, is heavily based on Burgess's experience in Banbury. Burgess has repeatedly told this story about how he got out of Banbury: one night, drunk and frustrated, he had completed and mailed an application to the Colonial Office for a civil service teaching position in Malaya. He had no recollection of this whatsoever until the Colonial Office in London actually showed him his application. But he was offered the post, and he accepted in 1954; Burgess was thirty-seven.

Burgess had now written two novels, *A Vision of Battlements* and *The Worm and the Ring,* but they had not been published. While not quite the pivot on which Burgess's literary career turns, the Malayan experience catalyzed his energies and greatly enriched the storehouse that he would draw on for his characteristic themes. In Gibraltar Burgess had found a sharp conflict (and some little confluence) of cultures; in Malaya, he would find the same, although on a grander scale. While Burgess himself observed deep conflicts of various sorts at intimately close range, he felt little uneasiness in his own personal relations with the Malays. To the chagrin and consternation of at least several fellow civil servants, he was soon speaking excellent Malay and involving himself in the politics of liberation. For a time he seriously considered converting to Islam. In 1956 his impressive Malayan novel, *Time for a Tiger,* was published by the London firm of William Heinemann. Because colonial servants were discouraged from publishing fiction, he used the name Anthony Burgess. He was thirty-nine, but his first novel was in print, and was about to receive good reviews.

Burgess says that inspiration flowed like sweat in the tropical heat. *The Enemy in the Blanket* appeared in 1958, and *Beds in the East* in 1959. The three novels were published under one cover in Britain as *The Malayan Trilogy* in 1964, and in America as *The Long Day Wanes* in 1965. Burgess began to be known in Britain for his rich, comic novels of life in Malaya, just at the time when colonials were leaving the newly independent Malaysia. Burgess, like others, was given a "golden handshake" and departed for a new job in Borneo as an English language specialist. While there, he was at work on a novel, *Devil of a State,* which, although set in a fictional African state, depicted a disguised version of Borneo. He had also begun *The Right to an Answer,* one of his most successful novels. It was then, though, that an event occurred that achieves almost mythic status in the Burgess story: he collapsed on a classroom floor while lecturing, was invalided to London, and was diagnosed (so Burgess has consistently claimed) as having a fatal brain tumor. Lynne told him that the neurologists were of the opinion that he had about a year to live.

Burgess's "terminal year" was his first year as a full-time writer, and it is an astonishing one by any standard. Anxious to provide some degree of financial security for Lynne, his prospective widow, he turned out five novels in that single year of 1960–61. That these were novels of high quality suggests that this was an annus mirabilis seldom matched in modern times (even if Burgess did have some plans or drafts stored away before the year began). Heinemann, the publisher, thought that such fecundity would turn the critics against Burgess, and thus induced Burgess to provide a pseudonym for two of the novels. Thus, *Inside Mr. Enderby* and *One Hand Clapping* appeared under the name "Joseph Kell." *The Worm and the Ring, The Doctor Is Sick,* and *The Wanting Seed* appeared under the name Anthony Burgess. The *Yorkshire Post,* which sometimes employed Burgess as a paid reviewer, sent him *Inside Mr. Enderby* to review, unaware of Kell's identity. Burgess reviewed his own book, later claiming he just "assumed that the editor wanted a bit of a joke."[7] The novel is, in fact, one of Burgess's best, and his own review did not begin to give it its due. Despite this, that an author had "deceitfully" reviewed his own book created a minor brouhaha. As a result, although Burgess was now suspect in some literary circles, he was better known to the public, which seemed to think his joke a good one. No sign of a brain tumor appeared in this year or ever again.

In 1962 Burgess published *A Clockwork Orange,* a novel "discovered" by many readers who had previously known nothing of Burgess. The release of Stanley Kubrick's film version of *A Clockwork Orange* in late 1971 catapulted Burgess to the uneasy status of literary celebrity. Although Burgess had sold the film rights years before for $500 and received only $2,500 more in ex gratia payments after the film's release, the sudden fame had its impact on Burgess, whether he liked it or not. He soon found himself on television talk shows, and he generally revealed an actor's presence as well as intelligence and wide knowledgeability. When given half a chance, as on "The Dick Cavett Show," he came across as a wit, a cynic, a showman, a fearsomely intelligent flayer of the vulgar and the banal, a renaissance man, a conversationalist par excellence, a lovable grouch, a heady puzzle of apparent contradiction. He seemed somewhat embarrassed that his novella, a slight thing in his own estimation, had brought him this kind of fame, but when he was pushed into the spotlight, he gave a bravura performance. Ever since the demand for Burgess as a literary journalist, reviewer, lecturer, visiting professor, symposium panelist, and cultural commentator has been steady and unremitting.

Several months after Lynne died in 1968 Burgess married Liliana Macellari, an Italian contessa then teaching in the linguistics department at Cambridge. Shortly thereafter, the Burgesses gave up residence in Britain, but not before Burgess had created a bit of a ruckus about British confiscatory taxation and insensitivity to writers. With their son, Andrea, the Burgesses have lived, apart from several extended stays in the United States, in Malta and Italy; they now divide their time between Monaco and Switzerland.

Little Wilson and Big God

The first volume of Burgess's autobiography, *Little Wilson and Big God,* was published on 25 February, 1987, Burgess's seventieth birthday. As one would expect, it provides much necessary information and a stylish narrative that zooms in, with fine selectivity, on exactly the right details, and then draws back to capture, in sharply focused wide angle, the backgrounds against which the personal events were played out. The evocation of the Manchester of the twenties and thirties, the British garrison at Gibraltar during the war, and the voices of the enlisted men are masterfully vivid. Still, Burgess is aware of, and admits to, playing a kind of game with the reader and with himself. His awareness that the boundaries between fiction and biography are nebulous is sophisticated, if unoriginal. The book has the feel of objectivity; it even has the benefit of a thorough and very useful index that someone has prepared. But this volume is really very much like one of Burgess's fictions in the strength of its ironies, comic portraiture, and linguistic energy. Only if we deliberate on the "factuality" of this book do we notice this oddity: everyone, except Wilson, can be—and is—reduced to a caricature.

Is Burgess aware of distortion? It would seem so. "Memories sometimes lie in relation to facts, but facts also lie in respect of memory" (*LWBG,* vii), he writes. It is, then, only through the eyes of a man condemned to chronic "emotional coldness" (*LWBG,* 88) that nearly everyone seems silly, reprehensible, or too trivial to be taken seriously. Burgess refuses to open the portals of his own heart or his own imagination, and he "thingifies" others. Is this what he primarily intends to convey by subtitling the book "Confessions"? (This subtitle appears in the British Heinemann edition.)

When Burgess had just received his university degree, he was hired, for a short time, as the tutor of an eleven-year-old boy. The boy, for no special reason, gave Burgess twenty-five pounds as a gift. Burgess seemed to have no qualms at all about taking, without the parents' knowledge, the boy's money at that time, nor any now as he reports it (*LWBG,* 235). He relates, matter-of-factly, that in Malaya he had "sexual encounters with Tamil women . . . including a girl who could not have been older than twelve" (*LWBG,* 386). Burgess's "Confessions" (called such also in the preface to the American edition) are not, ostensibly, very much like those of St. Augustine, who retrospectively flays himself for the boyhood theft of an apple from a farmer's tree. We cannot be sure that Burgess does not regard sex with a twelve-year-old as a token of being a sophisticated man of the world. At other times, readers must wonder if Burgess is aware, as he presents himself, that he often comes across as self-pitying, truculent, overly suspicious, and condescending. (Sufficient evidence seems to exist that the "real" Burgess is often somewhat less sour, contentious, and resentful than his autobiographical persona. As a book reviewer, he is characteristically generous, and to students and researchers he has been mostly courteous and cooperative.)

The answer to the question of whether or not Burgess presents himself truthfully might well be that he recognized that the process of writing the autobiography would be coincident with a coming-to-awareness that would occur with the attempt to present the "self" in an "objective" way. The "Wilson" that we meet is, like a character in a complex, ironic, modern fiction, one that is both rich and elusive. He refuses to be pinned down absolutely, because rigid self-definition is killing. The falsifications inherently involved in a justifying self-interpretation would not, on the other hand, produce any of the liberation that comes with true revelation. Thus, Burgess is frequently concealing even as he seems to be revealing, an unsurprising phenomenon given that irony is his usual métier in fiction. He knows that "objectivity" is impossible; one's own "truth" will shift and change. Fact and myth, past actuality and memory, often blur. Readers are virtually offered two versions of the pivotal "classroom collapse/brain tumor" story. One is that it was a "willed collapse," a tired and disgruntled man's decision just to lie down so that something would have to change. The other is that the collapse was all very real: why else would a man submit to profoundly discomforting neurological tests? We learn a very great deal about Burgess in *Little Wilson and Big God,* most of it as accurate as the material in any usual, good autobiography, but we are also reminded that he knows how to play some cunning games.

The Pianoplayers

Although published one year before *Little Wilson and Big God, The Pianoplayers* (1986) gives every indication of being a by-product of Burgess's careful rummaging through the memories of his own early years. The young Ellen Henshaw, narrator and protagonist, is, allowing for the sexual transposition, almost the young Burgess himself. Her father, Billy Henshaw, is modeled heavily on Joe Wilson, although the real and fictional characters perhaps knew each other: Henshaw drinks in the Golden Eagle of Miles Platting[8] and plays a piano accompaniment in the theater for "Wilson's the Tobacconist" (*P,* 28). Ellen attends the same Catholic elementary school that Burgess did, and so on.

As a novel *The Pianoplayers* is highly imperfect; as a superior form of entertainment it is nearly irresistible in its combination of mock memoir, nostalgic reflection, and unembarrassedly broad comedy. Burgess told Samuel Coale in 1978 that he had "written a little novel about his father called *Piano Players,* which I've not published yet. I think it's too short."[9] Apparently, Burgess decided he could lengthen his fiction by rather loosely tacking on an ending whose inspiration derived heavily from a short story he had published twenty years before in the small magazine

Mad River Review. The story, "An American Organ,"[10] is modified and elaborated in the novel to provide the fabliaulike ending—an extended mother-in-law joke about the difficult marriage of Robert, Ellen's grandson. This perfectly superfluous coda to the novel is added with such brazen nonchalance that some readers will be offended, others charmed.

But Burgess does get away with his ending, barely, because of the sparkle and naturalness (malapropisms and all) of Ellen's narrative. She is reminiscent, certainly, of Defoe's Moll Flanders, Cleland's Fanny Hill, Shaw's Mrs. Warren, and the heroine of Anita Loos's *Gentlemen Prefer Blondes.* The "Henshaw" is probably intended not only to point to Kittie Warren of George Bernard Shaw, but also to suggest D. H. Lawrence's "Cocksure Women and Hensure Men." Ellen is attractive simply because she does not allow a veneer of respectability to cover her basic earthiness. What is more, she has a remarkable memory for detail, one that allows her to conjure up the past with stunning vividness. Whether Ellen is describing what people in Lancashire used to eat in the thirties (*P,* 69–70), or the wonderfully corny vaudeville routines ("concert party programs") popular in the Blackpool of those years, she does so in a way that is at once lucid, entertaining, and natural. Ellen involves the reader in sights, sounds, smells, and tastes, and (her Catholic girlhood innocence lost at age thirteen), some of the special ways in which she was touched. Readers will remember the song titles: "She Was As Pure As Snow and She Drifted" and "You've Worked All Your Life for Me Mother Now Go out and Work for Yourself" (*P,* 82). The catalog of songs and selections (some 180 or more) her father plays in the fatal piano marathon (*P,* 127–136) dwarfs the length of lists even in most naturalistic novels, but is integral here since we can feel Billy sinking beneath their weight. And, of course, Burgess is providing his own marathon of words and memories.

One element in the novel suggests that Burgess had some doubts that a rich skein of nostalgia would be sufficient. Somewhat tentatively he floats the idea (*P,* 122 and 137) that Billy Henshaw is both a figure of Christ and of the modern artist. The suggestion is that he has been reduced to an object or a function—a playerpiano that will be scrapped when it is all played out. (Likewise, the young Ellen is a kind of machine for the provision of sexual pleasure.) Burgess is, quite unnecessarily, reaching here; the texture of the novel does not really permit it to be viewed as a parable of the true artist in a debased modern world—one plausible interpretation of Kafka's "A Hunger Artist." Perhaps his recording of the Starving Man entertainment at Blackpool (*P,* 113) started Burgess thinking of Kafka and the possibilities of allegory.

The Pianoplayers is a relatively minor Burgess work, but the most distinctive Burgess qualities—the humor and the zest for life and words, combined, in a way that is almost unique to Burgess, with a mature cynicism—are richly present to recommend it.

Chapter Two

Style, Strategy, and Themes

Burgess characteristically has an uncanny ability to arrest readers' attention, to draw them fully into his fiction, to delight them with his wit, exuberance, and inventiveness, and to give them, at the same time, some serious things to think about. Both reviewers and ordinary readers have long noted that these characteristics are salient qualities of Burgess's success; to a significant degree the elements that make for this success are analyzable.

Burgess the "Word Boy"

In *Little Wilson and Big God* we learn that when Burgess set off for active duty in World War II, he carried with him "Hopkins and Joyce in my rucksack but little else, not even a change of shirt" (*LWBG,* 239). There is nothing surprising in the young Burgess's passion for literature nor his choice of authors. Both Gerard Manley Hopkins, the Victorian Jesuit poet very far in advance of his time, and James Joyce, the foremost literary modernist and prose experimentalist, were men obsessed with words, writers who extended language to its limits. In *Nothing Like the Sun,* Burgess's fictional biography of Shakespeare, Burgess calls the kind of man who is intoxicated by language a "word-boy." Critics have long pointed to affinities between Burgess's writing and that of another wordsmith, Vladimir Nabokov. Burgess had admitted the general similarity but disclaimed any active influence, claiming that he had read very little Nabokov until he was well into his own career. Joyce, Hopkins, and Shakespeare, however, are there as influences Burgess frequently acknowledges, especially Joyce, whom he regards as a "supreme master."

Although an apparently lifelong temperamental gloom comes through in much of Burgess's fiction, it is most often counterbalanced by an exuberant exploration of language and a display of sheer linguistic power that comes from a well-established fascination with words. Burgess's writing is generally sprinkled with multilingual puns, neologisms, and various kinds of linguistic games (anagrams and acrostics, for example). Burgess seems excellently equipped for all of these. He is a voracious reader of English and American literature, and an intensely devoted nonacademic philologist. He has good to excellent command of at least eight languages other than English. These resources Burgess will generally put to use effectively, sometimes dazzlingly. Admittedly, however, he will occasionally get carried away and fall into mere technical display or some predictable forms of ostentatiousness.

Burgess has written that his obsession with words is, perhaps, "a debased aesthetic pleasure, infra-literary."[1] Elsewhere, though, he has indicated that because he kept an eye on his potential reading public he reined in his natural propensity for rich verbal play: "Unfortunately I've had to earn my living writing books—no priestly vocation like Hopkins, no munificent patroness like Harriet Shaw Weaver who helped to support Joyce. This means that I've had to compromise, avoiding overmuch word play and verbal oddity."[2] He is aware, though, that he has not always avoided "overmuch word play and verbal oddity": he admits that, at the beginning of his career, his "notion of giving the reader his money's worth was to throw difficult words and neologisms at him, to make the syntax involuted" (*LWBG,* 363). Of course, Burgess has no wish to deny himself the exploitation of the rich resources of language, and he opines elsewhere that "the development of a novelist like myself has to be in a greater concentration on the resources of my own language."[3] Whether or not Burgess sometimes gives way to sheer linguistic self-indulgence, his readers, first time or experienced, will not fail to notice the vigorous ways in which he handles language, revels in it, and invites them to share his joy and fascination.

Devices for Arresting the Reader

Anthony Burgess can certainly write a seriously flawed novel (he has written several), but he seems almost inherently unable to write a dull chapter, perhaps even a dull page. Lively of mind and naturally engaging in style, Burgess, "prodigally talented" (the phrase perhaps most frequently applied to him), probably does find his repeated conquests of dullness a relatively easy thing. Still, there is no doubt that he also works at it. Quite probably it was Burgess's sixteen years as a teacher that forcibly made him aware of the need to arrest and hold his audience's attention.

"It was the afternoon of my eighty-first birthday, and I was in bed with my catamite when Ali announced that the Archbishop had come to see me," is the opening sentence of Burgess's *Earthly Powers.* Is that a good first sentence, or is it very nearly a parody of the kind of opening sentence a hack writer might employ in an all too obvious attempt to "grab" the reader at any cost? The answer here is that both alternatives are true. If the reader likes this sentence, fine; if he is put off by it, he will be pleased to discover later in the novel some ironic signaling that reveals Burgess's recognition that he operated without shame when he wrote that sentence. Burgess tries to have his cake and eat it too. He invites his readers to play games with him, some of which involve questions of art, even novelistic strategies. The first sentence of *A Clockwork Orange,* "What's it going to be then, eh," is in keeping with Burgess's general inclination toward the sharply angled in medias res beginning. Readers almost feel themselves addressed by the question and wonder who is addressing them. Readers soon find that it is the "humble narrator," Alex, the fifteen-year-old punk protagonist, murderer, rapist, and perpetrator of atrocious assaults and the "old ultra-violence." Alex has his own demonic charm, however, and Burgess, by a series of cleverly designed strategies, allows the ingratiating Alex to sidle up so close to readers that they come to feel a kind of complicity in the outrages performed by Alex. This strategy provides a most effectively neat reinforcement of the thematic idea of man's strong predisposition toward evil; and the question, "What's it going to be then, eh?" (which opens all three sections of the book), a very natural but tidy indicator of the central theme: man can freely choose either good or evil, and the sacred right of choice must remain inviolate.

" 'A V C C,' said the big blonde Wren. 'I don't think I've ever seen them letters before,' " is the opener of Burgess's earliest novel, *A Vision of Battlements,* written in 1949. Like the Wren, readers might try to solve the puzzle of the abbreviation. When its wearer teasingly says that it means "Arma Virumque Cano Corps," just before indicating the true meaning, "Army Vocational and Cultural Corps," readers with a certain degree of prescience might already be contemplating whether they are beginning a war story modeled in some way on Virgil's *Aeneid.* Once Burgess has readers sufficiently in his grasp, he will usually hold them, primarily by a rapidly moving plot or by extremely colorful two-dimensional characterization, frequently of a Dickensian sort. There is, of course, nothing remarkable about an author's attempting to set in motion an engrossing plot or to employ vivid characterization. Burgess has an unusually strong ability, however, to make characters and situations resonate with meaning. Burgess's very sophisticated awareness of the use of myth and archetype certainly accounts for this ability to some degree. A common element in the reactions of many readers will be that very rudimentary response of wonder. What will happen as the naïf is forcibly plunged into the steaming and troubled cauldron of the-world-as-it-really-is? What makes the rogue-hero lovable even while he is reprehensible? Is he right to defy a society that is perhaps wicked or oppressive, or is he morally at fault himself—suffering perhaps from the perversions of egomania? Similar sorts of wonder are evoked by other Burgess archetypes such as Faustian supermen and totally dedicated artists.

The Clash of Opposites

Readers and reviewers alike have found it impossible to classify Burgess's fiction according to type. Multifaceted and multipronged, Burgess's rich fictions elude both labels and quick estimations of their worth. Their essence is best captured if we note the essential clash of opposites that lies at their very heart, generally imparting energy, depth, and complexity, although producing some occasional confusion among critics as well. Although no complete disjunction exists between Burgess the man and Burgess the literary artist, we find some intertwining of biographical and fictional paradoxes. Burgess "left" the Roman Catholic church when he was sixteen, yet the insistent theme in his fiction has been theological. A lapsed Catholic now for well over fifty years, Burgess castigates the Church for what he sees as its capitulation to dissolute modernizing forces that have put serious cracks in its foundation. Burgess tells the Church, which he no longer believes in, what its practices and beliefs should be, because, it might seem, he wants the luxury and nostalgia of continuing an old love/hate relationship exactly as it was. Burgess has animadverted frequently, in fiction and journalism, on the changes in the Church that occurred during and after the Second Vatican Council, but in *Earthly Powers* (1981), one of his greatest novels, the attack is central, sustained, and a little scurrilous. Burgess's themes suggest he is something of a philosopher-theologian, yet philosophically weighty themes are often present in the same books where there is some low comedy and even buffoonery. Gloomy in his view of man's nature and condition, he is as exuberant as a music hall chairman as he presents the human spectacle. Consciously aware of these dichotomies within himself, Burgess has written, "I see myself as a creature of gloom and sobriety, but my books reflect a sort of clown."[4] Showing again an awareness of the tug of opposites within himself, Burgess, in his urbane but very up-to-date handbook of the contemporary novel, *The Novel Now,* places his own fiction, in the chapter titled "On the Margin," in the margin, that is, between "serious fiction" and "entertainment." On the scales of highbrow to lowbrow, or high art to popular culture, Burgess is likewise most difficult to locate. A worshipful devotee of James Joyce and a strong admirer of T. S. Eliot (Burgess once translated *The Waste Land* into Malay), Burgess might well seem a literary modernist and elitist. That this is not quite so is seen in one of the few qualifications that Burgess had about Eliot—that is, that he never fulfilled the enormous potential that he had of combining the high and the low: "there was always a 'double standard' in Eliot's approach to popular art which forebode a serious synthesis of the high and the low."[5] And to Burgess, Joyce is not at essence the high priest of Art and Difficulty, but a "fun" writer full of the wisdom of the human heart. Burgess, author of two critical books on Joyce and editor of *A Shorter Finnegans Wake,* declared his intention of rescuing Joyce from "the professors." Elsewhere, he declares, "The appearance of difficulty is part of Joyce's big joke; the profundities are always expressed in good round Dublin terms; Joyce's heroes are humble men. If ever there was a writer for the people, Joyce was that writer."[6] Working from the other end of the spectrum, we can soon locate Dickens, another writer most highly regarded by Burgess and an influence on his work, as any reader of the Enderby novels who is familiar with Dickens will be likely to see quite readily. "Dickens's achievement was to create serious literary art out of pop material,"[7] writes Burgess. Burgess has pilloried a fair part of modern culture as debased and vapid and thus might be thought to detest, just as Evelyn Waugh (another certifiable influence on Burgess) did, almost everything distinctly belonging to this century. Yet his enthusiastic appreciation of the great modernist authors is one proof that this is not so. The experimental elements in novels like *MF* and *Napoleon Symphony* prove that he is not simply with our time but in the vanguard. As a pianist Burgess plays jazz and popular music most competently, and he has said, quite seriously, several times, that he could make a living as a cocktail pianist if he had to. Of course, he does not have to because another distinctly modern employment is keeping him lucratively busy of late—script writing for television and film.

Considering the seeming denunciations in a number of Burgess's novels (*The Clockwork Testament* and *1985,* for example), of various kinds of leveling influences in contemporary society—that is, the reduction of nearly everything to the least common denominator—we might expect that we could describe him, politically, with sufficient accuracy as a case-hardened conservative or even a crusty old reactionary. We see an entirely different emphasis in *A Clockwork Orange,* however, and, indeed, Burgess has put himself on record in writing, "My political views are mainly negative: I lean toward anarchy; I hate the State."[8]

Pelagianism/Augustinianism

The central, perhaps too insistent and oft-repeated conflict in Burgess is that of Augustinianism versus Pelagianism. Augustinianism takes its name from St. Augustine (354–430), Pelagianism from his contemporary Pelagius (ca. 355–ca. 425). Pelagius's career, one that led him to be declared a heretic, appears to have begun with a noble and even sensible impulse. He saw that many of his contemporaries were in a state of moral torpor; they were people somewhat depressed by evil, yet comfortable enough with it, used to the weight, as they saw it, of its inevitability. Pelagius wished to emphasize that man is the pilot of his own moral destiny. He enjoined his listeners to feel the power of their free will and to exercise it for the good. His emphasis on man's power to effect spiritual change, however, gradually became so great that he came to deny the necessity of God's grace, the doctrine of original sin, and the need for Christ's redemption. Excommunicated from the Church, Pelagius disappeared from history in about A.D. 418. The Pelagian doctrine described above (slightly simplistically because of space limitations) is largely equated, in Burgess's scheme of things, with twentieth-century style liberalism. It might be said (again, perhaps, in a somewhat simplistic formulation) that the liberal tends to deny the existence of real evil as an entity or as an active agency in the world. What is generally considered "evil," he feels, is merely the effect of some combination of ignorance, superstition, mistrust, and adherence to outmoded conventions. Thus, the liberal or Pelagian is optimistic about the possibilities and efficacy of change. That broad and deep reforms in the totality of the educational process could, especially over time, effectuate profound and beneficent societal changes is usually an article of faith in the liberal creed. Some argument may exist among liberals about the kind and degree of other forms of social engineering, but liberals and Pelagians are of the belief that education, coupled with legislation, can go a very long way toward remedying the ills of the world. Man, basically a beneficent creature, will come closer to a perfect world through intelligent actions set into motion by virtue of his greatest gift, his free will. The emphasis laid upon free will in the liberal or Pelagian doctrine is a strong attraction for Burgess.

Burgess's pull toward Augustinianism, the antithesis of Pelagianism, is, however, both stronger and more perceptible in both his fiction and his extraliterary statements. The liberal notion that man is perfectible is one that Burgess finds ludicrous, naïve, and dangerous. Burgess has, in fact, expressed this view with a ferocity that will strike many ears as a little forced and silly: "Once you start viewing man as a creature sinful only because of his environment and *[sic]* if you put the environment right, man will suddenly become good—when this sort of doctrine appears, I want to vomit."[9] Burgess, like his British contemporaries William Golding and Graham Greene, is a strong believer in original sin and, hence, man's innate predisposition toward evil. Attempts, then, to remove evil from the world are hopelessly bound to failure and can only have the effect of meddlesomely infringing upon the individual's right of choice.

That in the Pelagianism/Augustinianism conflict Burgess leans toward the latter cannot be disputed, but there is more pull toward Pelagianism than many commentators have noticed. God's grace (and, often, God Himself) are far removed from Burgess's works, giving them in that sense a definite Pelagian tincture. In *1985* Burgess writes, explicitly and quite sensibly, "We are all both Pelagian and Augustinian, either in cyclical phases or, through a kind of doublethink, at one and the same time."[10]

The Pelagianism/Augustinianism conflict is, as are all of the conflicts discussed above, not resolved. Conflict, of some sort, though, is the motivating force behind most, maybe all, art, and Burgess, quite wittingly, allows the dynamic forces of his tension of opposites to be the chief driving forces, both in form and in content, of his highly energized fiction.

The Persistent Manichaean Idea

Burgess, acutely aware that his novels are structured and powered by the creative force of conflicting opposites, has a name for it—Manichaeanism. Manichaeanism (also referred to as "Manicheeism" and "Manichaeism") was the heretical religion founded by the Persian Mani in the third century A.D. It seems probable that the impulse that inspired this widely disseminated faith was the need to explain the universally human question why does evil flourish so easily in our world? The basis of Manichaean belief—and that which Burgess finds most useful for his fictional purposes—is a belief that man inhabits a radically dualistic universe (in fact, then, a "duoverse"). The Manichaeans believed that right from the inception of all things, opposed coequal forces were set against each other in eternal conflict: Light–Darkness, Good–Evil. Matter, and hence the body, is viewed as base and of the power of darkness; it is the source of evil present in the world. Only spirit is good and comes from God. While it was the firm duty of every believer of the Manichaean church to strive for the Light, the spiritual, and thus, ideally, to lead rigidly ascetic lives, Manichaeans recognized that there was a nearly hopeless intermixture of Light and Dark elements on this earth. The larger, looser, more encompassing meaning of the word Manichaeanism, then, came to signify any of various dualistic beliefs that viewed evil as a positive agency emanating from a power coequal with the power of good. To know either one of these powers was, by opposition, to know something of the other. The interpenetration of good and evil is one of Burgess's main themes, as it is also for Graham Greene, who is an important influence on Burgess. Manichaeanism, then, is not a serious religious belief for Burgess, but a ready-made system symbolically very useful for explaining the dynamic of the universe.

The Necessity of Commitment

"Great sinners can become great saints," and "the corruption of the best is the worst." These old Christian paradoxes are given vigorous thematic play in Greene and in Burgess. Burgess frequently sounds the thematic note that the world is in a state of moral stagnation and cultural degeneration, not because it is beset by active agencies of evil, but rather because far too many citizens of our time are people uncommitted to good or evil. They are the pale neutrals, the "trimmers," of Dante's Inferno, whose totally fitting punishment is the eternal carrying of heavy banners on which nothing is written. This helps to explain, for example, why, in *A Clockwork Orange,* Alex's pee and em (father and mother) are given basically satiric characterizations, whereas Alex's violence seems to be romanticized. Burgess's themes frequently tend toward the excoriation of apathy, indifference, and moral neutrality, although his novels fully suggest how, with the grand wars of the opposites going on constantly around us, we may feel small, inert, and paralyzed. Apathy, torpor, and moral neutrality, Burgess insists, are the deadly and all-pervasive sins of our times. As we will see, England, his native country, seems best suited to his effective exemplification of these ideas.

The Sanctity of Free Will

The nature of the moral self, Burgess finds, is defined by the quality of its commitment to good or to evil, and good and evil, he wants us to understand, are terms that have meaning only in contradistinction to each other. Goodness cannot exist without evil; evil cannot exist without goodness. If a person ceases to choose between good and evil, his soul becomes moribund. The problem, though, is not just that countless individuals have, for somewhat mysterious reasons, surrendered their right of choice. Burgess, like many authors, feels that increasingly in our century, soul-sustaining avenues of choice are being closed, by Big Government (and the social engineers in its employ), by big business, and by big labor unions. Man is reduced to a cog in a machine, a mechanism, or "a clockwork orange." Eliminate man's ability to choose evil, and you destroy his moral self, the very essence of his humanity.

The Quest Motif

Modern man, greatly diminished, has a sense, sometimes vague, sometimes acute, that he is missing something vital—something that he thinks he might just achieve because his basic disquietude creates stirrings that seem, at optimistic moments, to propel him closer and closer to discovery. In general terms, Burgess's protagonists are very much like most of the characters of twentieth-century literature, all of them accurately enough described as "alienated," that necessarily overworked adjective of twentieth-century criticism. They are people who feel a sense of estrangement from themselves, their surroundings, their society, their culture, or even the world itself. Many of Burgess's protagonists are literal exiles, people who not only do not have a feeling of "at-homeness," but also people who are actually geographically and culturally far removed from their roots. Others are not at-home with their true selves because of gross, obvious violations of the sanctity of their individual personalities by the State or other nearly all-powerful forces, such violations including brutal psychological or pharmacological "reconditioning."

In Burgess's novels, as in most fictions where the quest motif can legitimately be discerned, the protagonist's search for self-knowledge, wholeness, and individuation is accompanied by, and signified by, a series of actual physical movements, with these movements frequently taking on mythic dimensions. In Burgess's novels, still not too unusually, the quest motif is conjoined with near picaresque forms. Burgess's questing and often rebellious antiheroes become quickly involved in a series of episodic and frenetic adventures in worlds that are seen to be either corrupt or tangles of such hopeless confusion that they portend some kind of chaos. As the reader comes to feel some of the satiric bite of the picaresque, he begins vividly to understand the protagonists' need to search for something else: people should not want to adjust to "crazy" or corrupted worlds.

The Uses of Myth and Literary Echoing Devices

In *Re Joyce,* one of his two critical books on Joyce, Burgess writes: "*Ulysses* is a story, and a simple story at that. It is a story about the need of people for each other, and Joyce regards this theme as so important that he has to borrow an epic form in which to tell it" (*RJ,* 87). The lesson of *Ulysses* was very much with Burgess as he began composing, in 1953, his first novel, *A Vision of Battlements.* Burgess relates that he "approved the ground bass of a myth for the novel I wanted to write. The novel was to be about the later days of my service in Gibraltar, and, as Joyce had made the *Odyssey* the substructure of his novel, so the *Aeneid* would be the underpinning of mine" (*LWBG,* 363). This novel interested the London publishing firm of William Heinemann (although they did not seem to notice the mythic substructure), but it was twelve years before the novel would appear. As Burgess began his second novel, he "felt it would be in order to apply myth once more to a realistic novel, and I chose the fourfold matrix of Wagner's *Ring of the Nibelungs*" (*LWBG,* 367–68). Given no hint, the great majority of readers simply will not discern the epic parallels in either work. When readers do discover these parallels, they very sensibly feel that Burgess is operating in the mock epic mode. He is, but not entirely. As Burgess remarks in *Re Joyce,* "The invocation of the *Odyssey* may reduce Ulysses to Bloom, but it also exalts Bloom to Ulysses" (*RJ,* 87).

The very heavy mythic scaffolding of the first two novels is greatly diminished in Burgess's succeeding novels, but elements of myth, and echoes of other works of literature, continue to resonate, sometimes to complex effect, in later Burgess fictions. Echoes of Joyce, Hopkins, and Eliot, especially Joyce, are rife in Burgess. My 1976 article "*Nothing Like the Sun:* The Faces in Bella Cohen's Mirror" is aimed at demonstrating that, quite remarkably, if puzzlingly, Burgess's fictionalized life of Shakespeare is scaffolded on the Shakespeare theory of Stephen Dedalus, presented in the library scene of *Ulysses.* Another critic has convincingly demonstrated the ways in which *Napoleon Symphony* is patterned on *Finnegans Wake.*[11] This is not the place even to begin to suggest the presence or function of other literary allusions, overt or buried, in Burgess. A reader of *Earthly Powers* might correctly suspect that a somewhat coy Burgess teases the reader by calling upon him to make some literary identifications, of both authors and works. But then, too, real people, including authors (Kipling, Joyce, Pound, Hemingway, and others) meet Burgess's fictional characters. An English reviewer (Francis King) has suggested that this was a trick copied from E. L. Doctorow's *Ragtime.* Perhaps, but it should be remembered that fictional characters meet real personages in *Ulysses.* Molly Bloom knows J. C. Doyle, and Stephen Dedalus converses with George Russell, the Irish poet known as AE. It is significant that the very same George Russell has a small but very memorable part in *Earthly Powers* and that his appearance in *Ulysses* is alluded to by the protagonist. Burgess seems fond of crisscrossing ironies and hall-of-mirrors effects.

Musical Forms in the Novels

Just as Burgess's novels are sometimes built on the frameworks of myth, so, too, are they sometimes constructed according to musical analogies. This should not be too surprising since he has consistently maintained that musical composition was his first vocation. In the biographical sketch he provided for himself for *World Authors, 1950–1970,* Burgess wrote that "at fourteen, I taught myself the piano and musical composition and, almost till the time of my first novel, I wrote full-length serious musical works—two symphonies, two concertos, sonatas, songs, incidental music for plays." In *The Long Day Wanes,* Burgess's Malayan trilogy (his third, fourth, and fifth novels), the musical correspondences, hinted at in the narrative itself, can be discerned. A. A. DeVitis discovered this early on, and puts it well: "Burgess's *Malayan Trilogy* is . . . not so much plotted as it is orchestrated. Themes are introduced, they are developed briefly, they appear later on somewhat varied, sometimes muted, but still insistent and vital."[12] In the novel itself, the reader is given a description of a symphony written by a brilliant young Chinese composer, Robert Loo,[13] and he might correctly suspect that certain structural qualities of Loo's symphony are actually sly pointers to the construction of the novel he is reading. In *Little Wilson and Big God* we learn that during his stay in Malaya Burgess was not only writing his three novels, he was also writing a symphony—the very one he ascribes to Robert Loo, he informs us (*LWBG,* 416). Burgess was approaching the same subject and imparting some of the same forms and techniques to it, in two different forms—novel and symphony.

One of Burgess's most experimental novels, *Napoleon Symphony,* concertedly and intricately derives its structure from Beethoven's *Eroica* symphony. Exegesis of this whole enterprise is, fortunately, rendered somewhat superfluous: the chapter "Bonaparte in E Flat" in Burgess's *This Man and Music* elucidates his intentions. Another chapter, "Oedipus Wrecks," comments on musical structures in *MF,* both less obvious and less important. Musical elements seem naturally to suggest themselves to Burgess's mind as he writes his novels, and a fairly lengthy study of musical forms in his novels could assuredly be done. Whether the uncovering of these forms would enhance most readers' appreciation of the novels, though, is probably arguable. Burgess himself, however, keenly appreciates others' success in this field. He has praise for Aldous Huxley's *Point Counterpoint* and, as might be predicted, is awed by Joyce's accomplishments, writing that "in the 'Sirens' episode of *Ulysses,* [he] comes as near to a genuine synthesis of literary and musical techniques as seems humanly possible."[14] That Burgess wrote the following relatively early in his career (1962), might well indicate that musical correspondences are to be found in many of the novels: "I still think that the novelist has much to learn from musical form: novels in sonata-form, rondo-form, fugue-form are perfectly feasible. There is much to be learnt also from mood-contrasts, tempo-contrasts in music: the novelist can have his slow movements and his scherzi. Music can also teach him how to modulate, how to recapitulate; the time for the formal presentation of his themes, the time for the free fantasia."[15]

Chapter Three

The Clash of Opposites: Some Confluence, More Paradox, Much Conflict

The Long Day Wanes (The Malayan Trilogy)

In "Epilogue: Conflict and Confluence," one of the essays in *Urgent Copy,* his first book of collected pieces of literary journalism, Burgess mentions how, relatively soon after his arrival in Malaya (in August 1954), he found the pungently exotic atmosphere was a natural stimulant to novel writing. He notes that "there were Malays, Chinese, Bengalis, Sikhs, Tamils, Eurasians. There were toddy-shops, Cantonese eating-halls, open-air *sateh*-stalls, *ronggeng*-dancers, and musical gong societies. There was conflict turned by the British into a confluence. At last I could write. In the oppressive heat of the afternoon the sweat flowed. It flowed on to paper, along with words. At last I had become a novelist."[1]

The results of this creative impulse were *Time for a Tiger* (1956), *The Enemy in the Blanket* (1958), and *Beds in the East* (1959). Although an obvious trilogy, these novels, each published in England but not in America, did not appear under a single cover until 1964—as *The Malayan Trilogy* in England, and in 1965 as *The Long Day Wanes* in the United States. The protagonist of the trilogy is a thirty-five-year-old Englishman named Victor Crabbe, a teacher of history, whose appointment and external circumstances match, fairly heavily, those of Burgess himself as he wrote the novels. Victor Crabbe is a romantic and a liberal humanist, but the ugly complexities of life in Malaya, and sometimes its ugly simple realities (ax murderers being readily available for cheap hire, for example), have begun to eat away at the corners of his optimism. The schools with which Crabbe is associated have the benefit of the stabilizing order brought by the British, who have ostensibly brought confluence out of conflict. This, though, is a confluence both factitious and temporary. The schools serve as a clear microcosm of Malaya, at the very least, and perhaps of all the world, either in past, present, or future. Consider the barely restrained chaos at the Mansor School where, at the beginning of the trilogy, Victor Crabbe is a housemaster and teacher: "The pupils themselves, through their prefects, pressed the advantages of a racial division. The Chinese feared that the Malays would run amok in the dormitories and use knives; the Malays said they did not like the smell of the Indians; the various Indian races preferred to conduct vendettas only among themselves. . . . The Chinese cried out for pork which, to the Muslims, was *haram* and disgusting; the Hindus would not eat meat at all. . . . The dormitories buzzed with different prayers in different tongues" (*LDW,* 34).

Crabbe (and Burgess) are, of course, in Malaya in the very twilight of the British Empire. Encyclopedias confirm Burgess's information that "the Federation of Malaya . . . was not quite a British colonial possession. There were three crown colonies—Penang, Malacca and Singapore—which were under direct British rule, and a number of territories under Islamic monarchs with a British adviser. . . . By 1957 all these territories, including the three crown Straits Settlements, were to be granted total independence" (*LWBG,* 377). The Malaya that is met in the trilogy, then, is a bubbling stewpot of nationalities, cultures, and religions, and Burgess's readers are implicitly invited to wonder if things will boil over as the forces of history turn up the temperature. Malaya is clearly represented as being in a state of transition owing to natural historic forces, and the novel seems to suggest that the operative patterns of history are circular.[2] Indeed, it seems possible that Burgess models his pattern of "cyclic history" on that of Giovanni Battista Vico, the early eighteenth-century Italian philosopher whose work strongly attracted Joyce.

At the most basic level Burgess does not suggest (as did some other of the novelists of Empire) that the English are innately superior to the native population; the deepest thematic suggestion is that humanity is one. What he does suggest, though, is that the British currently occupy a point far removed from that of the Malayans in the grand, ever-moving cycle of things. Readers of the trilogy will see, beneath or within the frenzy and turbulence of life in Malaya, smaller historical forces spinning away within larger historical patterns—wheels within wheels. Some of the forces will collide with exactly opposing forces so as to produce paradox as readily as conflict. For example, even as Malayans are involved in frenzy and turbulence, they frequently will be maintaining cultural, largely preintellectual patterns of acceptance and passivity. Opposing forces collide everywhere within the trilogy: the active and the passive, chaos and order, East and West, the old and the new, yin and yang, and many more.

Victor Crabbe, largely a thoughtful and sensitive observer of the rich human drama being played out all around him, is himself involved in a somewhat wrenching interior drama that results from the conflict of opposites. His first name, Victor, suggests conqueror and also suggests Victoria, the queen in whose long reign the full magnificence of the Empire was achieved. The name, though, also suggests victim. The long day of the Empire is waning (the title of the American edition comes from Tennyson's dramatic monologue "Ulysses") and, in fact, Crabbe's own day is waning as he approaches the literal death by drowning that actually awaits him at the conclusion of the trilogy. Crabbe, half the biblical three-score-and-ten, apprehends himself, in fact, as a creature halfway between life and death. With his obvious feelings of vulnerability and with a last name suggesting a crab, Crabbe is intended to remind the reader of Eliot's J. Alfred Prufrock whose almost comical hypersensitivity leads him to think, "I should have been a pair of ragged claws/Scuttling across the floors of silent seas." A sensitive man unable to adjust to the whirlwind of change in a period of historic transition, Crabbe is as exposed as the crustacean caught in the vulnerable stage of transition when it is without its hard shell. In his autobiography Burgess writes that Crabbe's "name has its own irony, suggesting the past imperial triumphs of the British and, at the same time, a backward scuttling into the sand of failure and eventual death" (*LWBG,* 400). Crabbe tries to protect himself by an increasing effort to withdraw safely behind a shell of cynicism (a frequent ploy of the disillusioned idealist), but that is not a sufficiently effective psychological strategy. The closely observant reader will see an almost step-by-step emotional deterioration in Crabbe.

This, though, is not to suggest that *The Long Day Wanes* provides, as its primary focus, a probing psychological portrait of a good and sensitive man in the throes of emotional and spiritual dissolution. Modestly, but sensibly, Burgess writes, apropos *Time for a Tiger,* that "a desire for information is what frequently sends [English readers] to a novel (*Hotel, Airport, Il nome della Rosa*) which retails information falsely but painlessly. *Time for a Tiger* went into its several printings not for the beauty of its prose or the vivacity of its characters: it gave painless information about a British territory which the British would soon be abandoning" (*LWBG,* 402). The style of the trilogy cannot properly be termed realistic, two-dimensional characterization and the propensity for the idiosyncratic detail or highly unusual event subsisting throughout. Burgess does, though, provide a rich abundance of vivid detail. He is more than willing to match intimate knowledge of his locale with that of any of the other writers of Empire—Kipling, Maugham, Forster, Orwell, Waugh, Greene. In 1965 Burgess wrote, with some degree of exaggeration, that his "point of view was from the inside of Malay, Tamil,

Chinese and Eurasian minds."[3] Because of the almost constant devolution toward comedy in the novels, we do not have probing psychological investigation or studied, consistent attempts at social realism, and readers are never quite "inside" those minds, inscrutable or not.

What does make the trilogy memorable, though, is Burgess's achievement of a strange blend of the sardonic and the ebullient, a most unusual combination that characterizes the style of much of his writing. Some reviewers and ordinary readers understandably feel that these elements identify satire as the dominant mode of the trilogy. If we employ any strict definition of satire, however, neither the intention nor the achievement qualify the trilogy as satire. Satire aims at moral improvement; it exposes foolishness or knavery in hopes that the uncovering will in some way bring about correction. Burgess sees some of his Malays as fools or knaves, but he also sees such negative characteristics as invariably a part of human life and thus not susceptible to any kind of meaningful correction. Burgess's achievement is rather basically a comedic one, and its appropriate vehicle is a seemingly relatively loose, somewhat episodic plot that is held together by an intelligent use of thematic point and counterpoint.

When the first novel, *Time for a Tiger,* opens, Crabbe and his beautiful second wife, Fenella, have been in Malaya six months. Fenella is bored and homesick, but Crabbe has already come to love Malaya and, beneficent idealist that he is, has the feeling that the country needs him. His marital situation, though, is further complicated by his feelings of guilt connected with the death of his first wife (she was killed in an auto accident when Crabbe was at the wheel), and by his currently keeping a young native mistress, Rahimah.

Crabbe's situation is counterpointed by that of Nabby Adams, a kind of Dickensian character who is larger than life not simply in portraiture, but in his physical size: Nabby is six feet eight inches tall. Like Crabbe's, his name has symbolic significance. As Burgess himself elucidates, the "name Nabby Adams turns him into the first of the Islamic prophets—*Nabi Adam*—or possibly Adam's son, whether Cain or Abel is not clear: he raises Cain and is able enough at drinking" (*LWBG,* 401). An alcoholic police lieutenant, Nabby Adams has achieved something that comes to have an almost irresistibly strong pull for Crabbe: absorption into the East. Adam's English is, in fact, threatened with disappearance because of disuse. As this first novel closes, Fenella is becoming increasingly unhappy, but Crabbe's enchantment with Malaya, despite the troubles caused by Communist insurgents and constant foul-ups with the schools, is becoming increasingly strong. Still he sometimes vaguely wonders if his growing wish to be absorbed is not a disguised but sustained death wish. Near the end of the novel, a fellow teacher, Mr. Raj, tells him pointedly that "the country will absorb you and you will cease to be Victor Crabbe. You will less and less find it possible to do the work for which you were sent here. You will lose function and identity. You will be swallowed up and become another kind of eccentric. . . . You will be ruined" (*LDW,* 160).

As *The Enemy in the Blanket* opens the Crabbes are in the imaginary state of Dahaga, on the opposite coast of Malaya, where Victor has received the headmastership of an English-speaking school. Victor and Fenella move farther apart. The real power in Dahaga is wielded not by its impotent sultan, but by the Abang ("Big Brother"), an upstart who feels that family position justifies his sexual conquests of a long string of blond women. The Abang (the title comically appropriate) rather quickly decides that Fenella ought to be his latest acquisition, and she, feeling emotionally neglected by Victor, is more than sufficiently flattered to go along with the Abang's plan. Meanwhile, Victor manages to assuage to some extent the long-standing guilt he has felt over his first wife's death by having an affair with a married woman, Ann Talbot, who bears a definite resemblance to his dead first wife.

In this novel Victor's situation is counterpointed by that of Rupert Hardman, an impoverished and rather inept English lawyer and expatriate. While Hardman contemplates marriage with 'Che Normah, a wealthy Islamic widow, he tries to deal with a nagging Catholic conscience by secretly confessing to a renegade priest, a Frenchman who is himself in the process of being absorbed by the East. Hardman finally marries 'Che Normah and they make a pilgrimage to Mecca, but, feeling swallowed by her possessiveness and voracious sexual appetite, he abandons her, even though she is pregnant. He flees back to a cozier, more stable (if more dull) England, feeling that even a low-paying teaching job there will provide him the basis for the emotional stability he needs. This merging of East and West is not total (despite the unborn child), nor is that of Fenella and the Abang. When Malaya achieves its independence, the Abang flees, pockets loaded down with plunder, into "exile" in Europe, accompanied by Fenella, who is ostensibly his secretary. The relationship does not endure very long, however, for Victor and the reader learn in the last novel that Fenella is back in England, living a literary and rather insular life on that largely homogeneous island—attending afternoon teas and publishing minor poetry in little magazines with titles like *The New Presbyter . . . Formerly the Old Priest.*

Beds in the East, the final volume, finds Crabbe, still clinging to his somewhat diminished idealism, doing what he can to prepare the people to meet effectively their new independence. Helping these divergent people to develop a sense of national self-pride and eliminate a destructive factionalism is the quixotic task that Crabbe persists in. Among the novel's many characters are found representatives of many national groups and even races, their mutual antagonisms microcosmically suggesting the near-impossibility of a successful future for the new nation. Crabbe makes it a special project to attempt to assist Robert Loo, a precocious Chinese adolescent who gives promise of extraordinary talent as a musical composer. Crabbe tries to promote Loo's talent, but, indicating the base suspicions endemic to the country, people assume Crabbe's real intent is pederastic. Actually, Crabbe has hopes that Loo will serve an extraordinarily valuable function, that of being a great national composer. "Music presents a sort of image of unity" (*LDW,* 355), Crabbe says. Not surprisingly, Crabbe's hopes prove delusory. Whatever talent Robert may have is corrupted somewhat when his father introduces into his store a gleaming new jukebox, and, more importantly, Robert is corrupted by his overwhelming infatuation with the beautiful Rosemary Michael.

This same Rosemary Michael is, in fact, a chief character in *Beds in the East.* Rosemary is acquainted with many beds, although she strongly prefers the beds of Westerners to those of other Easterners. Burgess is once again employing foil characterization with Rosemary: her superficiality, egocentricity, and brainlessness show up, by stark contrast, Crabbe's depth, altruism, and intelligence. Rosemary is a young teacher, a dark-pigmented Tamil, university educated in Liverpool, who hopes to use her voluptuous body to good advantage. An inveterate snob, Rosemary has a disdainfully superior attitude toward other Asians; her eyes are cast longingly toward Europe and a future with a European husband. Her combination of venality and prejudice is obviously intended to represent certain educated classes in Malaya, a decidedly ill omen for the new country.

Crabbe carries on nobly, however, his most concerted attempt at forging unity being a multiracial "bridge" party he gives at his home. He expresses his pleasure at "the sight of all the races of South-East Asia mixing freely and in obvious harmony" (*LDW,* 397). The Communists, Crabbe declares, for their own ends, have been disseminating rumors "about the prospect of racial discord in the new, independent Malaya" (*LDW,* 397). In a high-minded, exhortatory mode, Crabbe urges that "there must not merely be mixing, there must be fusion" (*LDW,* 398). "Confusion," one character loudly says, nodding agreement. Confusion is, of course, what will prevail, and Crabbe's "bridge" party's breaking up in a scuffle and disarray is but one sign of this.

Crabbe's most profound disillusionment comes with a sharp sting: he learns that his first wife, worshiped in memory since her death, had been adulterously involved with Costard, an English manager now also in Malaya. Stung by this news and literally stung on the leg by a scorpion, Crabbe finds progress difficult. In attempting to board a launch, he stumbles and drowns. His bed in the East is the riverbed. He achieves the absorption with Malaya toward which he had been drawn from the first.

Despite a pace that occasionally lags, especially in the subplots, *The Long Day Wanes* largely succeeds. It does so because it is written from more than sufficient depths of the author's very self: emotional, intellectual, and even spiritual. Like Crabbe, Burgess loved most of what he found in Malaya, but he found that the agonizing divisions in the country created a corresponding tear in his own fabric. It seems not too sententious to say that writing the novels was a way of trying to make himself whole. But, only honesty can produce wholeness, and thus, paradoxically, Burgess's honest artistic vision is one of conflict. (One easily sees the farcical and the satiric in this trilogy, but feels the underlying compassionate, nearly tragic, depths that would appear to run in the opposite direction. Tensions and conflicts do, in fact, give the trilogy its depth and memorability.) Burgess, expressing a minority view (but an unsurprising one given his "Manichaeanism"), feels that total resolutions of conflict are nearly as impossible in art as in life, but this he sees as desirable, for conflict is creative.

Devil of a State

Another novel of Empire, *Devil of a State* would seem to follow in a smooth, straight line from the trilogy. The similarities are strong, but this novel is a considerably lesser achievement. While the trilogy came from the guts, this novel was rather cold-bloodedly contrived. Burgess quite apparently set his mind on cultivating a literary manner, and, surprisingly, the manner that he cultivates turns out to be very heavily derivative. Some reviewers have noted the influence of Graham Greene (to whom the novel is dedicated) and others that of Evelyn Waugh. That both are sources is correct and fairly obvious. What is rather remarkable is that no one has commented on the utter improbability and inadvisability of Burgess's attempting to fuse the styles and themes of these very dissimilar authors, alike mostly just in their Catholicism. Evidence of flawed structure appears in other forms as well.

Devil of a State is an out-and-out comic novel—in fact, a farce—although definable elements of parable, satire, and even tragedy are present. (Burgess also may intend some parodic play in his uses of Waugh and

Greene but this is still puzzling and ill-advised.) The setting is Dunia, a newly independent, uranium-rich state in East Africa ruled by its Caliph, a chain-smoking Islamic pederast. To show proper obeisance to this Caliph anyone addressing him must, by custom, refer to himself in the third person as "Dog"; for example, "Dog begs your Highness's pardon?" A father-and-son pair, Paolo and Nando Tasca, are hotblooded Italian marble workers engaged in a terrific Oedipal conflict that regularly causes great comic explosions. The U.N. Advisor, James Tomlin, is very nearly deaf, which opens the gates wide for any number of comic misunderstandings. The novel gives us, then, relatively easily manufactured comic contrivances of plot enacted by cartoon characters. Much of this is still funny, but some of it is also forced.

The protagonist of the novel, a passport officer, Frank Lydgate, seems to have wandered into the Marx Brothers world of Dunia from Graham Greeneland. He is fifty and suffused with a Catholic sense of guilt about a first wife; the reader is made to feel the effect of heat, squalor, dust, alcohol, and boredom on his frayed nerves. Superficially a bit like Victor Crabbe, Lydgate lacks his intellect, altruism, and dimension. The reader cannot feel anything for Lydgate, but there are obvious signs of uncertainty on Burgess's part as to whether or not he wishes to have his reader register any response to Lydgate.

Despite the dedication to Greene, the novel is obviously far more indebted to Waugh. This is one time, though, when Burgess's mimetic abilities fail. Waugh is consistently in control of his styles and tone, giving a sense of effortless ease, the classical touch. Burgess here huffs and puffs to push his madcap plot forward at a frenetic pace, while picking up every joke along the way, and straining hard to reach some others not really graspable. Most Waugh devotees were severely disappointed by Terry Southern's screenplay for the film version of *The Loved One.* If Burgess is attempting his own emulation or "translation" of Waugh in *Devil of a State,* it must be said that he achieves only the same level as Southern, and for exactly the same reasons.

Some readers, noting that the novel seems to be about the dominion of chaos (the "devil" signifying primal disorder) in the world (which, allegorically it might be, *dunia* being Arabic for world), might feel that Burgess is logically excused from the usual sorts of authorial control and consistency. To read this novel in a very relaxed, decidedly uncritical way might well be to find it a delight, yet readers who know a better Burgess—or Waugh, or Greene—will probably experience a modicum of disappointment. While a mixture of modes and styles can certainly be effective, the proportions for the mixture are, in this case, not well considered. It is only fair to note, however, that the novel was a (British) Book Society choice when it appeared in 1961.

Honey for the Bears

Honey for the Bears is one of two successful novels (the other being *Tremor of Intent*) that had its impetus in a cruise Burgess and his first wife took to Leningrad in 1961. (In part the inspiration of *A Clockwork Orange* can also be found in this trip.) This trip strongly reinforced in Burgess's mind that humanity is all of a piece, East or West, Communist or capitalist. The characters of *Honey for the Bears* are also very close to learning this lesson at the end of the novel, but before they do, they are involved in a comic series of misadventures resulting from an incongruous failure to see what is right in front of their noses or inside their hearts. They are people tyrannized by abstractions and false categories, their movements throughout the novel constituting a mock mythic quest—for freedom and personal identity.

Burgess's protagonist is Paul Hussey, an English antiques dealer visiting Leningrad on a cruise with his sensuous American-born wife, Belinda. In England Paul had been rather uncritically satisfied with himself, almost smug, perhaps; he is particularly proud of having risen from working-class origins to genteel, suburban comfort and respectability (although he does not admit how much of this was due to Belinda's money). Belinda, daughter of a professor of English literature (an Alexander Pope specialist), had, at the time of her marriage to Paul twelve years earlier, been infatuated with nearly all things English. If she and Paul were able to forestall any recognition of blandness in their marriage, it was because they added a very modest dash of suburban spice—a bit of spouse swapping with their friends Robert and Sandra. Both, too, have been able to deny to themselves their basically homosexual orientations. Paul (one of Burgess's bloodless Englishmen) comes to admit he is not a highly sexed man and Belinda is not sexually satisfied, but he denies himself an admission of the truth—that it is his heterosexual drive that is not strong.

The Husseys' move toward illumination begins when their friend Robert dies of heart disease and they discover that, as a smuggler and black marketeer, he possessed "twenty dozen chemical fabric dresses" that he had arranged to have secretly delivered to Russia. Paul and Belinda agree to carry through the deal for the now nearly impoverished Sandra. Burgess has thus set the stage for a confrontation of what seems to be Manichaean opposites: soft-bellied capitalism/staunchly practiced communism; homosexuality/

heterosexuality; America/Russia; freedom/enslavement; neutrality/active commitment; English bloodlessness/dark Russian energy. These perceived polarities activate psychological and intellectual forces of attraction and repulsion, and these are what set the plot in motion and keep it humming. Only gradually do the characters come to understand that these supposedly opposed binary forces are not stable, meaningfully defined essences that people can confidently use as fixed stars to help themselves navigate toward good as opposed to evil, or reality as opposed to illusion. Life is as complex as it is precisely because the opposites constantly interpenetrate. A recognition of this alone, however, can be useful in slipping the bonds of ideological illusion and personal misidentification.

The "drilon" dresses, products of a Western technocratic and consumer-driven economy, are the honey the Russian bears are supposed to crave. The dresses give Paul great difficulty, however. When the arranged contact is not made, Paul tries to flog the dresses himself. Trouble comes for him, though, in several forms, including a police duo, Zverkov and Karamzin, nice guy/mean guy, who have Paul under surveillance. Just as he is about to conclude a deal for the dresses with a previously arranged contact on a crowded street, Paul sees the police closing in. Dismayed, but quick-witted, he disposes of the evidence: he bestows the dresses freely on astonished passersby, all the while proclaiming Anglo-Russian friendship.

Meanwhile, Belinda is in a Leningrad hospital with a seriously annoying skin disorder, which her female Soviet physician, Dr. Lazurkina, immediately thinks is psychogenic. The physician diagnoses the real trouble as an inner conflict resulting from Belinda's repressed hostility toward men and repressed preference for women. Imposing and authoritative with Paul, Dr. Lazurkina is, with Belinda, very warm, very close, very supportive. To Paul she says definitively, "So I explain what your wife has been doing by saying that it is all because you are homosexual and are not honest enough to admit it."[4] Out on his own, Paul has spent some time with Alexei Prutkov, Brooklyn-born son of émigré Russian parents, who has returned to the land of his fathers, carrying some American baggage with him, however. Prutkov has been trying hard to establish his own identity as a genuine Soviet hipster. When Paul temporarily moves in with Prutkov and his girlfriend, he comes closer to discovering something about his own sexual identity—he is more drawn to the young man than his attractive girlfriend. Paul thinks that he can confirm his heterosexuality by a kind of masculine display. In a scene reminiscent of one in *War and Peace,* Paul sits dangerously far out on a window sill and, watched by an alarmed Prutkov and his friends, drinks "a bottle of vodka straight off" (*HB,* 154). If that exhibition goes any distance at all, however, toward proving something about Paul's "normal" sexuality (and, of course, it does not), it would be vitiated by what happens when all that vodka takes effect: Paul proposes a homosexual orgy, happily suggesting to Prutkov's male friends "that we all strip ourselves stark ballock naked" (*HB,* 156).

Paul continues to be bedeviled by his problems with identity and his false categorizations, as well as the propensity of others to classify and divide both people and things in ways that deprive things of their full flavor and dimension and reduce human dignity and freedom. When the police team takes Paul in for interrogation, the thuggish Karamzin, Communist hardliner and chauvinist, punches Paul hard in the mouth, sending his false teeth bouncing across the floor. Although finally there is no exact boundary between the simulated and the real, Zverkov does seem genuinely shocked and dismayed at his partner's action, and later, a very human, if not quite tender, part of Karamzin is revealed. Categories melt and merge as even Paul earlier had seemed aware in thinking of "the Slav manic-depressive cycle," itself, of course, a broadly generalized categorization that does, however, point toward a slightly more complex "reality." The stupidity of division does, in fact, intrude itself more and more into the forefront of Paul's consciousness. To Prutkov he says, "As for America, that's just the same as Russia. You're no different. America and Russia would make a very nice marriage" (*HB,* 152). This is, indeed, one of the novel's stronger themes. The two superpowers are seen largely as mirror images of each other. Both seek material progress as an almost sacred goal. Both are seen as exalting the State, and thus severely diminishing the human individual. Americans have constitutionally guaranteed freedoms, but, perhaps out of a long-existent tyranny of the majority more recently combined with the intimidating effects of the near-psychosis of the cold war, they act as if they did not. The Russians have few freedoms, but, as if in compensation, they refuse to allow their burdened souls to be fully shackled. The book presents a vivid scene of *stillyagi,* young hoodlums somewhat like English teddy boys, freely roaming and ruling the night streets of Leningrad.

Both political and sexual identities cause no end of confusion, and the political and sexual themes are cleverly intertwined. They are most clearly tied together toward the end of the novel in a plot, in which Paul is the chief player, to smuggle out of Russia a young man Paul is told is the son of a great, disgraced Russian avant-garde composer, Opiskin, now an enemy of the state. A fellow cruise passenger, an endlessly mysterious, wheelchair-bound character called Dr. Tiresias (appropriately named, in fact, for "its" sex cannot be determined) persuades Paul to go along with his/her

"Angleruss" cultural exchange organization, not simply because of some sparks of idealism, but also because Paul needs both some human connection and a boost for his badly flagging self-esteem (Belinda has left for Rostov with Dr. Lazurkina to find a new life of lesbian fulfillment and love). Paul does what is planned. He gets the hairy, rather ugly "Opiskin" on board the cruise ship disguised as his wife, Belinda's absence thus serving a useful purpose. They make Finland safely, but Paul is met there by Zverkov and Karamzin who inform him that the man he has just helped to escape is not the son of Opiskin, but a hardened, long-standing, vicious criminal who has "worked as a sort of brutal man" (*HB,* 253) for drug smugglers. And, although Tiresias's sex is never established, it is definitely determined that he/she is a smooth, large-scale professional smuggler whose wheelchair contains secret cavities for the transport of drugs and jewels.

The idea of the interpenetration of opposites is given clever, ironic reinforcement when a strong thematic "truth" comes out of the mouth of Tiresias, a well-practiced liar: "I am tired of categories, of divisions, of opposites. Good, evil; male, female; positive, negative. That they interpenetrate is no real palliative, no ointment for the cut. What I seek is the continuum, the merging. Europe is all Manichees; Russia has become the most European of them all" (*HB,* 217). If Russia is strongly Manichaean, then so too is its fairly exact counterpart, America, with its sharp us/them attitude of the cold war era; America is afraid to reach out to make vital sustaining human contact with other peoples. That America chooses not to "marry" outside its own family might be seen as a kind of symbolic "incest" pointed to by the fact that Belinda's repressed hatred of men was caused by a pattern of incestuous behavior begun by her father when she was only seven.

Tiresias's specific remark about Manichaeanism is accompanied by enough similar statements to cause some readers to feel that the thematic design of the novel is too schematic, its fabric too boldly emblazoned with the insistent Manichaean idea. The Manichaean theme is so explicitly obvious that it mocks its own presence. This is a consistently comic novel of unerringly deft touch; Burgess in no way intends ponderous reflection on the part of his reader, only thoughtful attention to a few genuine, but playfully presented ironies. The reader should understand from the novel that the world is a place of great richness and ambiguity and that to be most free and to partake most fully of what life has to offer, people must do what is usually difficult: accept the very plenitude and ambiguity of human experience. Nothing else need be taken too seriously. Burgess is not making a weighty religious statement, nor is he, as some critics have thought, doing some conscious proselytizing for bisexual lifestyles.

Tremor of Intent

In *Tremor of Intent* another English protagonist takes a luxury cruise to the Soviet Union, is sorely tried and tempted by neutrals, and at the end comes to heightened self-awareness. On the surface mostly just a spoof of popular spy thrillers of the period, such as those of Ian Fleming, this novel, with its depths and polished contours, has, quite defensibly, generally been regarded as one of Burgess's five or six best. Both the Norton and Ballantine paperback editions place the phrase "eschatological spy novel" just above or below the title as if it were a subtitle, pointing toward the Greene-like Catholic themes that rise like hillocks on the surface of the novel. In evaluating this opulently comic thriller, critics and ordinary readers are prone to disagree only about whether the religious themes—whose convergence involves, again, overt references to Manichaeanism—are presented with full seriousness, and, if they are, whether they are meaningful, honestly integral, and possessed of real depth. The thought might even occur that Burgess is spoofing Greene as well as Fleming and John le Carré.

The plot is really quite simple. Denis Hillier, a British secret agent just entering mid-life, is sent to a Black Sea port city in the Soviet Union to recover, by persuasion or duress, a top rocket fuel scientist, Edwin Roper, who has defected to the Soviets. Hillier has been chosen not only because he speaks excellent Russian, but also because he and Roper have been friends ever since their days together at a Catholic boys boarding school in the northern English city of "Bradcaster." Like le Carré's Leamas, the spy who came in from the cold, Hillier is jaded and disgruntled, his moral life in dissolution; he has thus notified the agency that this will be his last mission. Hillier arrives in Yarylyuk, proceeds to the hotel housing the conference of Soviet scientists, and is easily able to isolate Roper.

No sooner has Hillier gotten Roper alone, though, than Wriste, his steward aboard the "gastronomic cruise" ship, arrives to execute both Hillier and Roper. Wriste behaves in good espionage novel fashion, graciously explaining why he is about to dispatch the two old friends. Wriste reveals that he is an independent agent, a specialist in execution who to corroborate the completion of his task takes a severed finger of each victim back to those who hired him. Some stratum of the British government that hired him for this job, he says, wants Hillier out of the way because he knows too much, and Roper must never be allowed to return to England because he could easily implicate a certain cabinet minister in a sexual affair that left him open for treasonous blackmail. The men are saved, though, by another cruise passenger, a thirteen-year-old boy named Alan Walters, who arrives in the nick of time to put a bullet straight through Wriste's eye and into his brain. But Roper refuses to return to England, so Hillier and Alan leave without him. Hillier rejoins the cruise, sails to Istanbul, and there sees to the death of another "bloody neutral," the independent espionage operator Mr. Theodorescu. In the book's concluding scene, which takes place one year later, we find that Hillier is living secretly in Ireland, and, that despite his Manichaean beliefs, he is now an ordained Jesuit priest.

Such a barebones summary in no way begins to do justice to this deliberately overfed novel that bursts with controlled, parodic excesses. Readers of the novel are apt to remember, as well as anything else, the figures of Mr. Theodorescu and his assistant, Miss Devi. Theodorescu, arch-neutral and larger than life villain, purveys secret information to the highest bidder. (He is, in his function, somewhat like the neutral cold war profiteer of *Honey for the Bears,* Dr. Tiresias, but he is in every way a larger figure than the wheelchair-bound androgyne.) Suave and ever-knowing, refined in the mastery of all the skills of his profitable trade, Theodorescu nonetheless has gross physical appetites—for food, drink, and young boys. This physically obese villain provides a fun house mirror reflection of Hillier who is himself afflicted, as he states in the opening paragraph of the novel, with "two chronic diseases of gluttony and satyriasis." Since each considers eating, drinking, and sexual conquest not only pleasureful but part of the great competitive game that is, in their view, life itself, it seems only natural that glutton should engage glutton in an eating contest. When Burgess sets up this "Trencherman's Stakes," he is able to indulge himself and the reader in a remarkably funny, absurdly inflated parody of all the scenes in which Fleming displays James Bond as grand gourmand. In the ship's dining room, Hillier and Theodorescu, in one entrail-exploding setting, ingest, amidst reported conversation and among other dishes "lobster medallions in a sauce cardinale," the lobster "poached in white wine and a court-bouillon made with the shells, then set alight in warm pernod"; "some red mullet and artichoke hearts"; "fillets of sole Queen Elizabeth, with sauce blonde"; "shellfish tart with sauce Newburg"; "*soufflé au foire gras*"; "avocado halves with caviar and a cold chiffon sauce"; "*filet mignon à la romana* and a little butterfly pasta and a few zucchini"; "roast lamb *persillée* and onion and gruyère casserole with green beans and celery julienne"; "pheasant with pecan stuffing. Bread sauce and game chips. Broccoli blossoms."[5] This, and more, is consumed long before they call for the dessert trolley to be wheeled to their table.

The Bond parody continues as Hillier shifts—the very same night—to another competitive field: the sexual. If James Bond is a sexual athlete and a connoisseur of beautiful women schooled in the provision of sexual delights, the hedonistic Hillier will enjoy as much as Bond does and much more. His partner is Theodorescu's employee, Miss Devi, a dusky Indian beauty. Burgess vividly describes her body, which is, in short, perfection, at least in the *Playboy* mold. No amateur or initiate, Miss Devi is an adept in the Eastern arts of lovemaking, having gone well beyond the *Kama Sutra* to more subtle and rewarding esoterica unknown in the West. No bookish theorist either, she has amazing energy and gymnastic capabilities. Miss Devi, in fact, provides Hillier with ecstasies that no ordinary language can describe, and so it is that Burgess employs extraordinary language, language pumped to bursting with Joycean mock epic catalogs of birds and ships, language shaken and aflame from eruptive bursts of preposterous metaphor that seem, marvellously enough, almost apt. It seems as if Burgess wishes to have those writers whose stock-in-trade is patented scenes of explicit sexuality to have their mouths gaping open in wonder and jealous dismay.

Most readers are—and it would be hard to say they are "wrong" in this—more impressed by the fun of the parodic elements in *Tremor of Intent* than they are by the serious religious-philosophical themes. The fun is heightened by the feeling that Burgess's parody is quite good-natured. Burgess's inclusion of Fleming's *Goldfinger* in his *99 Novels: The Best in English since 1939* (1984)[6] certainly supports this opinion, as does what he writes about the film translations of the James Bond novels in a 1987 piece for *Life* magazine, "Oh James, Don't Stop: The High-Tech Epic Continues with a Brand-New Bond"—that the Bond novels "may be considered now to be popular classics," and that "I regularly get through one or another in my bouts of insomnia."[7]

What is genuinely impressive about *Tremor of Intent* is that its carefully engineered design and energy make it not simply a parody of the spy thriller, but an excellent spy thriller in its own right. (That there are winking elements of self-parody in the James Bond novels also is undeniable, and is, in fact, no small part of their appeal.) Burgess's novel contains just about all the usual trappings and devices of the spy novel: the multiskilled, mostly unflappable protagonist; the beautiful ingénue in need of protection (here sixteen-year-old Clara Walters); the seductive fleshpot (Miss Devi) in league with a villain; a defector scientist (Roper); double agents (Theodorescu and Wriste); hairbreadth escapes; false identities; veiled hints and encoded messages of various kinds; forged passports; reversals; violent death; quick unravellings; ampoules of instantly deadly poison. Burgess mixes these ingredients together at least as well as, say, a Fleming, le Carré, or Ambler, and his pace is every bit as surefooted. What is more, his plot is slightly more plausible, and his characterization surely sharper and deeper. For highly literate and attentive readers, Burgess provides additional bonuses: buried literary allusions, puns, onomastic word play, and various kinds of linguistic game playing. Burgess even leaves his readers with an encoded message: "ZZWM DDHGEM EH IJNZ OJNMU F XWI OVU OVDP" (*TI,* 60). Readers who try but fail to break the code will find that an American critic has done it successfully for them.[8] Another critic finds, largely convincingly, what some readers may have suspected: that this novel, as other Burgess novels, is structured according to close musical analogy, in this case, a sonata.[9] Spy thriller fans who like their novels located somewhere near the border of detective fiction, and readers who like a bit of active puzzle solving are generally enamored of *Tremor of Intent.*

Whether the "serious" themes of the novel are sounded and incorporated in an unqualifiedly successful way is far more problematic. A. A. DeVitis, who sees Hillier as "Burgess's strongest protagonist," maintains that they are: "*Tremor of Intent* works on two levels: at one and the same time it is a suspenseful spy story and an allegory on the theme of responsibility and commitment. The two levels merge consistently and provocatively to make a novel that is both entertaining and theologically apt, always, however, within the general context of a Manichaean universe."[10] In his review of the novel when it first appeared, Lawrence Graver expressed an opposing viewpoint:

> Yet despite the fact that *Tremor of Intent* has more wit and comic invention than the books which it so boisterously ridicules, one is never quite convinced that the target is worth such lavish attention. Nor do Burgess' attempts to link these perishable materials to larger concerns provide much solace. From time to time—especially at the start and finish—the characters talk seriously about science, religion, and the nature of betrayal. But play is the thing; the ideas come on too casually and are never given sufficient articulation. Since the people fail to use above caricatures, their assertions are so much intellectual ballast.[11]

Patient, detailed (and somewhat necessarily lengthy) analysis can demonstrate that the truth lies slightly closer to DeVitis's position than Graver's. Graver's judgment that "the ideas come on too casually and are never given sufficient articulation" is puzzling. If anything, the ideas are all too clearly signalled from the outset and too programmatically developed. Not twenty pages into the book, for example, Hillier has laid out quite thoroughly (in the unmailed letter to a superior that forms a very large part of the narrative) the sharp differences that exist between Roper's view of the world and human nature and his own view. The opposing views reduce themselves very neatly to the Pelagian/Augustinian conflict that consistently provides a basis for Burgess's novels. Despite his attendance with Hillier at the Catholic boys' school in Bradcaster named St. Augustine, Roper is, and has long been, a Pelagian. Even at school Roper replied in this way to Hillier's question, "What about good and evil?" "I think it's all a matter of ignorance and the overcoming of ignorance. Evil comes out of ignorance" (*TI,* 13). Later he says, "It's all environment, all conditioning" (*TI,* 49). A scientist and a religious skeptic, Roper is a rationalist, an empiricist, and a meliorist. With his belief that "life can be better and man nobler" (*TI,* 2–3), he comes very close, in Hillier's (and Burgess's) view to being a heretic. On the other hand, Hillier, like Burgess, inclines to the Augustinian view and, also like Burgess, employs Manichaeanism to explain the ineradicable presence of evil in the world. To explain the nature of the Cold War to the thirteen-year-old quiz kid, Alan Walters, Hillier readily invokes his author's very familiar Manichaean philosophy:

> Beyond God . . . lies the concept of God. In the concept of God lies the concept of anti-God. Ultimate reality is a dualism or a game for two players. We—people like me and my counterparts on the other side—we reflect that game. It's a pale reflection. There used to be a much brighter one, in the days when the two signs represented what are known as good and evil. That was a tougher and more interesting game, because one's opponent wasn't on the other side of a conventional net or line. He wasn't marked off by a special jersey or colour or race or language or allegiance to a particular historico-geographical abstraction. But we don't believe in good and evil any more. That's why we play this silly and hopeless little game. (*TI,* 119).

Hillier's increasing recognition that he is a player in "a silly and hopeless little game" forms the basis for seeing the novel as something very close to an allegory on the need for moral self-awareness and regeneration in the modern world. A few references and several allusions to Dante encourage the reader to see the spiritually empty Hillier much in the way the narrator of the *Divine Comedy* sees himself before his spiritual journey—as a man lost in a dark wood. Aware as he is of his "two chronic diseases of gluttony and satyriasis" (*TI,* 1), seeing himself as merely a "technician," "a void, a dark sack crammed with skills" (*TI,* 4), Hillier is ripe for the spiritual journey he is about to begin. "I don't mind games, but when they get too dirty, I don't think I want to play any more," he writes in the unmailed letter to his superior (*TI,* 51). A fellow passenger on the ship, Clara Walters, a Beatrice figure, is a beautiful young virgin of sixteen, her first name suggesting a light and radiance that can direct Hillier, in pure and holy love, ever onward and upward toward her. (That, although technically a virgin, Clara possesses a traveling library of sex manuals, is a means, perhaps, of deflating any serious allegorical implications, although it might also be just another way of indicating what, because of the interpenetration of opposites, "a bloody Manichean mess life is" [*TI,* 22].) More play occurs with the name Miss Devi. Her name suggests devil, and in the torrid sexual encounter between her and Hillier, "his soreness was first cooled then anointed by the heat of a beneficent hell that (Dante was right) found its location at earth's centre" (89). In Hindu religion, though, Devi, a deity, is the consort of Shiva the Destroyer.[12] It would seem that Miss Devi represents both the nature of woman and the sempiternal forces: creation and destruction, God and devil, heaven and hell; these, in Manichaean fashion, are all entwined.

Hillier had come to see the cold war struggle of East and West as only a "game," no real struggle of good and evil. Commitment even to this struggle, though, he had perceived as far better than no commitment at all. As he says to Alan, "Don't you think we'd all rather see devil-worship than bland neutrality?" (*TI,* 238). At this point, though, psychological and theological elements coalesce. To maintain a commitment to something both intellectually and emotionally apprehended as a game is to make an impossible demand of one's spirit. At the end of the novel Father Hillier, ordained Jesuit, has rediscovered his true spiritual self, and it will live vitally in active commitment. Already possessed of guile and subtlety, the new Jesuit will, as he explains to Alan, be "sneaking into the Iron Curtain countries, spying, being subversive. But the war won't be cold any more. And it won't be just between East and West" (*TI,* 239). What Hillier says in his part of the dialogue with the Walters teenagers is really rather portentious and somewhat murky "Manichee stuff," as Alan puts it (*TI,* 238). Burgess seems to signal his reader that he does not have to take this all that seriously if he does not want to. Elaborate play is the thing; if the play involves the reader's pursuit of some slippery ideas or flashes of paradox, so much the better.

Exaggerated claims regarding Burgess's totally successful embodiment of profoundly serious themes in this novel will probably, in the long run, be damaging to his reputation. Within the limits of his form, Burgess does marvellously well to successfully evoke his big themes, to present them playfully and unpretentiously, and to integrate them as well as he does with his other materials. To claim, or to expect, lurking depths of truly significant and artistically realized meaning is hopelessly unrealistic. Most readers will find delight enough in the novel as espionage fiction and as a send-up of other espionage novels. Some readers will delight too in the discovery of all sorts of intricately laid and interlocking symbolic correspondences (not discussed here) involving most certainly names, literary allusions, and, very probably, even numbers that appear in the novel. The critic Samuel Coale has intelligently noted the general "ludic loves" of Burgess, finding that his "sense of the game pervades his fiction."[13] With *Tremor of Intent* the reader will feel at ease in choosing to play—or stop playing—Burgess's games at any point or level at which his inclinations dispose him. Burgess's cleverness, here largely unforced, enthralls all the more.

Chapter Four

Dystopias and Cacotopias

Any reasonably informed discussion of utopian and antiutopian fiction in our own century must soon involve the names of H. G. Wells and George Orwell. Wells, the cheerful apostle of rationalism, scientism, and technology, believed that the world's people, all basically benevolent by innate disposition, could, at some sufficient point of general enlightenment, produce a New Jerusalem on this earth. Wells believed, as Burgess writes in *The Novel Now,* that "there was no such thing as Original Sin; man was born free to build good—not to earn it or inherit it by divine grace. Wells believed that a Utopia was possible; he called himself a Utopiographer."[1] Burgess, of course, would call him a Pelagian. Burgess notes, correctly it would seem, that Wells "died a disappointed liberal." When we think of Orwell, we are apt to think of him as the exact antithesis of Wells: we remember the starkly brutal admonitory parable that is *Nineteen Eighty-four.* But Burgess is right again when, in an essay titled "After Ford," he notes that "Orwell exhibits the sickness of a disillusioned liberal."[2] In *The Novel Now,* Burgess gravely delivers his own oft-repeated warning: "Liberalism breeds disappointment. . . Accept that man is imperfect, that good and evil exist, and you will not, like Wells, expect too much from him" (39).

The Wanting Seed

A major blemish in Burgess's own loosely dystopian *The Wanting Seed* is that the ideational content is not only too rigidly schematized but also it is too explicitly articulated by the antihero, Tristram Foxe. Here, for example, is Foxe on the liberal or Pelagian dream: "What destroys it, eh? He suddenly big-drummed [his teacher's] desk, shouting in crescendo, 'Disappointment. *Disappointment.* DISAPPOINTMENT.' He beamed. 'The governors,' he said, in a reasonable tone, 'become disappointed when they find that men are not as good as they thought they were. Lapped in their dream of perfection, they are horrified when the seal is broken and they see people as they really are."[3] Foxe, this embittered schoolteacher, explains, a few pages later, the nature of the Pelagian/Augustinian conflict in such a way that it could well serve as a primer for readers going on to other Burgess novels and thus numerous reencounters with the same theme.

The troubles that beset the planet in *The Wanting Seed,* though, are not primarily caused by the crackbrained schemes of naïvely liberal ideologues. Two related plagues threaten the race—overpopulation and massive food shortages. England (a chief member of Enspun or the English-Speaking Union) is bursting at the seams to the extent that the southern coastal resort of Brighton is now part of London and is, in fact, the administrative locus. Life, such as it is, is lived by nuclear families of no more than husband, wife, and one child, in small apartments in featureless skyscrapers. Population control is vigorously pursued by both "positive" means (career advancement for homosexuals and castrati; the omnipresent slogan "It's Sapiens to be Homo"; "condolence" money paid out by the Ministry of Infertility to parents bringing in child cadavers); and by the more unabashedly negative (prison terms for those who illegally bear children; death in "wars" where "enemies" are never seen, that is in large-scale exterminations; tacit approval of cannibalism). In Pelagian periods at least, life is colorless and flavorless; best epitomized by the food available—synthetic and quite literally tasteless.

The general grayness and tyrannical dullness at the beginning of *The Wanting Seed* are strongly redolent of *Nineteen Eighty-four.* Burgess follows Orwell closely in setting up three superstates. Burgess calls his Enspun, Ruspun, and Chinspun, whereas Orwell had called his Oceania, Eurasia, and Eastasia. Other parallels are also obvious. Is *Nineteen Eighty-four* a prediction, a warning, or a satire of forces and tendencies that existed while or before Orwell wrote? The tendency has been to apply the term anti-utopian or (the same thing) dystopian to both *Nineteen Eighty-four* and *The Wanting Seed.* Some problems exist with the application of these terms even to *Nineteen Eighty-four* (although it serves no purpose to discuss them here) but they prove even more problematic when applied to Burgess's novel. An anti-utopia must, in strict definition, be a species of satire, the satiric target being, of course, some addlebrained notions for the creation of utopia that have actually been set in motion. The satirist exposes to ridicule the hopelessly naïve, crackbrained ideas of the would-be utopian reformers, people who usually grossly misestimate human nature or else, through social or biological engineering, or through brute force, attempt to deny it. Readers are intended to laugh at—or be horrified by—the gross human distortions that occur in the dystopian societies as a result of the naïveté of the utopian dreamers. The anti-utopian writer serves to provide a social corrective: he/

she warns us off reformers of the same cast that we might discover in our own midst.

In his novels Burgess issues warnings aplenty about the baleful results of Pelagianism, naïve faith in human goodness and belief in human perfectibility. The world of *The Wanting Seed* is, however, not just a disastrously inadequate Pelagian society that will be exposed. Instead, Burgess is intent on making the point that, human nature being what it is, an inevitable, endless alternation of Pelagian and Augustinian periods will occur, separated always by ghastly, violent periods of transition. Foxe explicates the inexorable process that follows the severe disappointment of the liberal that marks an end to the Pelagian phase or "Pelphase": "Disappointment opens up a vista of chaos. There is irrationality, there is panic. When the reason goes, the brute steps in. . . Beatings-up. Secret police. Torture in brightly lighted cellars. . . And all this because of disappointment. The Interphase" (*WS,* 19). One might suppose that the Augustinian-leaning Burgess is suggesting that disappointment and the atrocities attendant upon it could be avoided if only man, with a balanced and steady-eyed view of his own sinful nature, just permanently wedded himself to Augustinianism. This turns out, however, not to be the case. As I mentioned in chapter 2, Burgess is not quite an out-and-out Augustinian. Foxe again explains to his class:

> the Interphase cannot, of course, last for ever. . . . The governors become shocked at their own excesses. . . . They relax their sanctions and the result is complete chaos. But, by this time, disappointment cannot sink any deeper. Disappointment can no longer shock the state into repressive action, and a kind of philosophical pessimism supervenes. In other words, we drift into the Augustinian phase, the Gusphase. The orthodox view presents man as a sinful creature from whom no good at all may be expected. A different dream, gentlemen, a dream which again, outstrips the reality. It eventually appears that human social behavior is rather better than any Augustinian pessimist has a right to expect, and so a sort of optimism begins to emerge. And so Pelagianism is reinstated. We are back in the Pelphase again. The wheel has come full circle. (*WS,* 23)

Because most of Burgess's novels are based, to greater or lesser extent, on the paradigm that Foxe—only ironically said to be "not a good teacher" (*WS,* 9)—so carefully articulates, the paradigm has unusual value, but it points up a critical problem with *The Wanting Seed.* The cyclical pattern, adumbrated here by Burgess through his character, is one of historical necessity—inexorable and unchangeable. In strict definition, satire of the inevitable, that which proceeds from the basic human condition or other totally unalterable forces, is impossible because the purpose of moral correction—a necessary ingredient—is precluded. It might also be argued that satire should get its targets in very sharp focus; in *The Wanting Seed* the cause and nature of the corruption is not carefully enough identified. The rulers (of Pelphase as well as Gusphase) are not utopian visionaries. They are men who give way naturally to excess because they confront the very real problem of massive, worldwide starvation (natural Malthusian checks and balances having failed), a problem for which the novel suggests no solution.

The definition of dystopian suggested above, while useful for providing a clarifying focus, is not, it must be admitted, one that has met with universal agreement. Critics, as Matthew Hodgart notes in his excellent study, *Satire,* have not been able "to reach agreement on the strict definition of satire."[4] The judgment that *The Wanting Seed* fails as a dystopian novel, then, might seem entirely Procrustean. Still, because of a soft, diffused focus and a mixture of modes and effects, the novel poses real problems of interpretation and evaluation. A disparaging early reviewer put it this way: "Liberals are apparently damned, so are conservatives; sex is ridiculed, as is the denial of sex—if, that is, any such judgments are compatible with schoolboyish giggling. What's the point?"[5]

Some warrant exists for seeing this novel as a blackly comic, philosophical entertainment on sociopolitical swings of the pendulum from (to use the necessary shorthand) liberal phases to conservative, back to liberal, and so on endlessly. Readers in Western nations might generally remark how Burgess, albeit with the exaggeration proper for the satirist, has mirrored some of the shifts we have been personal witness to since 1962, when the novel was written. Burgess's view of the dynamic of change is comic yet compassionate, the drama it creates unfolding as we follow Tristram, his wife Beatrice-Joanna, and his brother Derek from Pelphase through Interphase to Gusphase. The sexually compliant, adulterous, fecund Beatrice-Joanna is a wily earth mother with strong natural appetites for life. Derek, high government official in charge of the Ministry of Infertility, provides superabundant evidence that he is the blatant, swishy sort of homosexual even his own brother believes him to be; actually, he is carrying on a vigorous clandestine affair with Beatrice-Joanna while reaping all the rewards the Pelagian state bestows on the homosexual. We follow the weighed-down scholar-teacher-pedant Tristram through most of the novel, as he is plunged from his own wise but insulated and inert world into a world of paroxysm and bloodletting. As he travels, searching for his wife from whom he has become separated, he becomes part of a crowded human canvas on which Burgess depicts the extraordinary twitches and gyrations of people just released from all restraint, or a bit later, back under severe restraint.

The human spectacle is here magnified and distorted, many will feel (despite Auschwitz, Hiroshima, and Cambodia), in favor of the base, the ugly, the monstrous, the depraved, the grotesque. Some reviewers questioned whether Burgess was affirming anything at all as superior to anything else, or whether the book was a product of a kind of sophomoric, smart-alecky cynicism. One thing that can at least be said is that, as usual, Burgess's tilt is toward Augustinianism. Burgess reprehends the soul-dulling constraints of the radical social engineering of the Pelagian phase; for all their very human but entirely repellent excesses, he still prefers the sudden soarings of the human spirit that come with the unfettering of instinct in the Interphase and early Augustinian periods. The English critic Walter Allen explained Graham Greene's preference for the Augustinian way back in 1943, long before Burgess had published his first book, but provided a quintessentially important understanding of a large part of Burgess's fiction:

> It is plain that, confronted with evil on a universal scale, as we see it to-day, the Augustinian is much better equipped to meet it and explain it than the Pelagian. To the Augustinian it comes as no surprise at all; he can always say "I told you so." In the understanding and assessment of the human situation in such an age of violence as our own the Augustinian, for whom evil is endemic in man's nature, is at a tremendous advantage. How tremendous may be seen if we compare the present age with an age of similar violence, the Elizabethan period and the first half of the seventeenth century. England had its burnings and its martyrdoms, its civil war, yet in comparison with continental Europe was relatively peaceful. But how the Englishman reacted to those years of violence may be seen in the plays of the great Elizabethans: Marlowe, Shakespeare, Jonson, Webster, Tourneur, Ford, are horrified but fascinated; yet they can assimilate the violence, the evil; it is part and parcel of their own emotional world; it is what happens to man when the order, natural and supernatural, that curbs him, is broken. It does not surprise them, because the jungle is, as it were, man's natural state.[6]

If Burgess had contented himself simply with the castigation of Pelagian näveté *The Wanting Seed* would have been a less complex novel. By making the novel a comment on the necessary circularity of human history, Burgess blurred and diluted his satiric force but extended the novel into a tragicomic celebration of life. The comic dimension of the novel has not generally been recognized, but Burgess is quoted in a 1984 lecture as saying that the book "was a comic effort . . . to be laughed at but it was not to be seen as either prophetic or genuinely cacotopian."[7] When Burgess's readers see the shrivelled selves of the characters in the Pelagian phase, their own souls seem to contract. When readers and characters enter the Interphase, they witness murder, torture, human barbecues, and sexual orgies ritualized as fertility rites; and there is in this, with Manichaean paradox, an Elizabethan sort of blood-throbbing expansion of the human spirit. Sparks from Dionysian combustions of emotional release light the tinders under Apollonian intellect. Readers, attracted and repulsed at nearly the same time, experience a relatively complex aesthetic effect.

The Wanting Seed, though, is not entirely successful. The intended effects cannot always be defined as complex; sometimes they are simply confused. If the novel is ultimately a kind of tragicomedy, the characters do not have to remain two-dimensional, a limitation appropriate to satire but not one necessarily appropriate here. The idea of the endlessly alternating cycles (Pelagian/Augustinian) is pushed hard and very expressly, but with not quite the intellectual vigor or depth we might expect in a novel that seems internally to signal the presence of formidable informing ideas. The situations, while extreme, are not quite sustained and coordinated enough to etch themselves indelibly into memory and achieve the mythic power of *Nineteen Eighty-four* or *A Clockwork Orange.*

A Clockwork Orange

The sheer memorability of *A Clockwork Orange* points to its successful achievement of the mythic dimension. Burgess, however, has frequently expressed slight chagrin that this is his best-known book, indicating his feeling that it is a didactic little book, and, elsewhere, that it "was very much a *jeu de spleen* when I wrote it."[8] He has grown wearied, and become annoyed, by questioners who, having in mind mostly the near notorious film version of Stanley Kubrick, seek to elicit his thoughts on the pornography of violence and his own presumed abdication of the artist's social responsibility. Discussions of the comparative merits of the British and American versions (the latter appearing, until 1987, without the last chapter) have also long ceased to hold any real interest for him. Burgess's ostensible disinterest (which is perhaps, genuine embarrassment) occurs despite, or maybe because of, the fact that this is the book that altered his career and profoundly affected his life.

The British (or, possibly, North American) society to which the reader is introduced at the beginning of the novel is dull, grey, and oppressive. Although the terms Pelagianism/Augustinianism are not used, it is apparent, employing Foxe's lesson in *The Wanting Seed,* that the society depicted is in a late Pelagian phase, like the one in the opening of that novel. All citizens not children, nor with child, nor ill, are compelled by state law to work.[9] People live in "municipal flatblocks"; this night they have been instructed to tune into a "worldcast" on their tellies. The sought-after homogeneity of this engineered, perhaps one-world society, is thwarted only by the presence of teenage rebels who rule the night streets. The protagonist and our "humble narrator," fifteen-year-old Alex, is the foremost rebel of those we meet. The *nadsat* (teenage) language of Alex and his *droogs* (gang members) is one sharp indicator of their effort (a product, it would seem, of both instinct and will) to resist mindless standardization. In nadsat, in fact, "to rabbit" is to work, to do as Alex's pee and em (father and mother) do every day because they are like timid animals who run in circles and live in hutches, or, noting the probable Slavic (here Czech) etymology, they are robots. Animals or automatons, they are in either case dehumanized. Alex, seemingly depraved, is very human. On the axis of paradoxes like this, the novel turns.

Alex, killer, rapist, sadist, and maker of general mayhem at age fifteen, is, in fact, one of the mouthpieces for Burgess's own ideas. Addressing the reader about people's shocked dismay when confronted with manifestations of evil, he expresses a rather amazingly sophisticated anti-Pelagian view:

> this biting of their toe-nails over what is the *cause* of badness is what turns me into a fine laughing malchick. They don't go into what is the cause of *goodness,* so why of the other shop? If lewdies are good that's because they like it, and I wouldn't ever interfere with their pleasures, and so of the other shop. And I was patronizing the other shop. More, badness is of the self, the one, the you or me on our oddy knockies and that self is made by old Bog or God and is his great pride and radosty. But the not-self cannot have the bad, meaning they of the government and the judges and the schools cannot allow the bad because they cannot allow the self. And is not our modern history my brothers, the story of brave malensky selves fighting these big machines? I am serious with you, brothers, over this. But what I do I do because I like to do. (*CO,* 46–47)

Burgess insists that Alex's actions, atrocious assaults and all, proceed from deliberate choices of his own free will. The question, "What's it going to be then, eh?," which opens all three parts of the novel (*CO,* 3, 87, 151), and the last chapter as well (*CO,* 206), reinforces the idea that people are free to choose their own actions. Some readers have felt that Burgess has to shout this point at them because it goes against the evidence. Alex is, in their view, something very much like a robot programmed for violence, or, if not quite that, a young man who acts out in disturbed fashion a universal need to assert life and independence in a tyrannously dull society. Their point is that whether he likes it or not, Alex's life has been heavily molded by his environment. If the environment were not so oppressively constrictive, Alex would not have the need to act out his rebellion so outrageously. Thus, environment has made Alex what he is, and it is the job of the behavioral psychologist to prescribe the means whereby emotional imbalances may be redressed. In insisting that Alex acts out of free choice, these readers maintain, Burgess has disregarded his own evidence. These are the readers, then, more inclined to accept the claims of Drs. Brodski, Branom, and cohorts to the effect that they are not doing something that goes against nature by conditioning Alex toward the good; rather, they are removing the "error" of some past conditioning that inclined Alex so heavily toward "the old ultra-violence." Actually, the freewill/determinism conflict in the work of Burgess, as in that of most writers, takes the reader down a dark, tricky, winding road.

Thematically, the behaviorists in the novel are portrayed as not particularly intelligent villains. Burgess's antibehaviorist stance in the novel is so pronounced that the print media have felt that Burgess cast himself as the bête noir of B. F. Skinner, thus virtually announcing himself as available on call to refute any proclamations of the renowned behaviorist about necessary abridgments of freedom and dignity. Burgess very unfairly stacks the deck against the behaviorists, say many who regard *A Clockwork Orange* as a thesis or philosophical novel. In the novel the behaviorists are pliant tools of a totalitarian state. They employ Ludovico's technique on Alex because the authorities need to get his type out of the prisons to accommodate hordes of political prisoners (the Interphase obviously having begun, liberal belief in basic goodness has apparently given way to sore disappointment because of the likes of Alex). The behavioral psychologists are seen as two-dimensional, uncultured shrinkers of the soul, clumsy in the application of procedures they themselves have devised. Dr. Brodsky says of music, "I know nothing about it myself. It's a useful emotional heightener, that's all I know" (*CO,* 131). He is unconcerned that the radical aversive conditioning process—Ludovico's technique—has destroyed Alex's enjoyment of Beethoven along with his ability to carry out violence.

Burgess's short novel inclines toward the fable, and it is unreasonable to expect that its sociophilosophical ideas are argued with the concentrated weight and scrupulous fairness with which they would be argued in an academic treatise. Burgess's novel did, though, so memorably strike some decidedly contemporary chords that it provided a ready reference point for certain social issues that were seriously, and heatedly, debated in the real world. By the mid-1970s aversive conditioning was making headway in the U.S. penal system: some inmates were given shots of apomorphine, inducing violent vomiting and dry retching; others were given Anectine, which produces agonizing sensations of suffocation and drowning; sex offenders were given electric shocks to the groin. Such practices were generally successfully opposed by the American Civil Liberties Union and other groups as "cruel and unusual punishment"; *A Clockwork Orange* was almost always at least mentioned in media reports about litigation connected with this troubling but ethically complex issue.

A Clockwork Orange stayed in the news because of the currency and vigor of its ideas, but it is a significant work of literature for other reasons. Burgess employs black humor and the grotesque—two highly favored forms of the late sixties—more integrally, and therefore more successfully, than any other writer of the period with the possible exceptions of Joseph Heller and Günter Grass. What might be referred to as the "violent grotesque" is employed at the very outset as the demonically engaging Alex recounts for us, his "brothers," with relish and a delicious savoring of detail, how he and his "droogies" (gangmates) perpetrated various nightly horrors: an old man returning from the library is insulted and assaulted; his false teeth are ripped from his mouth and crunched by the stomps of the teens' heavy boots; heavy-ringed knuckles slam into the old man's bared gums until his mouth is a riot of red; he is stripped and kicked for good measure. This is only the very beginning of violence that exceeds that of de Sade in intensity if not imaginativeness. Storekeepers, husband and wife, are brutally beaten and robbed; a writer's wife (Mrs. F. Alexander) is savagely gang raped in her home and her husband is forced to watch helplessly; two barely pubescent girls of ten are raped; an old woman (the Cat Lady), a well-to-do recluse, meets her death trying to defend herself and her valuables during a robbery. All this—and more—is accomplished by Alex, Dim, Pete, and George on the two consecutive days that comprise part 1, eighty-four pages of the novel.

The high level of Burgess's black comic craft is testified to by his ability to make us approach the vicious assault of an old lady with something very much like mirth and excitement. Burgess writes in his introduction to the New American Edition that his "intention in writing the work was to titillate the nastier propensities of my readers" (*CO,* x). He might be thought almost to prove his theological (Augustinian) point by the success with which he carries out his intention. Readers come to have ambivalent feelings only when their moral reactions, linguistically stupefied into unwatchfulness, suddenly rouse themselves and come panting up indignantly. By the near-miracle of his craft, particularly by his linguistic inventiveness, Burgess has succeeded in temporarily making his readers one with the wantonly brutal young assaulters:

> He [the old man returning from the library] looked a malenky bit poogly when he viddied the four of us . . . coming up so quiet and polite and smiling, but he said: "Yes? What is it?" in a very loud teacher-type goloss, as if he was trying to show us he wasn't poogly. . . . "You naughty old veck, you," I said, and then we began to filly about with him. Pete held his rookers and George sort of hooked his rot open for him and Dim yanked out his false zoobies, upper and lower. He threw these down on the pavement and then I treated them to the old boot-crush, though they were hard bastards like, being made of some new horrorshow plastic stuff. The old veck began to make sort of shumbling shooms—"wuf waf wof"—so Georgie let go of holding his goobers apart and just let him have one in the toothless rot with his ringy fist, and that made the old veck start moaning a lot then, then out comes the blood, my brothers, real beautiful. So all we did then was to pull his outer platties off, stripping him down to his vest and long underpants (very starry; Dim smecked his lead off near), and then Pete kicks him lovely in his pot, and we let him go. (*CO,* 9–10)

What forestalls reader revulsion at this basically realistic scene of violence is distancing through the use of invented language. "It is as if we were trying to read about violence in a foreign language and finding its near-incomprehensibility getting in the way of a clear image," Burgess says in a *New York Times* piece.[10] The distinct teenage language serves also to reawaken the reader's awareness of the anarchic impulse of the teenager and the instinct to be one with the herd, to regard other groups just as "other," utterly alien, in no way like the self. The original (British; now "New American") ending emphasizes that Alex and his droogs should be seen first as teenagers before they are seen as all men. These teenagers have their own language, *nadsat* (the Russian word for teen), a language that the reader, seeing the words repeatedly in context, will soon assimilate. In the novel Dr. Branom explains to Dr. Brodsky its provenance: "Odd bits of rhyming slang . . . , a bit of gipsy talk, too. But most of the roots are Slav. Propaganda. Subliminal penetration" (*CO,* 132). Actually, gypsy elements are virtually indiscernible; Cockney influences are quite noticeable, but not too important; words of Russian origin are heavily present and Burgess adapts them, with marvelous felicity, to various purposes. A few of the Burgess words convey a sharp sensory vividness through onomatopoeic effect. For example, in gang warfare, Dim's most skillfully employed weapon is his "oozy," his "real horrorshow length of chain" (*CO,* 20), twice round about his waist. As Geoffrey Aggeler remarks, a "bicycle chain. . . , its shiny coils shaken out along a sidewalk or whizzing through the night air, is so much more like an 'oozy' than a 'chain.' "[11] Or, we might take the word "horrorshow" from the same sentence. A believable anglicization of the Russian word *khorosho* (good, well, excellent), it conforms to Alex's propensities exactly, for to him nothing is more excellent than "a bit of the old ultra-violence," his personally choreographed "horror shows" that he puts on nearly every night. The most important function of the language is the softening of the otherwise unbearably repulsive violence, but the violence itself is thematically integral. Not at all pornographic, the grotesque violence is the means by which Burgess attacks the failures of rationalism. While it has proved difficult to define the grotesque precisely, many commentators seem to agree that it frequently involves the sudden subversion of the apparent world of order and form by the shocking appearance of the absurd, purely irrational, or primally chaotic. Naïve liberals and rationalists willfully shut their eyes to primal discords, but they are forced open by the "horror shows" staged by a Hitler or an Alex. Frequently used as a means of exposing the naïveté of excessive rationalism, the grotesque is associated with Conrad's Kurtz, the liberal humanist who, in quick descent, comes to preside over "unspeakable rites"; and Golding's Piggy, the bespectacled emissary of rationalism whose precious brain is spilled grotesquely out on a rock. Alex is a producer of the grotesque, but Alex is in all of us, which is the point that Burgess most cleverly gets across as he disorients his readers just enough by the language to cause them vicariously to share the thrill of cruelty.

Alex (his name seemingly suggesting "without law") is more an extraordinary teenage rebel than he is Satan or even Dionysus (as Burgess's own ending makes clear), but he has a winsome effect on the reader because, in a world of pale neutrals, he has energy and commitment. (By contrast, Alex's parents "rabbit" every day at mindless jobs, stare vacuously each evening at insipid programs on the telly, and retire to bed, sleeping pills in their bloodstreams, lest they be awakened by the blast of Alex's stereo.) From the beginning we sympathize with Alex because he is, in his own words, "our faithful narrator" and "brother." This is an old novelistic trick, readers tending to sympathize with anyone, save a total monster, who continually tells them about his life and makes them vicariously share it. Then, too, Alex has wit, some intelligence, a love of classical music, his gift of pungent language, and a kind of artistry in his violence. We react with sympathy and pathos when Alex falls into the clutches of the state, particularly when it attempts "rehabilitation" by reducing him to a "clockwork orange." This term is explained by F. Alexander, Burgess's mock double and another ironic mouthpiece, a pompous sort who has just completed a flatulently styled tome titled *A Clockwork Orange:* "The attempt to impose upon man, a creature of growth and capable of sweetness, to ooze juicily at the last round the bearded lips of God, to attempt to impose, I say, laws and conditions appropriate to a mechanical creation, against this I raise my sword-pen" (*CO,* 26–27).

Alex does become a clockwork orange temporarily when, in order to gain a much speedier release from prison, he assents to Ludovico's technique. The "therapy" consists of showing Alex atrocity films after he has been given a drug to induce pain and nausea. The association of violence and nausea incapacitates Alex from further violent action, any attempt instantaneously provoking literal wretchedness. Released, Alex finds himself quickly at the mercy of all those whom he had previously victimized. In a schematic plot framework almost parodically designed to show retributive justice in action, each of these victims pays back the now defenseless Alex. One of those who gets the satisfaction of a payback is F. Alexander, reputedly—and, in his own mind—an idealist and bastion of liberal values. His view of man had gone untested, however. An unsuspected part of himself powerfully leaps out when he discovers that Alex was one of the rapists responsible for his wife's death. Very much human, he is not above the philosophy of an eye for an eye. This is one of Burgess's "proofs" that evil is endemic in man, that it has always been there and always will be. Another proof is found in Alex's prison reading: the "big book," the Bible, in which he "read of these starry yahoodies tolchocking each other and then peeting their Hebrew vino and getting on to the bed with their wives' like handmaidens, real horrorshow" (*CO,* 91).

Alex suffers greatly—emotionally, mentally, and even physically—as a result of the Ludovico "therapy." Burgess's point is clear, since, in fact, it is presented somewhat didactically through a third spokesman in the novel, the prison Charlie; but Burgess's expression of it outside the novel is even clearer: "What my and Kubrick's parable tries to state is that it is preferable to have a world of violence undertaken in full awareness—violence chosen as an act of will—than a world conditioned to be good or harmless."[12] Not to be able to choose is not to be human. If evil were somehow to be eradicated, its opposite—goodness—would, having no meaning, cease to exist. "Life is sustained by the grinding opposition of moral entities," Burgess writes in the introduction (*CO,* ix) to the New American Edition. In most discussions that the book has generated this prime thematic point has generally been agreed with. The expostulations of B. F. Skinner have, though, given some listeners serious pause. Basically (most notably in *Beyond Freedom and Dignity*), Skinner argues that the very survival of the race depends upon the surrender of some freedom, as that term has been historically understood. No Augustinian, Skinner also pleads that we examine carefully the operant conditioning that underlies people's choices to behave poorly. He has made clear that his strong preference is always for positive reinforcement rather than aversive techniques to correct maladaptive behavior. Burgess likes to make the point that evil exists, and must exist, as a part of the human self; he is fond of pointing out that "live" is "evil" spelled backwards.

The novel's ending has always been problematic. Burgess's last chapter, the twenty-first, was deleted from the first American edition (Norton, 1963) and all subsequent American editions until 1987, although this chapter appeared in the British (Heinemann) edition and most foreign translations from the very first (1962). Burgess maintains that Norton insisted on the excision; Norton maintains it was only suggested as an artistic improvement. Kubrick's boldly imaginative film version (1971), which spiralled the novel to far greater fame, ended as the American version did. Persuasive arguments can be made for the superiority of either version. The twentieth chapter (chapter 6 of part 3) ends as the government authorities, under strong pressure from politically aroused public opinion, reverse the effects of the aversive therapy by deep "hypnopaedia," restoring Alex to his old self—he "viddies" himself "carving the whole litso of the creching world with my cut-throat britva" (205). Chapter 21—the famous deleted chapter—presents a mellowing, increasingly reflective, eighteen-year-old Alex who is coming to see that this previous violent behavior was childishly perverse. He thinks of marriage, stability, and the son he one day hopes to have. He contemplates explaining to his son all his own past crimes as an admonition, but then thinks that he "would not really be able to stop him [prevent his son from enacting similar crimes]. And nor would he be able to stop his own son" (*CO,* 218).

The truncated ending, which leaves the reader with a stark presentation of unregenerate evil, surely carries more impact. Burgess's own ending, besides having just a whiff of sentimentality about it, is easily exposed to ridicule. Detractors might say that it reduces the novel to a spectacular but largely meaningless comment on those oh-so-difficult teenagers and their problems of adjustment. Burgess prefers his own ending, with his own worldview, his own "theology." The truncated version, closing with a view of unregenerate human evil, would be a more fitting conclusion for a William Golding novel. With his own ending, Burgess implies a more nearly equal tug from the Pelagian and Augustinian poles, proving once again that he is not quite an Augustinian, and that he is a believer in eternally recurrent cycles. He writes that the Norton editors believed in 1962 that the last chapter "was bland" and "showed a Pelagian unwillingness to accept that a human being could be a model of unregenerable evil" (*CO,* ix). The truncated ("Augustinian") version, he says was "sensational," but not a "fair picture of human life" (*CO,* ix). No matter what the reader's perspective, *A Clockwork Orange* provides a picture that remains painted on the walls of the mind near the place where the conscious and subconscious meet.

1985

Burgess the always informed, consistently engaging, and altogether superior literary journalist combines with Burgess the novelist to produce the anti-utopian *1985*. The first 106 of this book's 272 pages are devoted to a lively, very particular, wide-ranging, and often incisive discussion of the best known of all anti-utopian books, George Orwell's *Nineteen Eighty-four.* The rest of the book (save for an epilogue) is Burgess's own fiction, which a large number of reviewers found pallid and unimaginative. Several deemed the expressly invited comparison of *1985* to *Nineteen Eighty-four* stunning foolhardiness on Burgess's part, since they saw Orwell as powerful, imaginative, and even politically sophisticated when contrasted with Burgess. They said *1985* lacks artistic vision, imaginative energy, and genuine political understanding. Not totally unreasonably, some thought the Burgess fiction mostly just a petulant, unimaginative compendium of his own personal irritants. Burgess actually tries—not quite successfully—to provide an effective blend of the fabulistic and realistic modes so as to make some telling comment on the present state of England.

Writing in 1978, Burgess was not attempting any daring forecast of a Britain only seven years in the future. He had to know well that he was taking no great imaginative leap. Rather, his point was more to illustrate that although the country was not rushing headlong toward the unmitigated horror of Big Brother in 1984 or 1985, it was already well caught in an undesirable drift. This drift would, in Burgess's view, carry the presently torpid British to a bad place, a cacotopia—not nightmare territory, but a bad enough place nonetheless.

In *1985* the United Kingdom has become Tucland, a failed workers' paradise in which the Trades Union Congress has accumulated so much power that the country is in the strangulating grasp of "holistic syndicalism." The antihero, Bev Jones (his first name suggesting Bevin or Bevan), has a wife in the hospital and a moderately retarded thirteen-year-old daughter at home, "a victim of bad medicine, bad air, bad food, farcical education, a despicable popular culture" (*1985,* 116). (Like Tristram Foxe of *The Wanting Seed,* Bev is a teacher of history who is able to establish a conceptual perspective most of the populace cannot.) Fire breaks out at the hospital where workers are on strike; fire fighters are already on a strike of their own; and police and army, with syndicalist solidarity, refuse to intervene. Ellen Jones is finally brought out dying; reaching to embrace her, Bev discovers "a handful of scorched skin and, under it, cooked meat" (*1985,* 113). Bev tears up his own union card. Vaguely subversive and recalcitrant, Bev is arrested and packed off to a T.U.C. Rehabilitation Center. Despite eventual release, and a few flickerings of hope—one kindled by his association with a mysterious Colonel Lawrence, leader of an armed resistance group—Bev finally succumbs to emotional beleaguerment and a feeling of emptiness. Rearrested, he throws himself up against an electrified fence and dies, although he had, until the end, spoken out bravely against "an insane morbid slothful State philosophy" (*1985,* 214).

Burgess's characterization in *1985* is two-dimensional. That comes, though, with the dystopian territory, and it comes also because the people of Tucland are thin, hollow creatures, starved even of a basic impulse to life. But as in *A Clockwork Orange,* a saving remnant of those who are committed to life does exist. The teenage gangs (*kumina,* as they are called, from the Swahili prefix that means teen) that prey upon the Londoners of Tucland bear some basic similarities to Alex and his droogs. For each group, the seemingly gratuitous acts of violence it constantly commits are its means of rebellion against a society that has institutionalized dullness and dehumanized its people. The kumina gang members perceive their intolerable grievance with an even greater clarity of vision than does Alex. Bev asks one gang member if his parents feel that the country is in a mess. His reply is, "They say nothing. They consume. But it's got to be a mess, because it's so fucking *dull*" (*1985,* 145). Burgess here, as elsewhere, associates dullness and hollowness with moral neutrality. In *1985* the state itself is the "Great Neutral." In the Manichaean duoverse conflict is creative. In the clash of the eternal opposites vitality is generated and man is invested with a sense of his full humanity. History is cyclical; nothing will ever stop completely the coming together of the opposites, because that is part of an inexorable process. In *1985,* however, we observe a situation in which the dynamic is severely retarded. It is as if there were an agglomeration of totally inert forces at the center of an electromagnetic field; no movement occurs because there is no gravitation toward either pole with the consequent energetic reaction that that would produce. In a passage central to the book's argument, Bev explains the temporary suspension of an essential part of the socioeconomic-political dynamic in this way to some kumina gang members:

> Now I come to the Great Contradiction. With a Socialist State you don't strictly need unions any more. Why not? Because the workers are officially in power, and who do they have to defend themselves against? East European Socialism has no unions, and that's logical. But British syndicalism, once started, has to go on existing. It needs its opposite still. Of course, there are still a few private bosses around, but the State is the main employer. You still have the old dichotomy of employer and employee. The workers have to regard their own political executive not as an aspect of themselves but as an entity they have to oppose. They oppose, and the opposition has to give in, because its wage demands are met and inflation flourishes. (*1985,* 146).

Since genuine opposition is needed for a true dynamic, we find in Tucland no true movements but only small spirals turned by men hard to differentiate from shadows. But while real movement can be retarded, it cannot be held back entirely; the forces of history are at work churning waves in what may have seemed to be stagnant ponds. In *1985* the tide of Islam in England becomes increasingly powerful, and because, as a driver who picks up the hitchhiking Bev says to him in words with which he agrees, "The big difference between Islam and the materialistic syndicalist states is the difference between God and a bottle of beer" (*1985,* 205), a sufficiently formidable opposition is created. History's wheel will spin, and the cacotopia of Tucland will pass.

Some will say that Burgess is a lightweight as a political economist and that the (to him) unforeseen, rapid turning of one of history's small wheels knocked him over. The coming to power of the Thatcher government in 1979 may be thought to have rendered obsolete Burgess's dire predictions just a year after they were made. Of course, Burgess's thoughts about the postwar English malaise were not original either: a familiar line of Tory thought and rhetoric runs parallel to the one Burgess charts here. In the essay portion of his book Burgess expends much effort in a partly successful attempt to convince the reader that *Nineteen Eighty-four* is, by and large, a "melodramatization" of Britain in 1948. *1985* is a "melodramatization" of Britain in 1978, an already pitiable place soon, Burgess thought, to become even worse. Although an expatriate, Burgess was apparently genuinely indignant about the current state of England, and mental muscles atwitch, felt the need to flagellate something. *1985* is a polemic, sometimes sputtering in its plot, and sometimes sanctimonious even in the delivery of a cliché.

Still, *1985* is a somewhat better novel than has generally been allowed. As any good dystopian novel should, it opposes certain life-denying forces that any reader—liberal or conservative—will agree should be opposed. It comes out in favor of "the right of man to loneliness, eccentricity, rebellion, genius; the superiority of man over men" (*1985,* 183). This has been said before, and in more fully imagined fables, making it sound slightly pious here. Burgess quotes the Savage in *Brave New World* in one of the essays in *Urgent Copy:* "I want God, I want poetry, I want real danger, I want freedom, I want goodness. I want sin."[13] This is exactly what Burgess wants. What he stands staunchly against in all three of his dystopian novels (and others) is any violation or abridgment of man's true freedom, particularly his freedom of moral choice, the essence and jewel of man's humanity. He is opposed to apathy, indifference, and moral neutrality, although his fiction fully suggests how, with the grand wars of the opposites going on constantly about us, we might very well feel small, inert, and paralyzed. Apathy—torpor, moral neutrality–Burgess insists, is the deadly and all-pervasive sin of our times, a not very surprising phenomenon given the continuing diminution of modern man and the constant, spiritually disheartening expansion of forces not easily susceptible to his control.

Chapter Five

Torpid, Vulgar, Debased and "Neutral": The Sad State of England

What might be termed the "condemnation of neutrality theme" is a persistent one in Burgess's novels. We have seen its presence not just in *1985,* but also in *Tremor of Intent, Honey for the Bears,* and even *The Long Day Wanes.* Its antecedents are in Conrad, Eliot (one should think of *The Waste Land* as well as "The Hollow Men"), and Greene, among others. Greene has also had a serious flirtation with Manichaeanism, and if his dualism, replete with its central good/evil paradox, finds its origins in Plato, Augustine, and Eliot, there is also, in his *The Heart of the Matter* (the title itself and the African setting providing clues to this) a deliberate devolution from Conrad's *Heart of Darkness,* which, in turn, gives off some carefully tuned echoes from Dante's "Inferno." Marlow's listeners on board the *Nellie*—the Director of Companies, the Lawyer, the Accountant, and the unnamed narrator—seem clearly intended as moral neutrals themselves, people consigned in death to Dante's Vestibule of Hell, a place specially prepared for the neutrals, the trimmers, the morally uncommitted, the forever lukewarm. Virgil describes them thusly to Dante (in John Ciardi's translation of the *Divine Comedy*):

> These are the nearly soulless
> whose lives concluded neither blame nor praise.
>
> They are mixed here with that despicable corps
> of angels who were neither for God nor Satan,
> but only for themselves. The High Creator
>
> scourged them from Heaven for its perfect beauty,
> and Hell will not receive them since the wicked
> might feel some glory over them.[1]

Although we cannot be certain, Dante very possibly finds warrant for his presentation of these opportunists or neutrals in St. John's deliberately jolting admonition to the proudly complacent and self-satisfied members of the church in Laodicea, a people who had relaxedly accommodated themselves, with broad assurance of their own favor, to the secular world around them: "Because thou art lukewarm, and neither cold nor hot, I will spew thee out of my mouth" (Revelation 3:16).

In *Heart of Darkness* Kurtz is, in Marlow's words, "the nightmare of my choice" because constant niggling self-deceit and hypocrisy, conscious or unconscious, have ceased to be a part of him. There is a kind of mad courage in his descent into his own primal, terrifying darkness. Kurtz is offered to us in stark contrast to the respectable and complacent businessmen on board the *Nellie* as well as the "papier-mâché Mephistopheles" who is the brickmaker and the "flabby, pretending, weak-eyed devil" of a manager. "Mistah Kurtz —he dead" is one of the two epigraphs to Eliot's "The Hollow Men" because in a world populated by timid wraiths, the Kurtzes are, for the most part, dead or nonexistent, and that is why it is suggested, in the concluding lines of the poem, that "the world ends / not with a bang but a whimper." Burgess, too, sees today's Western world as heavily populated by the timid and lukewarm. There are, of course, exceptions. Alex of *A Clockwork Orange* is the most notable, being a nightmare of Burgess's choice.

Time and again Burgess presents England as a tepid, lukewarm country, those adjectives frequently being expressly used. Burgess indicates that because he is "cradle Catholic," filled early with the drama of God/Devil, salvation/damnation, he always felt estranged from the English tepidity that (in his view) inheres in the Anglican church. In many of his novels Burgess thematically suggests that an equation exists between moral neutrality and cultural and spiritual atrophy. The spectrelike figures that populate the London of *The Waste Land,* Burgess finds in great abundance in post–World War II England.

The Right to an Answer

The Right to an Answer is clearly Burgess's best novel on "the post-war English mess." A number of this novel's scenes are set in a pub, but here, as everywhere, there is sterility. The pub, that venerable British institution, is no longer a place of conviviality and good fellowship, a place in which a man can release his innate and healthy vitality and expand his social nature. The habitués of the Black Swan pub wander in bleary-eyed from staring mindlessly for hours at their tellies, complaining only that a local church steeple interferes with their reception. Trying hard, with a force of desperation behind them, to discover a bit of fun, they succeed only in promoting some very stale and unexciting weekend adultery with people drifting as badly as themselves. Ted Arden, barkeep and owner, a literal descendant of Shakespeare, presides over all this with a trumped-up Elizabethan largesse. Almost ritualistically, he dispenses stout, as if it were the sacrament, to a congregation hungry for any sort of meaning to their lives, while all the while his cash register mind clicks away at the pounds and shillings he is taking in.

It is to this kind of life in the smug suburb of a large Midland city that the narrator and protagonist, J. W. Denham, returns for a visit after a long stay in the Far East where he works for a British firm. The querulous Denham does not at all like what he sees: a "great democratic mess in which there's no hierarchy, no scale of values, everything's as good—and therefore as bad—as everything else."[2] Denham sees tawdriness and corruption all about him, but his own behavior allows scarcely any distance between himself and the milieu he denounces. Burgess is fully aware of this irony, and it gives the book a dimension of moral complexity—coupled with good comedy—that books of reactionary sentiment such as *1985* or *The Clockwork Testament* do not have. The complexity is heightened by the introduction into this desiccated society of a Mr. Raj, a Ceylonese sociologist, himself a morally ambiguous figure as well as a catalytic force.

Raj, who had met Denham earlier in Ceylon, is writing a thesis titled *Popular Conceptions of Racial Differentiation* at a Midland university near the home Denham shares with his father. Raj takes an immediate liking to Denham's father and soon moves in with the elderly gentleman. Raj is the second "outsider" on the scene (the younger Denham, the narrator, being the first) and his perspective and reactions enrich the novel both thematically and tonally. Burgess had, in fact, remarked on the usefulness of the device of the outsider in this novel: "to look at England as an unusually knowledgeable foreigner might, to study its scene, its people, its way of life from the outside, at a certain ironic distance."[3] Additionally, though, the somewhat impenetrable Raj is a fascinatingly rich character. He is full of contradictions, yet he is totally believable. For example, he earnestly professes the necessity for universal brotherly love, yet he displays a pronounced antiblack prejudice. Almost comically self-assured at first, he gets most of what he wants by very clearly insinuating to people that any refusal is a shameful admission of prejudice. Encountering some real prejudice, he resorts to his fists. It begins to appear that the Ceylonese does not know the

West nearly so well as he had thought: he has, according to Denham, "an outstanding, astounding capacity for getting into trouble, a genius undreamed of, unthwartable by any number of good intentions" (*RTA*, 127).

Pathos and comedy begin to combine in the novel as the rather aggressive self-assurance of both Raj and the younger Denham begins to fade. Their increasing awareness of moral complexity (largely connected with the suburban spouse switching), imposes burdensome demands. Raj goes from a figure of fun to a villain of sorts, and then, simply, to a fellow human whose suffering is to be pitied. Love and honest human emotion bring Raj low. Raj prepares rich curries for the elder Denham who is amazed at his own gustatory delight. The old man's system, though, is shocked and unprepared, and he is soon dead. Denham cruelly attacks Raj for his father's death, even giving way to racial insult. The intense Raj is himself unprepared for any connection with the "bit of fun," the locals' term for their Saturday night spouse switching. To Raj's ear this is "bitter fun," and his misapprehension proves prophetic. Raj falls hopelessly in love with Alice Winterbottom, one of the swappers, and has no good idea how to proceed. Denham's sought-after advice proves inefficacious, and the result is disastrous. Raj kills Billy Winterbottom, the husband, and then, winking, fatally fires a pistol into his own head as Denham stands watching. Raj has been a victim of his own self-deceptions, but the self-deceptions of the society into which he innocently intrudes are responsible too. The complacent English have forgotten about both the power of unleashed human emotion and the deep, mostly logical sense that underlies the moral verities. The ultimate conflict is not that of East/West but of understanding/delusion.

Denham, also a complex figure both morally and psychologically, can also be summed up only at the risk of oversimplification. At the outset he is largely self-righteous. He condemns the casual sex of the Black Swan, but has long enjoyed the services of Asian women. Basically, he thinks he can afford to feel superior to the laughably messy entanglements of others because he has no entanglements of his own save his love for his father. He initially fails to see that his own detachment from a degraded world that he smugly thinks himself superior to is no sign of genuine superiority but only a selfish and sickly refusal to commit himself to life. He rationalizes his failure to engage life by trotting out a prepared bit of self-manufactured philosophy that holds that stability must be valued over freedom. It is having too much freedom that produces, he says, the passionless weekend adulteries. In actuality, though, Denham's lack of commitment reveals him to be no more than an intelligent and self-deceiving neutral, in self-imposed human exile wherever he goes. That Burgess's novel is slightly more than just a zany comedy or an emotionally arresting tragicomedy is proven by the modest but real movements toward moral self-awareness that Denham makes before the novel is through. *The Right to an Answer* is a highly flavored satire that provides, as satire should, the sustenance of moral comment.

The Doctor Is Sick

If Denham had been close to emotional ossification at the beginning of *A Right to an Answer,* so too is Edwin Spindrift, protagonist of *The Doctor Is Sick.* In outward circumstances, though, this lecturer in linguistics resembles Burgess far more closely than Denham. This is, in fact, one of Burgess's most highly autobiographical novels, its subject matter, a central part of a story Burgess has told so frequently that it has come to achieve near mythic dimension. In 1959 Burgess was invalided home from Brunei (where he had been an educational consultant) with a suspected brain tumor. With only the slightest of variations, Spindrift's story is Burgess's: Spindrift is "a lecturer on linguistics in a college in Burma who had one day, quite without warning, fallen on the lecture-room floor while lecturing on linguistics."[4] When the same thing happened to Burgess in Brunei, he was sent to the National Hospital for Nervous Diseases in London, and when the novel opens that certainly seems to be where Spindrift is too.

As the novel begins, Spindrift feels that he is in the process of being reduced to a thing. In *Little Wilson and Big God* Burgess gives us his own experience: "I was placed in a huge ward full of neurological ailments. The man in the next bed had a face fixed in an *homme qui rit* rictus. . . . 'We'll soon put that grin right,' said his doctor, who saw the face as merely another limb. . . . A patient in a bed opposite had been reduced to the mere fodder of apparatus like an octopus" (*LWBG,* 444). In the novel the very first words are given to a neurologist: " 'And what is *this* smell?' asked Dr. Railton. He thrust a sort of inkwell under Edwin's nose" (1). Burgess was tested exactly in this way. "How would you define *spiral?*" (*DIS,* 2), asks Dr. Railton. The same question was asked of Burgess by Dr. Roger Bannister, first man to crack the four-minute mile barrier (Burgess mistakenly credits him with a one-minute mile!). Railton too was famous in another arena: he was a trumpet player well-known to television audiences. (Is the "rail" of his name intentionally suggestive of Bannister?)

Illusion/reality confusions and problems of identity are two of twentieth-century literature's most common themes, and they are central ones in *The Doctor Is Sick,* which is a comic picaresque, but also more than that. Moral and psychological concerns mix. Like Denham, Spindrift is pushed into a quest for a more true identity and meaningful engagement with other people and the real world. It is meaningfully ironic that Dr. Spindrift (with his Ph.D. in linguistics, he is the doctor of the title) should have any thought about being "thingified" by the hospital. Brain tumor or not, this doctor was already sick. Narrow and obsessive specialist that he is, he has reduced himself to a thing. A problem with sexual potency is the physical manifestation of his emotional disengagement, but it causes Spindrift no concern. As his wife drifts away from him, he gives overwhelming concentration to a phonemic analysis of the bilabial fricative. Any knowledge of man's emotional nature is as dead in Spindrift as his libido. Testing once more, Railton asks, "What's the difference between *gay* and *melancholy?*" Spindrift replies, "One is monosyllabic, the other tetrasyllabic. One is of French, the other of Greek, derivation" (*DIS,* 16). Whether a partial cause or symptom of his emotionless state, Spindrift and his wife—like Burgess and his first wife—have an "open marriage": "He and Sheila had long ago agreed that sexual infidelity was not really infidelity at all. You could accept a drink or a cigarette from somebody, why not also an hour or two in bed" (*DIS,* 13)? It is probably significant that the idea was mostly Sheila's (as it was Lynne Burgess's).

Spindrift's spiritual/psychological quest begins in earnest as he undertakes a quite literal quest through nighttime London in search of the promiscuous Sheila. Resentful of the hospital's treatment and suddenly jealous of his wife's latest paramour, Spindrift, pajama-clad and with his head shaved for his operation, flees into the streets of Bloomsbury and Soho. A whole series of robust (if just slightly overworked) comic scenes follow. Comedy—zany, satiric, and black—clearly dominates, but Burgess frames it mythically. The plunge of the ivory-tower pedant into the murky pools of London is much like a journey to the underworld that confers, by the time of ascent, knowledge of life and of the self. Certain portions of these scenes are clearly redolent of the Circe (Ulysses in Nighttown) episode in *Ulysses.* Burgess, in fact, playfully alerts his readers to a Joycean parallel, alluding to Stephen Dedalus's idea about the umbilical telephone line: "Edwin picked up the telephone, dialled—remembering his James Joyce—EDEnville 0000, and asked for Adam" (*DIS,* 115). The few hours that the pedantic, word-obsessed Stephen spends with the practical, viscerally conscious Leopold Bloom carry heavy import in *Ulysses.* The pedantic Dr. Spindrift has his life changed when he encounters the robust but seamy side of London life, and is moved from his disembodied world of abstract conceptualization to a world of material phenomena that everywhere reaches out to contact him as he moves through it. Part of this physical world is a certain mobster, Bob Courage, kinkily obsessed with whips and chains, and masochistically desirous of being "contacted" by Spindrift. The world of things and of the flesh, personified in Courage and others, pursues Spindrift with furious—and mostly very funny—vigor.

Most readers will naturally question whether Spindrift did actually take flight from the hospital and find himself immersed in an hilariously improbable sequence of adventures. The whole tenor and tone of these scenes, together with their shifts, turns, and transmogrifications, locates them somewhere between the worlds of dream and reality. The reader attentive to the logic of dreams can find in many of the incidents and details of Spindrift's waking day the origins of the stuff of his dreams—if that is what they are. In Spindrift's mind nightmare and reality have conjoined. Like a Kafkan accused, he is made to feel helpless and guilty as he lies in his hospital bed and gives "wrong" answers to Dr. Railton, a condescending but threatening God-figure with the power forever to reduce him, via brain surgery, to a "thing." Dressed in striped pajamas like a death-camp inmate, and alternately bullied and treated like a child by nurses and technicians, Spindrift is certainly ripe for nightmares or labyrinthian dreams, even without his neurological impairment or the chemical interferences of his medication. Then, too, there is the effect of the hospital visits of his dutiful wife—Sheila bringing along nearly every time a newly made male "friend." Embedded in real life is plentiful material for nightmare.

Whether Spindrift's peregrinations of London are dream or reality (or part dream and part reality) is not pivotally important. In either case, their vivid imposition on Spindrift's mind recalls him from his near robotic world of phonetics and philology to the material world of flesh, blood, and even money. Leo and Harry Stone, Jewish twins on the fringe of the criminal underworld, provide Spindrift with a tutelage that is a humorous exaggeration of the effect that Bloom has on Dedalus. Spindrift's metamorphosis is marked by his involving himself in this dialogue with the raffish Harry Stone, which so clearly recalls Leopold Bloom's money-making schemes: "As they walked eastwards they talked of many things. Legitimate ways of making money: a small cigarette factory fed with picked-up dog-ends; conducted night tours for American tourists; Leo put out to stud; old bedsprings sold as radio aerials; face cream made out of horse fat; dust sold as snuff; ideas sold to great firms (a refrigerator with a back door, double-headed matches to save wood, a tickling machine, warm water sprays in W. C. pans); . . . street singing as blind and cripple respectively; . . . expensive scent-bottles filled with Soir de Stoke-on-Trent" (*DIS,* 203).

A question arises here. If (as in *The Right to an Answer*) Burgess is predisposed to view contemporary England as culturally and morally debased, why should some of the more obvious symptoms of that decay be responsible for a healing in Spindrift? The answer, of course, involves paradox and ambiguity, as well as proportionality and a differentiation of various kinds of decay. And, of course, it involves the Manichaean intermixture of opposites. Spindrift must be thoroughly involved with life—any sort of life—if he is to be restored. If the debased and degraded gain powerful ascendancy, they pick up a curious vitality that irresistibly reminds the observer that there exists somewhere the dignified and uplifting. Spindrift has been shaken out of his feeling of torpor and helplessness by the time that he wins (with his head shaved for surgery) the televised, vulgarly ridiculous competition for "Bald Adonis of Greater London." In his acceptance speech, Spindrift vitally asserts both his own dignity and finer values: " 'As a matter of fact, I feel somewhat ashamed at having been a party to all this. So typical, isn't it, of what passes for entertainment nowadays? Vulgarity with a streak of cruelty and perhaps a faint tinge of the perversely erotic. . . . Here's my message to the great viewing public.' He leaned forward and spat full into the microphone a vulgar, cruel, erotic word" (*DIS,* 217).

Dynamic interactions give Spindrift the charge that restores him to life. This dynamism is not apt to be found in ordinary English life, however. Burgess once told John Cullinan that "I'm limited by any place in the world so long as it's not England. This means that all my settings must be 'exotic.' " Cullinan asked, "Why do you consider England so dull a subject?" Burgess replied, "Dull for me if not for others. I like societies where there's a dynamism of conflict. . . . I may have a personal thing about England. . . . It may even be so simple a matter as liking extreme climates, fights in bars, exotic waterfronts, fish soup, a lot of garlic. I find it easier to imagine a surrealistic version of New Jersey than of old England."[5] In *The Doctor Is Sick* Burgess tried hard to discover the surrealistic and the pungent (if not quite exotic) among certain petty criminals, deviants, and odd character types of Soho, the East End, and Earl's Court. What he basically aims for—and achieves—is humor: the themes of identity and ontology are significant but secondary. Some of the humor (dialects, puns, predictably antic capers, jesting literary allusions) are too obviously contrived but will not bother the critically relaxed reader.

One Hand Clapping

One Hand Clapping, a minor Burgess novel, humorously presents the predicament facing the individual aware that he is one of a legion of parched souls in a cultural desert. Television and modern education are here, as elsewhere, the windows into the modern soullessness that Burgess provides.

Howard Shirley, twenty-seven, a Bradcaster used car salesman, is the one aware of sterility. His wife, Janet, twenty-three, is a supermarket clerk; a product of a secondary modern school where "none of the teachers knew very much about what they taught."[6] Janet gets most of her "ideas," such as they are, from television. What Burgess thinks of the "tube" is revealed in the title alone of a 1982 article he wrote for *TV Guide:* "A Warning to Pitiful America: TV Is Debasing Your Lives."[7] Janet is superficial, conformist, and mostly contented. Howard, although only slightly better educated than Janet, is tortured by, in his own words, the "cheapness, vulgarity, silliness, brutishness, nastiness of everything and everybody" (188). One might expect from this that authorial sympathy would reside with Howard. This is not the case. Burgess divides his sympathy and establishes a fine, ironic tension in the book that allows it to transcend what it otherwise may have been—a cut-and-dried little lament about modern crassness and emptiness. Janet is the narrator, and she is delightfully cheeky and engaging—something, in fact, of a life force. Able to come to terms fairly easily with human evil and social ills, she seems an Augustinian. Howard, a thoroughly disillusioned—almost crazed—idealist, appears a disappointed Pelagian. Burgess's sympathies cross, and so do the reader's.

Early in the novel Howard and Janet go to see a play titled *One Hand Clapping.* If this play is not actually John Osborne's *Look Back in Anger,* it must certainly be a clone. This is part of Janet's description: "When the curtain went up, what should it be but some young people in a very dirty-looking flat, with washing hanging up, and a girl ironing in her underclothes. And that scene didn't change once. . . . What the play was about was about everybody being very unhappy because they'd got their education paid for by the government, or something, and there was no war for anybody to fight in, or something like that" (*OHC,* 130). Burgess's jab at Osborne's play is mostly playful, however. At this time Burgess was largely predisposed to agree with the content of most of Jimmy Porter's denunciations, although not the rant and posturing of their presentation. Osborne's protagonist comes out strongly in favor of commitment and vitality; he opposes dullness and neutrality. Jimmy decries the homogenization that comes with the American influence: "I must say it's pretty dreary living in the American Age—unless you're an American of course."[8] Materialism, consumerism, and a leveling of taste are the postwar American inheritance according to many British writers, and in *One Hand Clapping* "English people turned into secondhand Americans" (*OHC,* 188). Burgess once reported plans for "a mad novella in which England has become a mere showplace run by America (a work never published).[9] When Howard, gifted with a photographic memory, wins big on a television quiz program and then uses his computerlike brain to make a modest fortune at the race-track, the Shirleys actually travel to America. They are drawn to the center of the vacuum.

The novel's title (as that of the play within it) offers the suggestion that the cultural wasteland that is the West might be fertilized by Eastern philosophy. Howard explains the title *One Hand Clapping* to Janet: "It's from Zen Buddhism. . . . It's a way of getting in touch with Reality, you see, proceeding by way of the absurd. . . . It's supposed to be a way of getting to God" (*OHC,* 129). Janet has not much ability to imagine, nor does she wish to. Even as she reports Howard's explanation of the Zen koan, her narrative is a blizzard of digressions. After Howard, urged on by Janet, wins his £1,000 on the fatuous quiz program, it is not Zen that he uses to attempt to save himself. From the beginning his despair has pushed him to the thought that "when all's said and done, there's not all that much to live for, is there?" (*OHC,* 10). Howard now decides to forgo suicide only if his money can bring him real satisfaction as he buys the best a hedonistic culture has to offer.

Inevitably, this test fails, but the surprise is that Howard fully expects that Janet will accompany him in suicide; if necessary, he is prepared to ensure that by force. Janet's commitment to life is far too strong, of course, for any of this demented idealism. Howard's murder-suicide attempt goes awry when Janet neatly deals him a fatal blow with a coal hammer. From this point to the end, the novel takes something of a darkly comic and fabliau-like turn that parallels the ending of the later *The Pianoplayers.* Janet and a recently acquired lover, the poet Redvers Glass (whom Howard had helped with a monetary grant), take off for France with Howard's body secretly in tow. With only the slightest of twinges at the thought of what has happened to a man she genuinely loved, Janet reports: "What Red Redvers says he's going to do is start sowing seeds on the big patch of land at the back, and he's going to prop poor old Howard's body as a scarecrow, saying that the crows will make short work of him" (*OHC,* 214).

Although at this point in the novel Burgess sacrifices, for the sake of some Hitchcockian fun, a bit of Janet's credibility and the reader's sympathy for her, he basically maintains a balance of attraction/repulsion. For all her inability to see the larger picture, and for all the ways in which she is manipulated (mostly through television) by a society both vulgarly corrupt and empty of real values, she has an unforced commitment to life, and she will, like Orwell's proles, survive. Burgess causes us to think she might well be right when she reflects that "Howard was just a handsome machine wanting to die" (*OHC,* 215). And he seems to challenge us to assess our own personal hierarchy of values when he gives us Janet's near-closing words: "All I want is to live a nice decent life, getting as much pleasure out of it as I can. That's what we're here for, when all's said and done" (*OHC,* 215). Perhaps there is a glancing allusion here to Jeremy Bentham and the purely utilitarian view that if a game of pushpin brings as much happiness as poetry, one has no more intrinsic worth than the other. In *The Eve of St. Venus,* the Victorian ancestor of Sir Benjamin Drayton is reported to have believed "that pushpin was *better* than poetry."[10] One strongly suspects, though, that Burgess does not agree; nor does he prefer, as Janet does, canned foods over fresh.

The Worm and the Ring

The Worm and the Ring, while not a superior Burgess product, is a far better, and eminently more discussable, novel than the many drab novels of social realism turned out by English writers of the fifties and early sixties. Burgess's novel may, in fact, seem at first merely to be social realism—a "school novel" set in a gray, damp Midland town. This feeling might be increased by Burgess keeping his general linguistic exuberance very much under restraint in this novel. Not surprisingly, though, Burgess attempts a great deal and manages to integrate divergent materials relatively successfully. Profitable discussion can proceed along the lines of the autobiographical basis of the novel, its Roman Catholic theme, its comments on the English educational system, its surprisingly intricate mythic framework, its Pelagian/Augustinian conflict, and its early adumbration of the oft-repeated Burgess theme of English lukewarmness and "neutrality."

The novel came from Burgess's own experience as a teacher at Banbury Grammar School, Oxfordshire. At least one person thought that the book proceeded *too* directly from his school experience there. A school secretary felt herself libelled, and Heinemann, the publisher, withdrew the first edition of 1961; it did not reappear until 1970 in a revised edition. Burgess himself explained in an *Encyclopaedia Britannica* article: "The law of libel (especially in Great Britain) presents insuperable problems to novelists who, innocent of libellous intent, are nevertheless sometimes charged with defamation by persons who claim to be the models for characters in works of fiction. . . . Many such libel cases are settled before they come to trial, and publishers will, for the sake of peace and in the interests of economy, make a cash payment to the plaintiff without considering the author's side. They will also, and herein lies the serious blow to the author, withdraw copies of a whole edition."[11] The nine-year lapse between editions does seem a major factor in the relative neglect of this interesting novel.

More than most Burgess novels, *The Worm and the Ring* is rooted in a particular time and place. For one thing, it is both obvious and important that the novel is set in the days before the Second Vatican Council. Early on we learn that the exact year is 1951, the year of the Festival of Britain. With its depiction of a Catholicism that seems, by today's standards, very narrow, parochial, and legalistic, it might appear that Burgess is operating wholly under the influence of Graham Greene. This, however, was probably not the case: most Catholics old enough will probably recall their own involvement with certain religious stringencies and appreciate the accuracy with which Burgess represents them. When the protagonist, Christopher Howorth, a nearly lapsed Catholic, praises Martin Luther to his son or serves him bacon on a Friday, these actions, trifling today, cause deep emotional-spiritual twinges for all concerned. Catholic sexual puritanism has produced frigidity in Howarth's wife, Veronica; and because of the Church's ban on birth control, and an uterine disorder that makes pregnancy dangerous, she withholds her sexual favors. Hers in the world of "the Agnus Dei on the wall and the crude crucifix."[12] When Burgess recently referred to himself as having been raised a "medieval Catholic," he was alluding to the enormity of the change that has been witnessed in the Catholic church in the last thirty years—change which, somewhat ironically, Burgess reprehends. That the novel deals so heavily with Catholic guilt was the reason for Heinemann's initial rejection of the book (even before the whiff of libel). Today, along with the novels of Greene and some of David Lodge, this book evokes memories of the oppressive weight of bygone guilt.

Christopher's relative impecuniousness as a teacher also causes a gradual flagging of the spirit, much like that which Burgess himself experienced. Burgess has spoken bitterly of his "eight bloody pounds a week,"[13] and his frustration as he saw students easily able to buy books he himself could not afford. Some of the ferocity of his own feeling, perhaps not quite adequately distanced, gets into the novel when Woolton, the enlightened head of the school, forcibly makes a case to the Board of Governors: "That the scholar is, unless he happens to be some technological demiurge, not merely suspect but actively reviled and scorned, remains a painful fact which contains the seeds of our eventual and inevitable decline as a civilized country. The salaries paid to our teachers are a national scandal. . . . Because the teacher is poor he is stigmatized as a tramp, a social outcast" (*W&R*, 250–51). Then, too, Christopher must face, every school day, many loutish, semiliterate delinquents. His own sensitive son Peter, a student at the school, is taunted as a member of a very small Catholic minority.

Although Christopher Howarth's familial difficulties are the chief focus in the novel, Woolton, the "liberal humanist" headmaster, also encounters difficulties with those who oppose him, chiefly the conscienceless pragmatist, Gardner. Burgess's almost patented Augustinian/Pelagian conflict subsumes the one surrounding Woolton, "the old argument, Pelagian versus Augustinian" (*W&R,* 68), directly announced. As Howorth notes, Woolton "doesn't believe in original sin" and is consistent in his "belief that every child is a good child" (*W&R* 92). Under Woolton's reign discipline and order have suffered, but he is a good and honorable man; and although he is a Pelagian, Burgess foregoes sounding any prolonged satiric note. The movement to have Woolton fired is played out through a number of petty intrigues and not-so-subtle treacheries obviously endemic in the provincial atmosphere. Although inclined toward the ridiculous, these episodes have the authentic ring of truth. This is the sort of place that satirizes itself, Burgess seems to suggest. An arch but basically realistic presentation captures the point quite well.

Woolton and Howarth—allies throughout nearly the whole novel—are decent, principled idealists; they are men, it would seem, bound for defeat in any realistic novel precisely because of their admirable qualities. And so, indeed, they are vanquished by the cynical Gardner, who has a natural instinct for the calm exercise of ruthlessness. Gardner shamelessly plagiarizes Howarth's Master's paper for his own doctoral dissertation, destroys the incriminating manuscript, and brazenly carries off this academic theft with total success. Likewise, Gardner enjoys success in subverting Woolton gradually and methodically; and at the end of the novel with his newly conferred doctoral degree, Gardner self-assuredly heads the school. His triumph seems complete, because the school is already undergoing large expansion into a comprehensive school for the district, and his few remaining opponents are easily bought off by such promises as those of enhanced facilities and more and better equipment. (One of these is the music master, Richard Ennis, protagonist of *A Vision of Battlements.*)

Although it might seem slightly surprising to most readers, Burgess thematically suggests that this is how it always is when idealists confront Machiavellians or even hard-nosed realists; this is how it must be; and this is as it should be. In a forceful resignation speech to the governors Woolton makes a disheartening but (in Burgess's mind) keenly accurate observation: "I did not appreciate that the qualities required in a civilized human being were opposed to those most desirable in a ruler. I see now that only the man incapable of completeness in himself can be accepted as a leader of others; only he can sink to the unexpected lowness of the governor's chair. For the art of government involves the stripping from the ruler's personality of those very attributes which it is the ambition of the civilized man to achieve" (*W&R,* 252). Some readers will find this unduly cynical, but it is largely consonant with Burgess's own ideas about the nature of political leadership. And it certainly seems that we are meant to accept Woolton's prediction, that under Gardner's governance, the "School will flourish" (*W&R,* 242).

Neither Howarth nor Woolton ends in the sad position of unmitigated defeat, however. In fact, somewhat unexpected easy resolutions to their difficulties appear, not quite out of thin air, but as sudden gifts that fall into their laps. Burgess provides for Howarth an almost *Lucky Jim* kind of outcome. That this is not the most artistically honest of endings is perhaps indicated by Burgess describing in *Little Wilson and Big God* the ending that he had originally intended and completely ignoring the one actually published. The published ending provides a climactic and somewhat melodramatic scene, in which young Peter Howarth, urged on by some of the tougher Protestant boys in the school, ascends the outside of the school building to a gutter of the sloped roof to retrieve a ball. His father is the teacher on school yard duty, but Christopher is busy in the children's library relieving pent-up sexual frustration with a compliant (although married) young teacher, Hilda Connor. The gutter gives way under Peter's weight, and his fall ends when he is impaled on a fence far below. Seen by the other children as a "new sort of animal" (*W&R,* 237), the patiently hanging Peter certainly seems to have met his end, one connecting him to both Christ and an Elizabethan martyr in the Howarth family who died for his Catholic faith. (Family tradition had it that there was an Elizabethan martyr in Burgess's [Wilson's] own family as there was for Edwin Roper in *Tremor of Intent.*) In *Little Wilson and Big God* Burgess writes that Peter "dies in agony," and that "the father's guilt is so extreme as to be near-comic" (369). This, though, is simply not the published ending. Burgess has written to the present author that the original "gloomy ending . . . annoyed the editor at Heinemann,"[14] and that, as a result, he [Burgess] changed it. It is interesting to note that, in this case, Burgess yielded to the pressure of a British editor to soften a stark ending, and that, in the case of *A Clockwork Orange,* he acceded to the pressure of an American publisher to allow an ending more stark than he had intended.

In the published conclusion, Peter has somehow recovered. Christopher's life will be very much different because of a lucky accident. While chaperoning (with Hilda) a school trip to Paris, Christopher had run across an American officer he knew in the war. This man, Muller, is now a vintner with his own fields in Italy, and he has offered Christopher a very good job as a traveling representative, a position Christopher has now decided to accept. Veronica Howarth has finally had a hysterectomy and no longer spurns sex. Christopher feels that, with the Catholic heritage that is almost in the marrow of his bones, he will be more comfortably at home in Mediterranean lands than he ever was in England. Only the slightest of ironies snatches this from the realm of the fairytale ending. Veronica suddenly recognizes that "the Church was a man's Church, that it was unfair to women" (*W&R,* 183). She even begins to skip Mass and become "Englishly lukewarm at last" (*W&R,* 258). She and Peter express some preference for remaining in England. Some ambivalence about Christopher's future exists too because of the novel's moral dimension. An idealist and a good teacher, he is seen at the end of the novel selling his books to go to work for the playboy bachelor Muller. The smothering of idealism by the world as it is leaves us with a twinge of regret not present in Lucky Jim Dixon's going to work for Gore-Urquhart.

Woolton has a whole series of somewhat too obviously devised recognition scenes that bring him to a firm understanding that the Platonic idealist and liberal humanitarian will always know suffering because of naïve good intentions. Burgess heavily underscores these ideas by putting them right in Woolton's mouth in his final speech to the Board of Governors. We also recall Burgess's epigraph, his translation from Plato's *Apologia* on the end of Socrates: "condemned on the charges of corrupting youth and substituting false gods for the gods of the borough." Woolton, though, is not personally shattered. His mother has died, leaving him with an unexpectedly large inheritance. Not totally quixotically, he plans a continuation of a basic part of his effort: he will establish his own school, where he will "teach the humanities to a very few. 'I go to cultivate my garden' " (*W&R,* 252), he says.

It seems that Burgess realized that a potential artistic shortcoming with this novel was that he was not adequately transmuting his own personal experience of teaching at Banbury. One way of averting the danger—and of achieving other goals as well—would be to impose on himself a kind of external discipline. He erects the realistic elements of his novel on a mythic framework, the method he had employed with his first novel, *A Vision of Battlements.* He indicates that it simply seemed natural for him to again employ the mythic method, and to choose Wagner's *The Ring of the Nibelungs* for the mythic underpinning. In "Wagner's *The Ring,*" a 1964 piece he wrote for the *Listener,* Burgess recalls how it used to be for the young people of Manchester: "We had Wagner in the bloodstream, and if we never saw *The Ring* at least we had a rich subliminal indoctrination in its mythological content and its symbolism. When I wrote my first serious novel with an English *mise-en-scène* it seemed natural to base it on *The Ring* cycle and even call the book *The Worm and the Ring.*"[15] A. A. DeVitis and, later, Geoffrey Aggeler thoroughly traced the mythic identifications and their import. In *Little Wilson and Big God* Burgess states that "the realism overcame the symbolism" (368). That may be, but it seems more probably that the myth was an effort to control the realism, to give shape to the materials and to elevate them to a higher level of significance. Whichever way it was, Burgess describes his mythscape:

> I chose the fourfold matrix of Wagner's *Ring of the Nibelungs.* This was not altogether arbitrary. The hierarchy of gods, heroes and dwarfs found a parallel in a grammar school. The gods had their specializations, just like teachers. If Loge was the god of fire, Lodge could be the name of a chemistry master. . . . Wotan could be Woolton, the headmaster. The possibilities were interesting. . . . The golden ring stolen from the Rhine daughters could be something dangerous like a schoolgirl's diary, crammed with sexual fantasies involving members of the staff. Possession of this would confer power. It was not possible to find an easy parallel for Fafner the dragon or *Wurm,* except in an ambitious deputy headmaster who would use the diary to topple his principal Woolton. The name Gardner—that of a detestable Banbury shop owner—would do, with its Fafner suffix and its palinlogue of *drag* from *dragon.* And Siegfried? Perhaps an heroic teacher of German [Howarth] having an affair with a brown-haired mathematics mistress named Hilda. (*LWBG,* 368)

The Worm and the Ring is set in 1951, the "year of commemorated British achievement" (*W&R*, 20), the Festival of Britain. Economically and spiritually still depressed, Britons were only beginning to see an end to wartime rationing. The festival was an obvious attempt to pull a people out of the spiritual doldrums, to issue a renewed call to a sense of national pride and purpose, and to foster a sense of economic confidence. Burgess obviously agreed with many commentators who noted the British malaise, but he was not at all sanguine about a remedy. He referred to the Festival of Britain as "an official and marvelous dramatization of the Pelagian idea."[16] His point was that the nation's illness was not one that could be cured merely by edict or some neat bit of sociopolitical engineering. The moral inertia of the neutrals—exemplified in the novel, in slightly different manifestations by Gardner and Hilda Connor—is not easily broken. If Burgess had any answer to the problem, it lay in a general coming-to-awareness of deep religious truth. Still, he announces (rather like Stephen Dedalus) that Catholicism is intolerable, and all alternatives illusory and absurd.[17] In the novel Burgess provides no solutions, and no Brunonian reconciliation of opposites or Hegelian synthesis. He does, though, provide nicely textured ambiguities, and a strong, honestly felt and finely balanced (although unsubtle) sense of the Augustinian/Pelagian opposition. Modestly and candidly he has written that "*The Ring* is symbolism, and only artists who are not sure what they believe indulge in it, since symbols are good at reconciling archetypes which lie too deep to be disturbed by human self-division."[18]

The Eve of St. Venus

The Eve of St. Venus was written, Burgess says, in 1950, a glum period in England. It was not published then (Burgess states) because the time was not right for this delightful little entertainment and exemplum, a *jeu d'espirit* originally written as an opera libretto.[19] Published as a novella in England in 1964, it reveals itself to be a good-natured parody of English drawing room farce and the verse plays of Christopher Fry, popular in the late forties and early fifties. The novel gives us an aristocratic English country house, replete with all the stock characters we usually find there in most dramatic literature and certain species of novels. Grounded in some reality, this world exists, of course, more on the stage or page than in actuality. In his foreword to the American edition Burgess writes that this novella "depends for its effects largely on an understanding of the insular and conservative English character, especially as manifested in a silly, ingrown, mainly non-existent rural aristocracy."[20] Generally, American audiences who have stereotyped notions of what the English are like will find them all confirmed in Burgess's rich pastiche.

Burgess takes the basis of his tale from Robert Burton's *Anatomy of Melancholy* (a source also employed by Fry in his *A Phoenix Too Frequent*), Burton's vignette involving a young man who accidentally weds the very goddess of love. In Burgess's rendition, the young man is a quite decent, just slightly insipid structural engineer named Ambrose Rutterkin. He is on the estate of Sir Benjamin Drayton, whose headstrong daughter Diana he is to wed the next day. Nervous about getting the wedding ring properly on Diana's finger the following day, Ambrose, testingly, slips it on the finger of a statue of Venus in the garden. The stone goddess curls her finger back, refuses to release the ring, and that night comes fully to life to claim the riches of love from her new "husband." Not surprisingly, the local Anglican vicar mistakes Venus's life-giving warmth for the fires of hell, but Venus works her healing spell on all, even the would-be exorcist, before she is through. The characters sing, before the novella is through, the anonymous "Pervigilium Veneris," Latin hymn to the goddess, in Burgess's own translation. Although whimsically but delectably comic, the novella is also really something of a paean to love, particularly sexual love. Burgess clearly suggests that the vital spirit of Aphrodite has something to rouse people from the collective anesthesia induced by the welfare state. Burgess, of course, is not thematically alone in presenting the awakening of the old gods and what they represent—primal wonder, a vivifying sense of mystery, and a reverence for Nature—as antidotes to sterility. One thinks first of D. H. Lawrence, but might also remember the ironic "Oedipus at Colonus" of E. M. Forster. On stage Fry himself has given us *Venus Observed;* and, as an indication of the commonness of the Greek vitality/modern lifelessness idea, we might recall its sensational (if somewhat meretricious presentation) in Peter Shaffer's *Equus.*

Sir Benjamin is a comically fulminating Tory of the old school, a country baronet with a genius for inventive, if rather ridiculous, invective. He sees the country going to the dogs: "God help us. The country's sinking in a sea of giggles of girls in late-night buses. We're suffocating in a mound of cardboard pies with a spoonful of wormy-minced guts inside them. . . . I shudder to think what visions coil up from the fumes of the tea in the in-trays of these dentured myopic executives who are already working on the first draft of the millennium. Pardon. With its hearty pipe stuck into rotting teeth, table tennis for all and fishpaste sandwiches, and scoutmaster yarns about clean living" (*ESV,* 30). Despite the heart of gold that beats beneath his volcanic exterior, Sir Benjamin is genuinely cynical, for he sincerely believes that real life existed only in the past. He is a stock comic figure, and Burgess intends to engender no serious sympathies either for or against him. It is interesting, though, and somewhat ironic, that this figure, most comic when he is excoriating the vulgarity and debasement of the present, should call to mind such later Burgess characters as Bev Jones of *1985* and Enderby of *The Clockwork Testament* who do much the same thing. Sir Benjamin, however, conceived in 1950, is merely part of a well-oiled comic machine, very much distanced from the author himself. Jones and Enderby sometimes seem unnervingly close to Burgess himself as they issue their diatribes. In this transit Burgess slightly suggests the movement of his friend Kingsley Amis from politically disinterested (or even slightly left-leaning) social comedy to a kind of reactionary, if still very funny, personal grumpiness. Both probably hold the sad state of modern England more than sufficiently responsible.

Chapter Six
Artists, Creators, and Prometheans

From Richard Ennis of his first novel, *A Vision of Battlements,* to Billy Henshaw of *The Pianoplayers,* his twenty-ninth, Burgess has filled his novels with men who are either artists or movers or shapers of human destiny. Unlike Ennis and Henshaw, who have intimately close connections to Burgess's own life, many are historic personages: Shakespeare, Napoleon, Jesus, Keats, Freud, and Trotsky. The reasons behind Burgess's use of artist figures are several, apart from his personal identification with them. First, the artist figure allows Burgess to represent very centrally, with pathos, irony, or both, the radical human dualisms always present in his best work. The artist, struggling to give shape to the insubstantial visions of his spirit, can never divorce himself from the world of matter. In Burgess's work, artistic creativity is sometimes spurred by the libido. The artist's desire to reconcile the apparent opposites is, somewhat paradoxically, often what provides the motive force for his art, but it also makes his personal life very difficult.

The fictionalized biographies of creative men allow Burgess to do something else as well. The artist, a creator of form and a conduit of myth, provides the form and order that give life a sense of manageability. Every possibility exists, however, that this form and order is illusory, a mere product of individual or collective imagination. One way that Burgess raises this issue is to impart to his fictions about artists a degree of artifice that is pronounced, even if not immediately noticeable. *Nothing Like the Sun,* the fictional biography of Shakespeare, is modeled heavily on the library scene in *Ulysses. Napoleon Symphony* is built on lines parallel to Beethoven's *Eroica,* and is indebted to *Finnegans Wake* as well. Shakespeare and Napoleon, men far larger than life, are reduced to very human dimensions by being stripped of the false embellishment of myth, almost at the same time that Burgess, in other subtle ways, is directing the reader's attention to the problems of myth in relation to reality, history in relation to truth. *MF,* Burgess's most experimental novel with the exception of *Napoleon Symphony,* teasingly demands that the reader think about these and related questions.

As we will see, strong differences exist among the men who form this group of creators. The quest for the kind of order that one man thinks will bring fulfillment is very different from the quest another is pursuing. Burgess does not fit his characters into molds, and his Shakespeare and his Napoleon, although both demythologized, are worlds apart. Both provide memorable exemplifications of the essential human paradox: the opposites constantly clash, but, often, in collision, can temporarily merge to produce what is remarkable and dramatic, but, ultimately, very human.

A Vision of Battlements

A Vision of Battlements, written, Burgess claims, in 1949, but not published until 1965, is a partial and partially ironic self-portrait of Burgess as a young artist. Richard Ennis, the novel's antihero is, Burgess writes, "a failed musician like myself" (*LWBG,* 363). Burgess, like Ennis, spent most of the war on "the Rock," the British garrison of Gibraltar, as a sergeant-major. Ennis, a lapsed Catholic, has a background largely similar to his creator's, including some of the basic details about his father and mother. Ennis says of his father, "He was a very fine pianist. I associate him with big pounding chords on the piano; the piano used to stagger with the force of them."[1] Of his mother, long dead, he says, "she was on the stage. A very Junoesque woman, though she was billed for a time, in her early days, that is, as The Blonde Venus or something ridiculous like that" (44). That an author's first novel should be highly autobiographical is hardly surprising. That it should have been undertaken as a means of self-therapy is not unusual either: "There was [a] submerged motive for writing and that was to see if I could clear my head of the dead weight of Gibraltar. I had lived with it so long that it still lay in my skull, a chronic migraine: a work of fiction seemed the best way of breaking it up, pulverizing it, sweeping it away" (*VOB,* vii). Burgess writes, though, that the act of composition, carried to completion, "served only to call back pain and loneliness that refused to be exorcised" (*VOB,* vii).

Ennis, intelligent and high-minded, is also a bit callow, emotionally adolescent, and "bloody-minded." Reginald Jones of *Any Old Iron,* also stationed on Gibraltar, is most of these things; and the picture that we get of Sergeant-Major Wilson (Burgess) in *Little Wilson and Big God* strongly suggests that he, too, generally fit this description. Ennis is very much an alienated twentieth-century man; the alienation is greatly increased by enforced circumstance, basic temperament, and a strong commitment to art. "Ennis comes from a Celtic root meaning an island," Burgess writes

(*LWBG,* 363). And Gibraltar itself (despite being the girlhood home of Molly Bloom) is a bleak place that basically isolates the individual in his own heavy tedium. The great war that is raging—although not on Gibraltar—almost invariably will produce in Ennis's type something approaching cosmic alienation. The great, universal enemy—disorder—seems to be prevailing: "Ennis, in his ecstasy of execration, could not tell who the enemies were, but a number of faces had coalesced into a single image—the destroyer, the anti-builder, a Proteus capable of being time, the sea, the state, war, or all at once. It wanted cities down, love broken, music scrambled. Ennis the builder cursed and wept in the ruins" (*VOB,* 15).

Although "safe" from the war on Gibraltar, Ennis is not safe from the sense of existential futility that is, for the sensitive or independent soul, very nearly a necessary by-product of army life. Boredom, hard to overestimate, either paralyzes or causes frenzy; pettifogging regulations frustrate and madden; officers, inept bumblers or martinets, are capable of producing a panoply of negative emotions. Ennis is not the Yossarian of Joseph Heller's *Catch-22,* but his situation causes him to ponder not only the cosmic triumph of the forces of dissolution, but also the collective insanities that inhere in social institutions such as the army. Ennis, an instructor in the Army Vocational and Cultural Corps, has been ordered at one point to give a group of Italian POWs "a forty-minute talk every week" (*VOB,* 25). When Ennis dismisses the men after five minutes, Major Muir accuses him of "fragrantly" violating instructions. Ennis remonstrates, "Look, sir. The only prisoners up there at the moment are Italian Pioneers. The only Italian I know is musical Italian. You can't make a lecture out of *andante* and *lento ma non troppo*. I tried giving a talk in English about Mussolini, thinking that at least they'd recognize the name. They started cheering, and the meeting was broken up. It's absurd" (*VOB,* 25). "It is your duty," says Major Muir, "to obey instructions. If I tell you to lecture a squad of Hottentots, then you must do that" (*VOB,* 25).

If an artist is a person spurred to creativity by a rage for order, his total immersion in largely perfect disorder must have interesting results. In Burgess's work the conflict of opposites almost always results in creativity, but here the pull of the opposed forces would threaten the protagonist's destruction were he not possessed of saving streaks of natural rebelliousness and youthful self-contradictions that allow some natural bending. If Ennis slightly anticipates Yossarian, he anticipates Jimmy Porter, likewise a self-contradictory rebel, somewhat more. Burgess strongly hints at this himself in his introduction: "In point of public appearance, he (Ennis) limps after the known and established rebels; in point of creation he comes pretty early.

It's as well to remember that the Welfare State rebels were anticipated by the Army rebels" (*VOB,* viii–ix). The rebel and the artist are conjoined in Ennis. In one of his lectures, he finds himself stirringly declaiming to an already dissentient group from an antiaircraft unit that " 'Beethoven cared nothing for politics. He snapped his fingers at the thunder, he snapped his fingers at Napoleon. He had absolutely no respect for authority. He was a man who would not cringe to the powerful. He was independent, fearless, alone, no base crawler. . . .' The men cheered" (*VOB,* 155). Ennis's youthfully romantic conceptions of art and the artist usually afford him sufficient psychological fortification. As he is, at another point, being severely, and mostly unjustly, dressed down by Major Muir, Ennis is thinking to himself, "Then the shackled Lucifer was seen with his *Non serviam,* then Prometheus the brave fire stealer, pecked by eagles on the stark rock" (*VOB,* 55). Although the name R. Ennis is probably, despite Burgess's disclaimers, meant to spell "sinner" backwards, Ennis is certainly more a profoundly disaffected noncom than a genuine Luciferan figure. His *non serviam,* though, very probably allies him with Stephen Dedalus, another young man who uttered that phrase, and who considered an artistic vocation every bit as sacred as a religious one. The idea that Ennis sees himself as artist-as-priest is apparently reinforced when Mrs. Carraway, the fortune-teller, sees him as a priest (*VOB,* 169–70). It would not seem that, like Hillier, of *Tremor of Intent,* Ennis becomes a priest of the Church, since later he is, as a very minor character in *The Worm and the Ring,* music master at the school where Christopher Howarth also teaches.

Ennis's commitment to his musical vocation is strong, whatever level of talent he possesses. A cultured woman tells him that his musical compositions reveal only meager abilities (*VOB,* 137), but the reader has no way of confirming or rejecting her judgment. Although Ennis is the very first in a now quite long line of Burgess characters who are artists or types of the artist, his views heavily coincide with most of those who follow, and with those of Burgess himself. Like the (literally) nearsighted wordsmith Burgess, Ennis argues strongly for the dominance of the aural over the visual: "I don't think I approve of this visual bias that's creeping into education. Our civilization is, surely, based on the ear—the dialectics of Socrates, Shakespeare, and his illiterate audience, the peripatetic sermons of Christ" (*VOB,* 77). Although they are, of course, not original, most of Ennis's views about art and the artist show up in later Burgess novels, either as part of a thematic conception or as ideas actually specified by his characters, for example: "All artists are hermaphrodites" (*VOB* 115); "lust could be transmuted into creative energy" (*VOB* 116); and (a character agreeing with what Ennis has said), "immense artistic vigor is related to strong sexuality" (*VOB* 142). And to "sensible" realists such as Major Muir who feel that art is mostly a pleasant indulgence of the idle, Ennis argues for "the full life, sir, the total sensibility. Values, civilized living, the contact with the bigger reality" (*VOB,* 53). Although Ennis experiences abundant internal conflict, he has not yet quite consciously formed an aesthetic that holds that art has its genesis in elemental oppositions. He is, however, becoming aware of the dialectic of opposites to which he has already adjusted himself: "Ennis had become a Manichee, at home in a world of perpetual war. It did not matter what the flags or badges were; he looked only for the essential opposition—Wet and Dry, Left Hand and Right Hand, Yin and Yang, X and Y" (*VOB,* 55). Although by no means fully developed, the recurrent themes of art, love, responsibility, Catholic guilt, the search for a personal theology, and the clash of cultures are present here in stages well past the embryonic.

Although Ennis is an artist still in a stage of late apprenticeship, in a most inhospitable environment, it would nonetheless be unsensible to conclude that *A Vision of Battlements* is a novel of the artist. Basically, it is a realistic novel that does moderately well those things a realistic novel ought to do. Beginning with no insistent a priori ideas, it is an honest attempt to capture a "truth" Burgess personally experienced. The novel is full of the particulars of voice, word, gesture, and nuance that are absolutely convincing. The language and mind-set of the common troops are especially well captured. The reader can, very honestly, feel, from the inside, what it was like to be in the British Army in the early to mid-forties; and, most particularly, what it was like to be stationed on Gibraltar. Burgess felt uneasy, though, about making straightforward realism, however great its verisimilitude, his sole achievement. Burgess tries additional ways to please and tease; to add depth and reverberation. Ennis is, for one thing, a composer whose major work, a passacaglia, teasingly mirrors, to some fair extent, the form of the novel of which it is a part. Ennis is not just a put-upon antihero with suggested psychological depths, nor is he just a mock–Prometheus. He is also Aeneas. Burgess has said that setting the novel within the mythic framework of the *Aeneid* "was not mere pedantic wantonness, nor was it solely a little tribute to James Joyce; it was a tyro's method of giving his story a backbone" (*VOB,* viii). Burgess was apparently gratified with the result since, as we discussed earlier, he used Wagner's *The Ring of the Nibelungs* to much the same purposes in this second novel he wrote, *The Worm and the Ring.*

Although a reader can have the feeling, at times, that Burgess's writing can descend to facile contrivances, the care with which he works out parallels (whether a mere sign of obsessive cleverness or not) belies the charge that a novel is for him a product of rapid manufacture. In modeling *A Vision of Battlements* really fairly closely on both epic and musical parallels, Burgess, while perhaps slightly awestruck by his own daring in following his master, Joyce, is also laying down for himself the challenge of discipline. The method need not at all be deemed the somewhat frivolous indulgence of an overgrown, pedantic schoolboy.

In the past it was frequently said that surprisingly few truly significant novels came out of World War II. Later, sensibly, it was concluded that this phenomenon was no surprise at all—reality had beggared fiction. There was simply no way of artistically capturing between the covers of a book the sheer enormity and monumental horror that had been witnessed. Burgess's effort to employ the weight of classical literature and myth seems a more sensible attempt than many others. Because the Trojan War produced emotively rich echoes that sounded for well over two millennia, Burgess used this event to make manageable a degree of conflict the Greeks and the Trojans never dreamed of. There is artistic and psychological sense behind the basic parallel. *The Aeneid* deals with a man's attempt to restructure his life and the lives of those he leads after they were devastated in the consuming ten years' war that ended in ruinous defeat. Burgess writes of a time when millions of people across the world were trying to reorder their own lives familiarly, psychologically, spiritually, and economically.

The mythic parallels are serious but also ironic. As an instructor in the fictitious Army Vocational and Cultural Corps (a parallel of the real Army Educational Corps in which Burgess served), it is Ennis's job "to prepare for the future, you see. It's to get the men ready for when this lot's all over. To teach them how to build a new world" (*VOB,* 11). At the same time, though, the foundations of Ennis's personal life have been shaken. With his wife in the last days of embarkation leave, Ennis thought their love "a Troy that a ten-thousand-year siege could not shatter" (*VOB,* 14). The reader, however, learns this only in Ennis's retrospective view; as the novel begins, some twelve months later, he is earnestly declaring his love to Concepcion, a dark-skinned Gibraltese widow, the analogue of Virgil's Dido. True to her name, Concepcion is soon pregnant by Ennis. They separate, she not seeing any future with the passionate but slightly bumptious Ennis, who is, with his Catholic guilt, not ready for any commitment. She marries a suitor, Barasi, the analogue of Virgil's Iarbas, "his name anagrammatized," as Burgess tells his reader (*VOB,* viii). The innocent Barasi, meeting Ennis, tells him that Concepcion has died of a miscarriage suffered late in her pregnancy. What the reader soon comes to understand, however, is that Burgess does not strain either to meet mythic parallels or involve the reader in melodrama. World War II provided a large stage onto which were propelled countless people who, inspired by the high emotional pitch of the times, were enacting their roles in ways that would have surprised their ordinary selves. (In *Little Wilson and Big God* and *Any Old Iron* Burgess captures well, his exaggeration only slight, the feelings of wartime when adultery was so very common.) Ennis, like Aeneas, has left a burning city (a blitzed London), a dead father (killed by a Nazi bomb), and a wife he loved. To find these circumstances even slightly extraordinary is to forget the situation of many English cities in the period from late 1940 onward. Aeneas was perhaps still extraordinary, but not because of the sources of his sorrow. Neither were Troilus and Cressida extraordinary, for Ennis "thought uneasily of Troilus and Cressida, classical lovers remade by the Middle Ages, eternal symbols of the war-sundered grown unfaithful" (*VOB,* 15). The mythic and literary allusions bring with them a kind of shock: characters in books, felt for and wept over for over many hundreds of years, do not demand, by their situations alone, any more sympathy than do millions of real people of the period 1939–45. The archetypes (nonobtrusive though they be) can be both sustaining and jolting, ironic and genuine, in this very good, if not quite excellent first novel.

Nothing Like the Sun

Richard Ennis, a modern antihero who is a victim of dullness, and the spiritual near-bankruptcy of contemporary civilization, may be an inconsiderable artist. Despite what might appear to be the energizing presence of the almost embodied forces of evil—the Nazis—just across the Spanish frontier, the Rock is still seen as a wasteland. Congruent with Eliot's *The Waste Land,* Burgess's work customarily draws a sharp modern/ Elizabethan contrast. He sees, as does Eliot, the late sixteenth and early seventeenth centuries as far from perfect, but he sees them as alive with intense vitality. Elizabethans and Jacobeans recognize evil as an entity that exists abroad in the world and in their own selves. The abundant clash of good and evil and the other eternal opposites produces a vitalizing energy that invests all with adventure and significance. One of the chief beneficiaries of this spiritually vibrant age is the artist. In *Nothing Like the Sun* Burgess presents his reader with the greatest of these, the character "WS" (William Shakespeare), an intensely alive but victimized human, and artist triumphant. Published in 1964, the novel is a rich celebration of the four-hundredth anniversary of Shakespeare's birth.

More division of opinion on the merits of this novel exists than for any other Burgess novel, it seems. Several academic critics rank it as one of the best—if not the very best—of all of Burgess's novels. Several reviewers and at least two prominent British critics, however, have found it re-creates the Elizabethan world in bogus fashion and that it is far too reminiscent of a very familiar kind of costume drama. The British poet-critic D. J. Enright complains of "the sexual melodramatic or copulative grandguignolesque"[2] elements in the novel. Christopher Ricks, a distinguished British academic and prominent reviewer, one of the most astute commentators on Burgess's early work, has nonetheless pointed to this general tendency in Burgess, deprecating his "horror comedy, the mingling of black realistic violence and comic lightness,"[3] not just in this novel, but in Burgess's work generally. Today, other readers see black comedy largely as an outdated sixties sort of modishness. Whatever the judgment on it may be, it must be admitted that black comedy and the grotesque are indeed principal elements of the novel.

Although the subtitle is "A Story of Shakespeare's Love Life," the novel is remembered at least equally for the wonderful richness of its language and its employment of grotesque violence. In this tour de force the darkly comic and the graphically violent are present not only to inject marvellous Elizabethan pith and color, but also to underscore the thematic conception in an integral way. Quite simply put, the novel's theme revolves closely around the monumental struggle between flesh and spirit in the man Shakespeare. That is no simple conflict, for Manichaean belief holds that things of the body and soul are hopelessly mixed in this world: desires of the flesh, for example, may be directed into art to produce great triumphs of the human spirit. Burgess's WS is excruciatingly racked by the pain of being human, and out of his incessantly bursting humanness his art is created. WS is a Hamlet-like figure, a man great in emotion and intellect; he is vulnerable precisely because of that greatness. In short, WS is a magnified embodiment of all that it means to be human; if every man sometimes has clear intimations of the comic, tragic, or grotesque nature of existence, Shakespeare will have them all the more powerfully.

The sharply felt sense of human dichotomy informs the whole of *Nothing Like the Sun*.[4] If the novel then is sometimes incongruous in effect (WS tossing off the treasures of English literature in a fury of inspiration surrounded by smashed pates, broken teeth, and tossed chamberpots) and baroque in style (burstingly overinflated Elizabethan language), this is only so much to the good because the novel demonstrates, as does even blacker comedy, the grand incongruities of human existence. At the same time, because of the historical distancing, and because we are used to this type of coloration in literature of and about the Elizabethan period, the craft and technique themselves do not jar. Burgess largely convinces the reader that the grotesque world was in Shakespeare's day the everyday world. The grotesque and the realistic mix shockingly in an account of the public execution at Tyburn Common of Dr. Roderigo Lopez and two others. The horrifically barbaric hanging, drawing, and quartering (all graphically described by Burgess) is but holiday sport and spectacle to those of the populace fortunate enough to be present (*NLTS,* 124–28).

A significant paradox is that Burgess's Elizabethans appear more human precisely because they are represented as more vitally animal. They are people who live in an un-self-conscious celebration of the life urge; they are whole, robust persons far removed from the fragmented selves of contemporary fiction. WS is a partial but very major exception to this characterization. WS is of his own time, and yet not of it altogether. Success testifies that he knows his age and is in one sense well suited to it; his active life, his total immersion in affairs both of business and of passion seems certainly to confirm this. At the same time, as a giant of thought, feeling, and sensibility, he is prone to experience the agonies of man's human situation in any age. In the supercharged atmosphere of his own time, it seems that his agonies are increased. And so they are, but not as much as would have been the case had he wallowed in melancholic reflection. WS is no Prufrock, nor is he even a Hamlet. Being a man of blood rather than choler, he lives his life more than he reflects on it. For WS, the frustrations of the human paradox are relieved in the actions of living, while the actions of his life itself provide a telling illustration of that same human paradox. On a deep level his art proceeds from a need to heal self-divisions. On a more surface level it comes from a candid, bourgeois desire for money and social advancement.

The complications of WS's life as portrayed by Burgess are a combination of relatively few facts, Warwickshire legend, previous biographical speculation, and Burgess's own vigorously imaginative reconstruction. Since Burgess feels that Shakespeare put the incidents of his own life, only slightly transmuted, into some of the plays, Burgess works back in the other direction: he takes images and incidents from the plays and makes them part of WS's life. Anne Hathaway is a highly sexed woman, eight years older than WS, who virtually rapes him at a first meeting, and then, pregnant, easily inveigles him into marriage. The natural emotional complications that follow are heightened by WS's bisexual inclinations. A pederastic incident causes him to lose a teaching job in Stratford, but his muse or "goddess" has made him restless with Stratford anyway. In London WS soon meets Mr. W. H., known to us as the person to whom Shakespeare dedicated the sonnets. Burgess identifies him (as have many others) as Henry Wriothesley, earl of Southampton. The young, attractive Southampton, also bisexual, has a relationship with WS that extends beyond that of patron/sponsor. Soon, though, WS meets the dark-skinned Fatimah, also known as "Lucy Negro," a prostitute from the East Indies. (The Shakespearean scholar G. M. Harrison has suggested that the Dark Lady of the Sonnets was a black prostitute.) WS either confuses her with, or recognizes her as (things of this world always being mixed), the "dark goddess" of whom he has always dreamed. She is identified with the muse, a kind of sacred inspiration, but she is also very much of the flesh, and carries with her all of the weakness to which the flesh is heir. WS's love for her causes a sundering with Southampton who loves her too. Moreover, it proves fatal, for one of the things she brings with her is syphilis. Burgess celebrates the agony and the ecstasy of being human: *Nothing Like the Sun* is very essentially a romantic novel. The lives of Christopher Marlowe and Robert Greene, deftly worked into the background fabric in a small way, testify to the same sense of what human life is in the magnifying mirror of Elizabethan times. WS is a man of great mind and soul, but he seems only a puppet fabricated of flesh and blood, caught in an uncertain world halfway between good and evil, light and darkness, the sublime and the grotesque. An awareness of "what a dreadful Manichaean mess life is" provides the rage for order, for bringing confluence out of conflict. Manichaeanism and romanticism intersect as we see man achieving triumph in his tragedy.

This should not quite convey the impression, however, that the novel is all swirling romanticism or philosophical play with the grotesque. The evocation of London at the turn of the seventeenth century is effective because it has a historically accurate basis. Burgess writes about building "a framework of historical data to support the structures of fancy. . . . What I had to do . . . was to relate documented events to the conjectural development of WS' character."[5] Burgess, here a very careful craftsman, does this quite successfully, and he does so in richly filliped and filigreed fashion. Burgess, however, also does something that is as unlikely as it is fascinating. Harold Bloom recently remarked that in *Nothing Like the Sun* "Burgess's Shakespeare is overtly Joyce's Shakespeare."[6] Professor Bloom refers to the elaborate artifice that lies within Burgess's building most of the life of WS on the speculation of that pedantic young man Stephen Dedalus who presents his ideas about Shakespeare in the Scylla and Charybdis episode (the "library scene") of *Ulysses. Nothing Like the Sun,* through its whole frame, form, and content, challenges the reader to test Stephen's theory that art and nature are interchangeable. Stephen and Leopold Bloom are identified with Shakespeare, and Burgess, only half playfully, identifies himself with all of them and with Joyce.[7] Burgess wants his reader to question the relation of art to reality, fiction to biography, myth to history, literary character to creator. *Nothing Like the Sun* begins to move Burgess much nearer to the postmodernist frontier (although Burgess is apt to find the term *postmodernist* somewhat foolishly vague), and makes his foray into structuralism in *MF* not so surprising.

The Enderby Novels

Enderby WS, good businessman and consummate artist, is a man of the world and yet not of it altogether. F. X. Enderby, a minor but gifted contemporary poet, is, when first met, a comically reclusive naïf frightened by the outside world. Bad nerves, combined with the constant eating of greasy and other unhealthy foods, are responsible for producing in Enderby the characteristic for which most readers remember him most clearly—disturbances of the digestive and intestinal tracts and constant, noisy flatulence. A "PFFFRRRUMMMP," in fact, is what opens the novel. The flabbily fat poet spends a good part of each of his days in the bathroom. He sits on the toilet and composes his poetry, dropping completed sheets into a bathtub never used for its intended purpose. With bodily and inspirational winds breaking and moving, the method works. Poetry—good poetry (some of which the reader gets to see)—is produced.

As his name, Enderby, suggests, the forty-five-year-old poet retreats to the bathroom to take care of fundamental matters—the demands of the physical organism. In another sense, though (both motives and things mixing in this Manichaean duoverse), he goes there to flee base matter—everything connected with the repulsive stepmother who raised him. This woman had, when frightened one night by lightning, climbed into bed with the boy Enderby, who, gorge rising with disgust, dashed to the sanctuary of the bathroom. Thus, a psychological connection was made. This fiercesomely repulsive woman is described in a bravura passage so vivid that the American novelist Paul Theroux claims to have committed it to memory:[8]

> Oh, she had been graceless and coarse, that one. A hundred-weight of ringed and brooched blubber, smelling to high heaven of female smells, rank as long-hung hare or blown beef, her bedroom strewn with soiled bloomers, crumby combinations, malodorous bust-bodices. She had swollen finger-joints, puffy palms, wrists girdled with fat, slug-white upper arms that, when naked, showed indecent as thighs. . . . Her wind was loud, even in public places. . . . She picked her teeth with old tram-tickets, cleaned out her ears with hairclips in whose U-bend earwax was

> trapped to darken and harden, scratched her private parts through her clothes with a matchbox-rasping noise audible two rooms away . . . cut her meat with scissors, spat chewed bacon-rind or pork-crackling back on the plate, excavated beef-fibres from her cavernous molars and held them up for all the world to see, . . . belched like a ship in the fog, . . . tromboned vigorously in the lavatory.[9]

In *Little Wilson and Big God* we learn that Burgess's stepmother was not entirely unlike Enderby's in personal habits or appearance (48). In outer circumstance, Enderby is much like Burgess: both had mothers who died when they were very young (Enderby's dying giving birth to him); both had fathers who quickly remarried; both had fathers who were wholesale tobacconists; both Burgess and Enderby assumed their real mothers' maiden names; Burgess has several times complained in print of the numerous physical and psychological ailments that beset the writer; both are lapsed Catholics. So great are these external similarities that a few Burgess commentators have supposed that Enderby and Burgess are virtually one. Burgess sensibly denies this in *Little Wilson and Big God,* admitting, though, that he gave Enderby some of his own poems (85). Enderby, however, has nothing of Burgess's finely tuned awareness of contemporary social or cultural landscapes and very little of his humor or irony.

Enderby is full of paradoxes and self-contradictions. At the beginning of the novel, he is each day growing more slovenly; more and more like the stepmother he loathed. He abhors disorder, and the kind of gross physicality that he identified as its harbinger. In the bathroom he creates his own worlds of beauty and order; safe from the messy world outside. For this man of deeply regressive tendencies, the bathroom is clearly something of a womb. Still, the bathroom is a strange place to retreat to escape the demeaning physicality of the body. "Swift's Scatophobia," the horrified disgust at human excremental function from which Dean Swift could not free himself, is mentioned on the first page of the novel. In Swift's poem "The Lady's Dressing Room" the speaker cries as if in continued surprise and outrage, "Oh! Celia, Celia, Celia shits!" (l. 118). And, indeed, Enderby might well be said to share the emotional immaturity and psychosexual infantilism sometimes imputed to Swift. Enderby tends to see all women as his stepmother: repositories of all bodily lowliness. One woman is excepted: his long-dead mother, idealized and freed of the corruption of the body. Enderby more and more identifies her with his muse. One of the forces behind his poetry seems to be an attempt to recover the mother he never knew.

The socially inept, emotionally arrested Enderby—a man happy only in his art—calls to mind both Edwin Spindrift of *The Doctor Is Sick* and

J. Alfred Prufrock. The latter, flatteringly comparing himself to Hamlet (but instantaneously rejecting the comparison) wonders if he was meant "to be" or to continue "to be." Enderby's name, almost certainly, suggests the same: end or be. Can a person psychologically survive if he lives solipsistically in a world of his own creation—even if that world is a beautiful world? Is life without change possible or supportable in a mixed, finite world? Can a person survive in the cold lonely hell of Enderby Land—a real Antarctic territory? On the other hand, if this person "remakes" himself and becomes socially adaptable, will he have killed the self—that which makes him both what he is and an artist? For a time, there does seem to be an end to Enderby. An overbearing psychiatrist, Dr. Wapenshaw (who is only a somewhat lesser Dr. Brodsky or Branom of *A Clockwork Orange*), transforms Enderby into Piggy Hogg, useful citizen with "normal" values. The theme of identity is further developed as a plagiarizing poet, Rawcliffe, steals not only Enderby's major poetic work, but also something of his identity; a reversal, however, occurs much later when, upon Rawcliffe's death, Enderby inherits his property and identity. At an earlier point, though, fearing his poetic gift has gone forever, Enderby had indeed attempted suicide.

Enderby, however, is clearly not intended as a study in psychopathology, nor even as a deep, consistent probe into the question of the origins of art in neurosis. It is more genuinely a comic treatment of the familiar theme of "the problems of the artist," that being more true in book 1 (beginning to page 217). (Burgess has stated that the book was always a unity in his mind, but the two "books" of *Enderby* were published separately as *Inside Mr. Enderby* [under the pseudonym "Joseph Kell" in 1963] and *Enderby Outside* [1968].) Picaresque satire soon joins comedy as the dyspeptic poet, who is religiously dedicated to his art, is delivered (called forth to receive a major poetry award) from the fetal security of his lavatory to the flamboyant, and vulgar outer world of London of the mid-sixties. Enderby, astonished, sees this with more than Pickwickian innocence, but he soon becomes nearly overwhelmed by the all-pervasive crassness, tawdriness, and pretentiousness of contemporary life.

There is a corresponding shift in technique as Enderby proceeds from inner to outer world, from lonely autoeroticism to disastrous marriage. The first part of the novel is full of linguistic inventiveness and literary allusions and echoing points. The second half of the novel is rich in visual detail and quick-moving action—even chase sequences of an almost cinematic sort. The author who writes fully competent poems "in the tradition" for his character, suddenly plunges us into the world of Charlie Chaplin, Mack Sennett, and (remarkably, perhaps) the Beatles' films. (Burgess is—or at least was—like Joyce, a knowledgeable devotee of silent film.) At this point the incidents and contrivances of plot tumble over each other without particular rhyme or reason, and bizarre characters begin to loom up everywhere. Moods, tones, and effects shift rapidly. Some reviewers remark on a loss of control and purpose in this part of the book, and, to some extent, they are correct. In another sense, though, Burgess can be seen to be enjoying the dispensation of a "new sensibility," widely referred to in the late sixties. Although he wrote his piece before the second book of *Enderby* appeared, Kingsley Amis, in "What We Need Now Is Savage Laughter," offers some comment that is strikingly apropos to Burgess. In tracing the influence of *Tom Jones* on some "young" English writers, he observes that they are "alike in their evident feeling that the novel of a consistent tone, moving through a recognized and restricted cycle of emotional keys was outdated . . . their attempt has been to combine the violent and the absurd, the grotesque and the romantic, the farcical and the horrific within a single novel."[10] By deliberately upsetting the reader's equilibrium of ordinary literary expectation, the writer is able to tilt him into postures well-angled for new insights.

The Clockwork Testament Midway through the second part of *Enderby,* the naive but smartening poet flees England and arrives in Tangier, where he remains, nursing the dying Rawcliffe, the plagiarist guilty of the theft of Enderby's poetic opus *The Pet Beast.* Burgess lived for a short while in Tangier (where he was friends with the American novelist William Burroughs). Autobiographical elements are present in *Enderby,* but they are, in the alchemy of Burgess's comic art, thoroughly transmuted into self-sustaining fiction. In *The Clockwork Testament* the distance between Burgess and Enderby has greatly shrunk, and the autobiographical bases for the fiction are transparent and near at hand. In the 1972–73 academic year Burgess was teaching at the City College of New York as a visiting distinguished professor of English. During this period the siege of journalists on Burgess was just beginning to abate. Their importunities came as a result of the furor created by Stanley Kubrick's 1971 film version of *A Clockwork Orange.* They came armed with questions about the glorification of violence and the social responsibility of the artist. Burgess found it necessary to make, time and again, this kind of statement: "What hurts me . . . is the allegation . . . that there is a gratuitous indulgence in violence which turns an intended homiletic work into a pornographic one."[11]

Enderby's situation in *The Clockwork Testament* is a relatively precise reflection of Burgess's. Because he had been led to provide a "film treatment" for Hopkins's *The Wreck of the Deutschland,* Enderby has stumbled into notoriety. He finds himself, as one result, teaching at the (fictitious) University of Manhattan for a year. But, as another result, he finds himself vilified, for the filmmakers have, beyond his power, transformed his script into a debased and absurd vehicle of sex and sadism. Crass traders in what they think is very marketable pornography of a sadistic sort, the movie people have pulled Hopkins's nineteenth-century nuns (leaving Germany because of the oppressive Faulk laws) into the Nazi era and made them into graphically suffering victims of rape by teenage storm troopers. The trashy film is a succès de scandale, and it is reported to have provoked several instances of nun raping. Enderby, himself artistically and financially raped by the sharp and vulgar moviemakers, is held morally accountable for all of the deleterious social effects of the film.

Burgess uses his novel, to which he imparts the sharp satiric edge of exaggeration with a point, to get off his chest some of the frustration and bitterness he felt over the whole Kubrick film affair. This is, for the most part, both funny and effective. That the filmmakers are, as expected, Americans and that Enderby is now in America allows Burgess some very funny (even if predictable) development of the collision of cultures theme. This follows the general lines of the cultured Englishman in barbarous America theme that is, to many Americans, pleasingly familiar. Waugh and G. B. Shaw, among many other Britons, knew that a fair number of literate, book-reading Americans thoroughly enjoyed a mostly feigned English condescension toward nearly all things American. But many of these same readers took—understandably—some umbrage with *The Clockwork Testament,* their feeling being that Burgess probably meant exactly what Enderby said here and what the whole thematic drift implied. Aside from some easy potshots at New York City street and subway violence, Burgess shoots at open admissions policies and, seemingly, at minorities in general. Somewhat anticipating Alan Bloom's surprisingly best-selling polemic of 1987–88, *The Closing of the American Mind,* Burgess had, in a published letter to his City College students, complained that "it disturbs me that you want to study Vonnegut and Kesey and, God help us, even my own work."[12] Invited the same year to give a commencement address at Fordham, Burgess was prompted to castigate all that went with "having to hear *Godspell* and watching people reach-out-and-touch at what should have been a dignified ceremony."[13] In a letter later published in the [London] *Times Literary Supplement* a Fordham dean charged Burgess with unforgivable rudeness on that occasion.[14] Likewise, many *Enderby* fans were disappointed to find that the titular hero, valiant, last-ditch defender of language and literary art, had become both enervated and predictable in his denunciations of television commercials, insipid talk shows, citizen noninvolvement during the commission of crimes, young people's willful ignorance of the past, women's lib, the debasement of language, total cultural relativism, shibboleths uttered in favor of minority rights. A British reviewer summed up well what many readers felt had gone wrong: "It is sad to watch [Enderby's] stature shrink in this alien setting. The egotism, the slovenliness, the indifferent poetry, which were all such fun in earlier volumes, seem rather dispiriting now that their possessor is actually proposing himself as an arbiter, even a model, of cultural excellence. And more seriously, Enderby's insularity and his racism . . . seem merely contemptible now that he has been translated from the easy-going bigotries of his native turf to this tense, angry city."[15]

Nevertheless, the novel is genuinely funny; its comedic technique is both usual and easily defensible. The incongruity necessary to comedy is almost invariably abetted by exaggeration. Here, then, all the negative features of the New York (and American) landscape are magnified, as are Enderby's bad temper and rambunctiousness. The matter of aesthetic distance between author and character is frequently a tricky one, but it must be noted that the "public" Burgess, like the "public" Waugh, is more than a little bit the actor who knows how to get audience response. Enderby, too, proves himself both an improvisational actor and creator—Elizabethan-inspired in each case—in both subway and classroom. In the subway he routs, with a sword that had been concealed in his walking stick, some punks intent on assaulting a terrified matron.[16] In the classroom—in one of the funniest scenes in the novel—he indulges himself in a lecturer's tour de force: he extemporizes for his sullen, gullible class on the life and works of the Elizabethan dramatist Gervase Whitelady. The man is a fiction, the product of a second's inspiration, created before our eyes in the tapestry of language and imagination. Surprisingly, but then again, not so surprisingly, the reader begins to discern a similarity between the once shy, involuted exponent of a bygone culture and Alex of *A Clockwork Orange*. Enderby feels an attraction to the Elizabethans because of the intensity of their lives—"a matter of being *integer vitae*" (*CT,* 117). Enderby even questions himself: "Die with Beethoven's Ninth howling and crashing away or live in a safe world of silly clockwork music?" (*CT,* 117).

Enderby offers his own (slightly woodenly insistent) reprise of the themes of *A Clockwork Orange*. The once emotionally adolescent poet has found his own level of personal maturity and he has fought, although quixotically, his own good fight in Manhattan. He does not capitulate to the "safe world of silly clockwork music" (*CT,* 117), but felled by a third heart attack in his sublet Manhattan apartment, he dies, thoughts of the Augustinian/ Pelagian conflict racing through his mind to the end.

Enderby's Dark Lady In *Enderby's Dark Lady* (or No End to Enderby) the poet turns out not to be dead at all. "Composed to placate kind readers of *The Clockwork Testament,* or Enderby's End, who objected to my casually killing my hero" is the short explanation Burgess places immediately below his title. Enderby died only if the reader accepted the hypothesis that he went to teach in Manhattan. Burgess tells us that Enderby did come to America, but not to New York; he journeyed to Indiana "to write the libretto for a ridiculous musical about Shakespeare in a fictitious theatre in Indianapolis."[17]

While *The Clockwork Testament* explicitly (and somewhat redundantly) restates the theme of *A Clockwork Orange, Enderby's Dark Lady* clearly harkens back to *Nothing Like the Sun.* Not only has Enderby written the book for the Indiana musical (which the producer and director hope will soon make its way to Broadway), but he is also now indulging himself in some rich fantasizing about Shakespeare. In this he is like Burgess himself, once called (in 1968) by Warner Brothers to Hollywood to assist in the writing of *The Bawdy Bard,* the working title of a musical about Shakespeare's life that was never produced. In the novel Burgess sets up several more than just playful parallels between Shakespeare, Enderby, and himself (Burgess). When the leading actor, drunk, is unable to perform on opening night, Enderby himself, now Shakeserby or Enderspeare, is enjoined to perform the part of Will. (The temporary melding of Dedalus and Bloom into Blephen and Stoom in the Ithaca section of *Ulysses*[18] is obviously in Burgess's mind.) Each of the members of this entwined triumvirate feels in some way the force of the conflict of artistic integrity/commercial success, but it is clearly Enderby, an unwilling compromiser and a last apostle among modern philistines, who feels it the most.

Comedy is in the forefront as Enderby grapples with show biz types, vulgarians, and half-cultured charlatans in a featureless Indiana city. The reader will feel some genuine pathos, though, for the poet with the problems of loose dentures, cholesterol buildup in a leg (like Burgess), vulgar antagonists, and strong sexual desires joined, unfortunately, to minimal capacities. He will also feel some genuine admiration for Enderby's spunk, integrity, and basic decency. Most readers, too, will feel a genuine attraction for the two stories Enderby has written—stories we are given whole, which sandwich the entire Indiana misadventure. The first of these, "Will and Testament," was written gratis for a struggling Canadian university–sponsored magazine, and its publication was what caused the Indiana theater people to beckon Enderby from Tangier. This seems almost, if not totally, identical to *Will and Testament: A Fragment of Biography,* a work Burgess had published with the Plain Wrapper Press of Verona, Italy, in 1977. Enderby's other story, which concludes the book, is titled "The Muse" and is the very story that Burgess had published in 1968 in the *Hudson Review* as "The Muse: A Sort of SF Story."[19] It would not be fair, however, to deem that Burgess pulled these stories out of a file cabinet to plump up an otherwise thin novel. The stories frame the Enderby-in-Indiana narrative in ways that are aesthetically interesting and thematically germane.

"Will and Testament," the somewhat lesser of the two stories, gives us a flavorful Gunpowder Plot and a tale about Shakespeare's contribution (in an Enderby/Burgess theory) to the King James Bible—thus the pun of the title. Shakespeare's friend and fellow poet, Ben Jonson, is seen in 1606 as a court undercover agent; a man who pretends to conspire with Guy Fawkes and his coconspirators so as to report on them to the Protestant Establishment. Shakespeare mostly looks on, but he does pass on a message from Jonson that saves Parliament from being blown sky-high on that near fateful Fifth of November. Shakespeare and Jonson are met again in 1610. Jonson tells Will of the commission he, Donne, Marston, Dekker, Beaumont, and Fletcher have been given: lending poetic embellishment to the recently translated Authorized Version. Shakespeare has been left out because not only has he failed to offer James due respect, but he is also in poetic decline. Jonson, though, throws his friend the flavorful bone of the forty-sixth psalm. Will notes the coincidence of his being forty-six years of age at the time. Shakespeare alters the forty-sixth word of the psalm from "tremble" to "shake"; the forty-sixth word from the end he changes from "sword" to "speare" (32). Burgess had previously made this suggestion in his nonfiction, coffee table *Shakespeare,*[20] and, in fact, he has long been fascinated—perhaps inordinately—by this sort of play. He is well aware that in the Scylla and Charybdis episode of *Ulysses* Stephen Dedalus claims that Shakespeare "has hidden his own name, a fair name, William, in the plays, a super here, a clown there, as a painter of Old Italy set a face in a dark corner of his canvas."[21] Burgess hides his own name (Wilson, usually) in many of his novels, sometimes not very deeply. In fact, Burgess once complained, in writing about *Nothing Like the Sun,* that "the novel's first reviewers failed to notice the author's personal monograms sewn into the fabric of the work."[22]

In 1976 Enderby is at the Peter Brook Theatre in "Terrebasse" to "write not only verse but mock Tudor dialogue" (36) for a musical that will celebrate the three hundred and sixtieth anniversary of Shakespeare's death and the second American centennial. Enderby, with Shakespeare's known abilities at pleasing the groundlings probably in mind, tries hard to please the producer and director by writing lyrics designed to please the contemporary American audience. Part of what he writes, in fact, is "Give the people what they wish / Something trite and tawdry, / Balladry and bawdry— / Give the people what they wish" (*EDL,* 53). While Enderby's "Will and Testament" is an effective imitation of Elizabethan style, the musical (whose working title is either *Will!* or *A Dark Lady's Will*), provides Burgess with several opportunities for humor. Earnest Enderby does his level best to deliver as promised on his commission and still remain true to art and faithful to Shakespeare. Much of the fun arises as text, lyrics, and even basic conception are perforce altered to meet the demands of a martinet director (decisive, competent, and intelligent but unburdened by any notion of artistic purity), prima donna actors (one scornfully and repeatedly called a fag), and a savvy, jive-talking, beautiful black American pop star named April Elgar (cast as the Dark Lady). As rehearsals proceed, Enderby struggles with rewrites and the cast struggles with the materials and each other: there is parody, pastiche, bitchiness, cross-purposed intentions, and open, comic (but just believably realistic) hostility. In Enderby's book for the play Will is involved in a homosexual relationship with the bisexual Southampton (*EDL,* 80), as in *Nothing Like the Sun;* and the actor playing Will has his wife leave him when she—and everyone else—sees him paying much too explicit attention to his understudy. Enderby's identification with Shakespeare becomes increasingly compelling, and his own Dark Lady is April, the actress enacting that role. Lesser parallels are tucked away.

The Enderby of this novel has a bit more balance and dimension, and a good deal less prejudice than his hypothetical other self of *The Clockwork Testament.* His nerves are steadier and he is less prone to sermonize. Burgess gives, in fact, some of his American antagonists both a bit of wit and hints of a third dimension. The cultural clash is still starkly presented, but it is presented more realistically. The novel lacks something of the straight-ahead satiric intensity of *The Clockwork Testament,* but it compensates for this by the presence of humor that is slightly more subtle. As if to make up for what many readers took to be a revelation of some antiblack prejudice in *The Clockwork Testament,* Burgess here presents his black Americans as both morally worthy and well balanced. Enderby is so infatuated with April Elgar that his heart, blood, and brain activity all enjoy immediate increase. She has down-home wisdom (she is from Chapel Hill, North Carolina), street smarts, elegant sophistication, amazing presence on and off stage, and a knowledge of Kantian philosophy. Her family in North Carolina (Enderby accompanies her there for a Christmas visit) are seen as simple, very decent, religious people with some homely wisdom. Perhaps the only disturbing note is the name that Burgess chooses for the wealthy Indiana widow who, possessed of both cultural hollowness and self-important pretentiousness, sponsors the Shakespeare enterprise. Her name is Mrs. Schoenbaum, and one can only conjecture about whether this is some personal arrow aimed (puzzlingly) at Samuel Schoenbaum, a foremost and justifiably respected American Shakespeare authority. One wonders if perhaps Burgess is needling Schoenbaum because he once called *Nothing Like the Sun* "an absurd gallimaufry of invention and (to put it mildly) dubious biographical theorizing."[23]

As Enderby explains something of the rationale behind the theatrical conception to the cast, he provides as well a kind of pithy gloss on *Nothing Like the Sun.* So that the cast can note the psychological/spiritual weight of the sex scenes, Enderby explains that the Elizabethans tended to see the sexual act in cosmic terms (*EDL,* 77). To explain Will's homosexual relationship with Southampton, Enderby asseverates that Elizabethan "sexuality was so intense it expressed itself in many forms" (*EDL,* 80). Enderby, who comes to feel very close to Shakespeare, "enWills" himself to be one with the Bard, and certainly he feels his own intense passion when near April Elgar. Since, though, he is still something of the old Enderby, his form of sexual expression is autoerotic release, which he enacts three times, in fact, the day that he first feels April's powerful presence. Still slightly self-pitying, Enderby identifies not only with Will, but with Lucy Negro, the Dark Lady, who was sold into slavery. An artist among philistines, Enderby has come to feel that he has sold himself into a slavery of sorts by accepting a contract with the Indiana commission. And, his infatuation with April complete, he freely compromises his own art by heeding an "evil muse, a conflatrix of the spirit of bemerded Will's poetaster enemies" (*EDL,* 101) that dictates some new lyrics on the situation of Lucy Negro: "Know you not where the future lies? Look westward, sister / from this derelict / island, a blister / soon to be pricked. I speak for the future, madam, Cleopatran New Rome, I speak of black power, / that's what we'll get; / although I lack power, / I'll get it yet" (*EDL,* 101). With such sins against art on his conscience, Enderby comes to feel that a series of small accidents he incurs are most probably fulfillments of the curse that Shakespeare placed against those who disturbed his bones. Although Enderby, impressed at the last moment to play the part of Will, gives a creditable performance in the foreshortened play (a representative of the actor's union coming on, whistle in mouth, to end the performance), the modern poet/playwright is more certain than ever that the whole enterprise has been a mistake. His concluding words are, "poetry has to go on. Nobody wants it, but we have to have it. There's something else I have to write first, though. A little story. *Leave Well Alone* or *Leave Will Alone,* some such title. About Shakespeare. If he'll allow it" (*EDL,* 141).

Enderby writes his "little story," and although it is titled "The Muse," it has "leave Will alone" as its informing, ironic idea. This story, in addition to its qualities of vivid, magical strangeness, and its crisp, ironic ending, has some interesting epistemological play to recommend it. A young literary historian, Paley, either voyages to an alternate universe presently in the Elizabethan age or journeys back, by way of a time warp, to Elizabethan times on this earth. This young scholar, of the year 2064, hopes to have a momentous meeting with Shakespeare that will perform the important function of historically authenticating both the man and his works. The very day the time traveler lands, however, he finds his way fraught with peril. Unnervingly, these Elizabethans have additional eyes in strange parts of their bodies, or at least it seems so to Paley. He has to summon the utmost concentration in himself so that people and rooms do not dissolve or transmogrify themselves right before him. Paley suspects his perceptual problems might be due to some defect in the fine-tuning of the time travel, but he cannot be sure. He finds Shakespeare easily enough, but disconcertingly, the playwright is not at all surprised to be visited by a time traveler, for he indicates he has encountered them before. Moreover, Shakespeare makes an unmistakable homosexual pass at him. We come to understand, in the final irony that reveals the full meaning of the title, that Paley, like the other visitors from the future, is Shakespeare's muse. The playwright from Stratford-upon-Avon, it turns out, is a hack. The plays he has written himself are *Heliogubalus, A Word to Fright a Whoremaster, The Sad Reign of Harold First and Last,* and *The Devil in Dulwich.* He has begun to make much, though, of the manuscripts brought to him by the "muses" who visit him out of the future. He thus takes Paley's "Shakespeare" plays with satisfied nonchalance, and we understand that he will blithely copy them out in his own hand and present them as his own. Coolly, he has Paley trundled off to a madhouse.

To some extent, Burgess answers, half-playfully, half-seriously, those scholars who expressed the opinion that in *Nothing Like the Sun* he had taken presumptuous liberties with what little we actually know about Shakespeare's private life. In *Enderby's Dark Lady* Paley is dismayed to see "standing before him a fictional character called 'William Shakespeare,' an actor acting the part. Why could he not get in touch with the *Ding an sich,* the Kantian noumenon? But that was the trouble—the thing-in-itself was changed by the observer into whatsoever phenomenon the categories of time and space and sense imposed" (*EDL,* 156). April Elgar's mention of the "noumenon and phenomenon" in Kant (*EDL,* 88) had most specifically prepared the way for epistemological problems, as had, in a lesser way, her not being April Elgar at all, but rather one May Johnson, who named herself for the British composer of an admired work called, she had thought, "Pompous Circus Dance." Because the definable essence is forever elusive, Burgess perhaps wishes to remind Samuel Schoenbaum and others that he modestly titled his earlier novel *Nothing Like the Sun* (from Sonnet 130) to emphasize "the impossibility of conveying the authentic effulgence."[24] The ending suggests that artists are inspired by muses sometimes strange even to themselves, a phenomenon apparent in both *Nothing Like the Sun* and *Enderby.* Rivulets of the foul, the sublime, and the ridiculous run together to form the wellsprings of the art of an Enderby, or even a WS.

MF Starting relatively early in his career, more than a few Burgess critics and reviewers have been of the opinion that he is basically an artistic novelist whose cleverness and gift of language give him the potential for becoming one of the great novelists of the century. In the stream of critical approval, however, there has often flowed an undercurrent of slight dissatisfaction—a feeling that in no single work has Burgess reached the level of achievement for which his abilities have clearly prepared him. Some have shared in the near prevalent view that he writes too quickly, and some have felt that he is frequently distracted from his basic artistry—that at just the wrong moment he cocks an eye in the direction of commercial success. Many of Burgess's early followers were probably heartened, then, by this statement he made in a 1968 interview with *Life* magazine: "The sort of things I write will be more and more involuted, more and more difficult, less and less salable. This just has to be. You get fed up with existing technique. You have to do something more daring."[25]

It is a correct, if somewhat overworked, observation that English novelists of the last fifty years have tended to be not at all daring. In general, they have been content with the relatively small, well-controlled canvas of social realism or social satire. They have generally avoided the "big" or cosmic themes of the American or Russian novel and have shied away from technical experimentation. In the latter regard, a number of British novelists felt that, in only one generation (that of 1910–39) the spirit of technical innovation was understandably exhausted. In *Finnegans Wake* particularly, many felt Joyce had reached a point beyond which it was simply impossible to go, and more than a few considered the trip an egocentric bit of pretentious self-indulgence anyway. Burgess, much more international in sensibility and a Joyce aficionado, did not at all agree. In 1964 he urged further exploration of regions first charted by his master. "We should all now be writing novels like *Finnegans Wake,* not necessarily so obscure or so large, but starting on the way Joyce has shown in exploring the resources of the language."[26] In 1978 his outlook was still constant. He told Samuel Coale, "We've got a hell of a long way to go with modernism. Some people think *Finnegans Wake* is the end of modernism. . . . I think we're still in a modernist phase."[27]

In *MF* (1971) and *Napoleon Symphony* (1974) Burgess makes large efforts to do something new, to extend the boundaries of the novel form. In 1973 he told Charles Bunting that "when people deliberately turn their backs on experimentation, then they are violating the essential principle of the novel, i.e., that it is novel; it is something new."[28] Although his prediction that it would not be salable proved true, Burgess expressed self-satisfaction with the innovative character of *MF.* "*MF,* believe it or not, is a completely original experiment,"[29] he declared to John Cullinan in 1973. In *MF* itself, the narrator/protagonist, Miles Faber, a long way into a most curious adventure, suddenly addresses the reader: "What, incidentally, are you like? Yawning and idle, looking for a *good read,* have you picked this idly from a public library shelf or remainder table or barrowload of dogeared joblot hasbeens . . . ?"[30] It is not, though, just the "yawning and idle" who will be puzzled, disappointed, or even infuriated by *MF;* any reader who is rather rigid in his conventional expectations of what a novel should be, is bound, no matter how experienced or sophisticated a reader he otherwise is, to feel frustration and annoyance when confronted with a truly experimental novel.

Burgess gives every indication of preparing both himself and his reader for his *MF* enterprise with the kind of statements he was making about the novel form in 1970. In writing of what the novel would be like "in 2000, A.D.," he slyly described what he himself would be doing in *MF* and *Napoleon Symphony.* He writes that the novel of the future will be one of "semantic richness (a *récit* of delicious complexity)," and that some of it will consist of pages "of prose as elaborately and painfully composed as a piece of 12-part counterpoint for strings."[31] And in another statement that dimly echoes Eliot's thoughts about a literary artist's creating the taste by which he himself will be appreciated, Burgess writes that "one can be truly creative if one creates not merely a subject but the medium in which the subject moves."[32]

Burgess goes further than this, though, in attempting to provide his readers with some pointed, preliminary instruction in how to read *MF.* Very probably, he identifies with the dismay that Joyce must have felt when, after the publication of *Ulysses,* he had to provide his readers with a key or two to the mythic framework, employing his friends Gilbert and Budgen as interpreter-messengers. Burgess gave the key away in an interview published just prior to the novel: "I want to write a structuralist novel. The first of the structuralist novels, I hope, based on the Lévi-Strauss theatre of the correlation between language and social forms. So that I want to exploit the Algonquin legend, the boy who was bound to commit incest because he could answer all the riddles correctly, which is a direct tie-up with Oedipus."[33] Burgess took the idea that provides the whole basis of *MF* from Claude Lévi-Strauss's *The Scope of Anthropology,* a book that he had reviewed for the *Washington Post Book World* in 1967.

Burgess's *Book World* review, "If Oedipus Had Read His Lévi-Strauss" (reprinted in *Urgent Copy*), shows Burgess's fascination with archetypal myth; an unsurprising interest given his abiding reverence for *Ulysses* and *Finnegans Wake,* novels heavy with archetypes. Burgess notes that Lévi-Strauss reports (as had cultural anthropologists before him) that societies far distant from each other in time and geography share certain basic myths. Lévi-Strauss discovered that in Algonquin and Iroquois Indian legends there is a close connection between riddling and incest, just as there is in the myth of Oedipus. Burgess writes in the review that "If Oedipus [after correctly answering the riddle of the Sphinx] had read his Lévi-Strauss, he would have known that incest was on its way. The man who solves the insoluble puzzle has, symbolically, disrupted nature. Since incest is the ultimate perversion of nature, nature is shocked to death."[34] Burgess goes on to examine a somewhat disguised riddle/incest motif in *Finnegans Wake,* finding that Earwicker is in love with his own daughter and that his son Shem is prevented from committing incest with his sister by his inability to answer a riddle.

Burgess also indicates a less consequential germ for *MF* (or *M/F;* Burgess indicates that the title may appear either way). He noted that several years before, "William Conrad, the robust actor who played Cannon in the television series, expressed a half-serious desire to make an all-black film on Oedipus, calling it *Mother Fucker.*"[35] In addition to this obscenely incestuous reference, the title seems to stand for male/female, mother/father, as well as Miles Faber, the protagonist. In Latin *miles* means soldier, and *faber* means craftsman or maker. The name, then, might suggest destruction/creation, or it might suggest a soldier who fights for culture or civilization.

The title is merely the first of countless puzzles or riddles in this most unconventional novel. *MF* will really be enjoyed only by those readers fascinated by puzzles and riddles. Readers not at least somewhat inclined will find *MF* taxing and trivial. Against the charge of triviality, however, Burgess would surely call the structuralists to his defense; he would ask his reader to reflect on the deep interconnectedness of patterns within our culture. Ties between our linguistic system and our socioeconomic systems are so old and buried so deep that we fail to discern their presence. Burgess's novel is, then, a play with form in the deepest sense: in its seeming formlessness and disparateness it contains, nonetheless, some of the very clues that will allow us to uncover surprising patterns of unity—or, at least, highly patterned principles of duality.

Understandably, since it mirrors human life in a highly fragmented world (the world of today, particularly), the novel is full of division. A few of these divisions have a basis in nature, but most do not. Inherent in culture is the need to classify and systematize, but many of our taxonomies are false. The first of the novel's three epigraphs points to one such false, or insignificant, structural division: "In his *Linguistic Atlas of the United States and Canada* Hans Kurath recognizes no isogloss coincident with the political border along Latitude 49 degrees N." This quotation from Simeon Potter—about a real atlas—points out that American English does not halt at a political frontier: the United States/Canada division is an insignificant structure. In the novel as well there are a number of false or insignificant classifications. An important one is race, and Burgess employs a neatly effective way of indicating that racial division is nonessential and, in fact, trivial: it is not until the very end of the novel that Miles Faber reveals he is black. Miles thinks of himself just as himself, a human being. To him race is an irrelevance.

The tension of opposites in *MF* is strong in conception, theme, and general execution. Burgess issues himself the challenge of making *MF* seem a reasonably conventional, straightforward, realistic novel while he is actually engaged in the artifice of employing the Algonquin legend as a paradigm. Readers, of course, would have no notion (even with the few slender clues embedded in the novel itself) that Burgess is following, fairly closely, the Algonquin riddle-incest story unless they have read *The Scope of Anthropology.* Here is Lévi-Strauss's account of the story:

> The Iroquois and Algonquin Indians tell the story of a young girl subjected to the amorous leanings of a nocturnal visitor whom she believes to be her brother. Everything seems to point to the guilty one: physical appearance, clothing, and the scratched cheek which bears witness to the heroine's virtue. Formally accused by

her, the brother reveals he has a counterpart or, more exactly, a double, for the tie between them is so strong that any accident befalling one is automatically transmitted to the other. To convince his incredulous sister, the young man kills his double before her, but at the same time he condemns himself, since their destinies are linked.

. . . of course, the mother of the victim will want to avenge her son. As it happens, she is a powerful sorceress, the mistress of the owls. There is only one way of misleading her: that the sister marry her brother, the latter passing for the double he has killed. Incest is so inconceivable that the old woman never suspects the hoax. The owls are not fooled and denounce the guilty ones, but they succeed in escaping. The Western listener easily perceives in this myth a theme established by the Oedipus legend: the very precautions taken to avoid incest in fact make it inevitable.[36]

Lévi-Strauss continues to explain that among the Pueblo Indians of the southwestern United States there is a connection between riddles and incest, and that "among the Algonquins themselves . . . there are myths in which owls, or sometimes the ancestor of owls, set riddles to the hero which he must answer under pain of death. Consequently, in America, too, riddles present a double Oedipal character: by way of incest, on the one hand, and by way of the owl, in which we are led to see a transposed form of the sphinx, on the other."[37]

Readers of *MF* will see that Burgess, while interpolating some plot elements of his own, follows somewhat closely (especially in the latter half of the novel) all the main ingredients of the Algonquin myth. When Burgess defers so heavily to a structure (the Indian myth) superimposed from without, he is, in a sense, establishing a dialectic of the artificial and the "real" that somewhat mirrors the culture/nature dichotomy of the structural anthropologist. Culture is the product of the innate human need for order—a way of organizing the "real" so as to make it comprehensible. Man's processes of classification and organization, however, usually prove distortions of the "real"; their perceived unities factitious, and thus fallacious. Miles Faber's strong rebellious instincts proceed from a keen awareness of social absurdities, most of these the products of false taxonomies. Miles, though, goes too far in his protests—not merely in the act of public copulation that has gotten him expelled from college, but also in his youthfully impetuous denial of some unities of both nature and culture that result from the interpenetration of opposites. At the outset, Miles seems more soldier than maker, more destroyer than creator, although—all things interpenetrating—this dichotomized judgment is itself partially fallacious. In any event, Miles, something of an existentialist rebel, does have a yearning for "the death of form and shipwreck of order" (*MF,* 64). A Professor Keteki (whose name means "riddle" in Sanskrit) has introduced Miles to the work of an obscure poet, Sib Legeru, and, as Miles says, "Sib Legeru's work was exciting to me because of its elevation of the useless, unviable, unclassifiable" (*MF,* 5). A reader who knows (as Miles does not) that *siblegeru* means incest (the word, meaning "to lie with one's sibling," having been used by the Anglo-Saxon bishop Wulfstan to uphold the near-universal taboo) will rightly suspect that Burgess has already prepared for the unleashing of some powerful ironies.

Miles, gifted with a formidable Oedipal talent as a riddle solver, is strangely unaware that he is an artist of sorts—that in supplying missing intellectual links he is an unwitting apostle of order and form. He does not realize at this point that man's rage for order is innate. Stronger within him is the conflicting universal urge to rebel: the impulse to achieve freedom by resisting the imprisonment of generalizations and taxonomies. At the end of the novel, he is able to say "that a mania for total liberty is really a mania for prison, and you'll get there by way of incest" (*MF,* 241). And, a bit earlier, he supplies a reflection that articulates one of the novel's most important themes: "For order has both to be and not to be challenged, this being the anomalous condition of the sustention of the cosmos. Rebel becomes hero; witch becomes saint. Exogamy means disruption and also stability; incest means stability and also disruption. You've got to have it both ways, man" (*MF,* 214). One recognizes the freedom/stability opposition as the thematic basis of several Burgess novels, but, most notably, *A Clockwork Orange.*

Just as Miles "wants to have it both ways," so too does Burgess, his creator. *MF* is, in part, a parable about art. In the sense that art tends toward endless series of couplings of the creator's own solipsistic ideas, it can be seen as incestuous. (In the Enderby books, as the literal masturbator Enderby spends his self-stimulated passion and emotion in private, Burgess emphasizes the masturbatory tendencies of art. Neither metaphor, of course, is original with Burgess.) The true artist must be both incestuous and exogamous. Burgess's play with the novel's form suggests this. The character Zoon Fonanta (a man whose name means "talking animal" in Greek and who turns out to be Miles's grandfather) might seem to speak for Burgess when he deprecates Sib Legeru's poetry to Miles thus: "The pseudoliterary works are based on the meanest and most irrelevant of taxonomies, they derive their structures from the alphabetic arrangements of encyclopedias and dictionaries" (*MF,* 234). In interviews, however, Burgess has several times indicated his attraction for precisely such an endeavor; and we can learn (but only because he informs us outside of the book) that he strategically yields to this growing impulse in *MF*. Burgess writes that, as Miles enters a hotel, "he notes the decor of the lobby, the garden without, a group of card-players, and hears a girl ask on the telephone for the number 113 and Mr. R. J. Wilkinson. He does not see the connection between these things. R. J. Wilkinson compiled a classic dictionary—Malay (or Indonesian)-English—and the entire scene is made out of the words on page 113 of that work."[38] Once readers learn this, they can surely find it a more than sufficiently neat illustration of the incestuous.

Most readers of *MF*, propelled forward by the narrative energy and fascinated by what lies beneath the shroud of mystery and strangeness woven by the elements of plot, will enjoy the novel. But those readers who feel challenged, rather than burdened, by linguistic puzzles, recondite allusions, and various kinds of intellectual byplay will find it still more satisfying. Some readers might have to struggle to adjust their habits and expectations when reading such a novel; readers of Joyce, Borges, Nabokov, or perhaps Thomas Pynchon, would seem to have a decided advantage. *MF* does have a strong general correspondence with many of the most serious, "experimental" works of American fiction of the last twenty-five years or so. *MF* is so self-consciously concerned with form and textures because any way of getting beneath these—to discover some "objective truth"—is considered highly problematic. Although Burgess does not flirt with nihilism, he is here entwined in radical skepticism. His narrator/protagonist, Miles, steps stage forward to deliver to the reader some words of advice that, in large part, both parody and mock intellectual/academic enterprise: "The story I've told is more true than plausible; at least I admit that the veridicality can, so to speak, be viewed relatively. . . . Don't try distilling a message from it, not even an espresso cupful of meaningful epitome or a Sambuca glass of abridgment, *con la mosca*. For separable meaning go to the professors, whose job it is to make a meaning out of anything. Professor Keteki, for instance, with his *Volitional Solecisms in Melville*" (*MF*, 240–41). In the very real sense that it questions both the nature of art and the novel as a form, *MF* is like other "reflexive" novels or works of "metafiction"—fictions that provide provocative play with the nature and processes of the story form itself. In the structuralist/experimental endeavor that is *MF*, Burgess "finds" deep patterns of unity amid cultural disarray and the accidents of a mostly random universe. But then, at the end of the novel he seems to withdraw his "discovery," or at least invite his reader to deconstruct his meaning. *MF* can thus be read as either a structuralist or poststructuralist novel; modernist or postmodernist. In either case, it provides bracing play with the most important questions of form and meaning. The novel's deepest riddles do not cease to puzzle when the reading is done.

It is a sign of a natural emotional letdown, but not artistic failure, that Burgess, in view of general critical and popular incomprehension, chose to explain, in some detail, his own novel. Burgess's essay "Oedipus Wrecks," a chapter in *This Man and Music,* provides extremely useful interpretive elucidation (probably invaluable, in fact, to readers who have not read the rewarding commentaries of Geoffrey Aggeler or Jean Kennard). Burgess naturally explains the whole basis of the novel in Lévi-Strauss and provides as well readable and tidily cogent explanations of the riddles, name symbolism, and allusions. Readers will be convinced of the importance of most and doubtful about a few. He informs us that once, when Miles wakes up in inexplicable terror, "his watch has stopped at 19:17 (the year of the birth of Jack Wilson)."[39] This sort of self-referentiality, playful or otherwise, is a quite common feature of the postmodernist novel. Here, perhaps, it is not unimportant, but another deliberate indication of the incestuous nature of art. Burgess is entirely convincing when he concludes, "I do not think it is possible to write many novels of this kind, but I do believe, and I think the little book proves it, that it is possible to juggle with the free will of fictional characters and the predestination of an imposed structure."[40] Those words remind one of a number of contemporary "experimental" novels, but most particularly, perhaps, of John Fowles's *The French Lieutenant's Woman* (1969). Fowles's far less genuinely experimental novel did, though, have rich historical coloration and far more realized characters, bringing it great popular as well as critical success. Burgess, though, was planning the even grander experiment of *Napoleon Symphony.*

Napoleon Symphony *Napoleon Symphony* is a novel that, with a kind of willed rambunctiousness, hurls its considerable weight and energy against the conventional boundaries of the novel form. Without much question, it is the most concertedly intelligent effort in English to use musical forms to give shape to a novel. Burgess seemed concerned, though (not too surprisingly, given the incomprehension or hostility met by *MF*), that he both instruct and disarm potential detractors of the new novel. At the end of *Napoleon Symphony* Burgess includes "An Epistle to the Reader"—a winsome, seemingly effortless, highly clever, and economic series of remarks in verse, which combines one hundred eighty lines of natural diction and heroic couplets. With convincing frankness, Burgess informs his reader that "ever since I chose/The novelist's métier one mad idea / Has haunted me, and I fulfill it here / Or try to—it is this: somehow to give / Symphonic shape to verbal narrative, / Impose on life, though nerves scream and resist, / The abstract pattern of the symphonist".[41] The novel is, in fact, fairly elaborately patterned on Beethoven's *Eroica,* the Symphony No. 3 in E Flat, Opus 55—the work Beethoven had originally dedicated to Napoleon. This work, Beethoven's favorite symphony, and, in its own day, a startlingly successful piece of innovation in its own right, obviously attracted Burgess because its powerfully explosive forces were given careful release in a daring but highly ordered pattern new to the composer just beginning his "middle period." Burgess, always fascinated by the collision of opposites, was most probably awed by this symphony's emphasis on points taut with tension, and the fine balance of tension and release that challenged emulation in a novel.

The virtuosity the reader encounters in *Napoleon Symphony* is entirely to be expected since the novel provides Burgess the natural opportunity to indulge his major loves: music; a display of linguistic skills that include rhymes, puns, and jokes in several languages; a skillful playing off of the lofty against the demotic; and ironic portraiture of a man who tends to be a homme moyen sensuel as well as a myth. Evident here as well is Burgess's characteristically eager willingness to do research for authentic (or at least pungent) backgrounds and details usable in his own artistic process of historic alchemy. To touch all the necessary historical bases while ensuring that the novel follows the model of the *Eroica* is the kind of challenge to form that Burgess relishes. In following Beethoven Burgess had to find a way of synthesizing Napoleon and Prometheus, another formal requirement that obviously had immediate appeal to a modernist like Burgess, for whom elaborate mythic design is a highly privileged strategy.

A systematically deep probe into Napoleon's "psychology" is not what the novel attempts. The suggestion of complexity in Napoleon's character is very definitely here, however. The reader is given a fair degree of latitude for the interpretation of Napoleon's character. In its imitation of symphonic form (albeit certainly not slavish), the novel necessarily provides a highly elliptical representation of events, and a jagged, cracked-mirror sort of reflection of character. These may be limitations, but Burgess turns them, at least in part, to his advantage. Is Napoleon an absurdly megalomaniacal little corporal? Is he an earlier, Corsican version of Hitler? Does he become an "ensanguinated tyrant"? Is he Prometheus? Is he Christ? Is he, like sufferers of the complex to which he gives his name, a severe victim of his own delusions? All of these questions (if not the answers) have clear and definite warrant in the novel itself. Some answers seem better than others, but viewpoints do shift. Readers should remember, perhaps, that Beethoven's view of Napoleon was somewhat ambivalent from the first and that shortly after his completion of the *Eroica,* his view shifted pronouncedly. Beethoven had been a fervent supporter of the French revolutionary ideals, and then of Napoleon, the First Consul of France. He was clearly inspired by Napoleon's charismatic potency but, as a resident of Vienna, had some premonitions that the First Consul could become despotic and the most dangerous of enemies. In 1803 his fascination with Napoleon was still great enough that he decided to dedicate his newly completed Symphony No. 3 in E Flat to him. It is said, though, that when Beethoven learned, in May 1804, that Napoleon had declared himself emperor, he furiously ripped out the title page with its dedication. (In the novel, just after "N" has been crowned emperor, a rippinglike "orchestral" noise is heard: most likely, a playful representation of Beethoven's destruction of his title page.) Beethoven now called his composition "Heroic symphony to celebrate the memory of a great man," Bonaparte now being sufficiently effaced so that the hero could be any great man. One such incarnation of the heroic spirit is Prometheus, and in his finale Beethoven incorporates themes from his own earlier completed ballet on Prometheus (*The Creatures of Prometheus,* op. 43). In Burgess's own finale—his part 4—"Promethapoleon," who finds himself suffering from a severe liver ailment on St. Helena, assumes Christ-like identities.

At a number of points in the novel Napoleon might appear to be the Burgessian sort of heroic vitalist—a man unstintingly engaged in the full processes of life. Burgess, however, indicated in an interview that he might be better viewed "as a great demonic force, and essentially as a very modern man, really a very contemporary man, because he's . . . half animal and half computer. . . . His head was a computer. His body was the body of an ape. His chest was preternaturally big. His lungs were preternaturally large. And he was over-oxygenated . . . over-energetic, even sexually so."[42] This biologically deterministic view (which is based on reported observations by Bonaparte's contemporaries) is articulated by a character (Cambaceres) in the novel itself: "He's not really human. Intellect and animality. A machine on top of an animal. He has a chest like an orangutan, have you seen him breathe in? . . . He dances up and down like a monkey when he's in a rage. . . . Swives like a rattlesnake, so they tell me" (*NS,* 73). Thematically, of course, the novel suggests far more than the very partial truth that simple biological difference is destiny. A corollary of sorts of the simple deterministic view is offered later in the novel by Talleyrand. He looks closely at a literal "young orangutan, neatly dressed in muslin" and remarks that "the copious oxygen it inhales feeds no great engine of organization. The subhuman and the superhuman are alike in that neither is human" (*NS,* 224). If Burgess is suggesting that Napoleon, a kind of computer-directed orang-utan, is a clockwork orange, he seems to invite us to consider that the times we live in can easily propel all of us to that condition. He might even expect us to remember a Malay word learned in *The Long Day Wanes: orang,* which means man.

Although possessed of a cold, brilliant, chesslike mind, N is more frequently reminiscent of Leopold Bloom than Ulysses, a wily but true warrior. Indeed, the mock heroic is mostly in the ascendant in the book. N is the victim of a bad liver, hemorrhoids, halitosis, hypochondria, and chronic heartburn, this latter malady (the reason for his keeping his hand inside his coat) caused or exacerbated by his constantly eating too quickly. Although he is always importunate to thrust—as in battle—his lovemaking is also quick and soon finished, a main reason for his being cuckolded (like Bloom and unlike Ulysses). N is but one of a long line of Burgess antiheroes who are inadequate lovers or cuckolds. It is largely through such afflictions as hemorrhoids and wifely betrayal that N is humanized. Otherwise, what the reader sees is monumental egotism, moral insensitivity, lack of artistic judgment, and elaborate self-delusion. A literary diagnosis of Napoleon's overbearing need for military conquest is attributed by a café lounger to Mme de Staël: "The conduct of war was, to him, a highly extravagant mode of self-stimulation. It is conceivable that Austerlitz contrived for him a modest ejaculation, but the massive slaughter and suffering of the Russian campaign must, one hopes, have procured a truly satisfying orgasm—else, what waste" (*NS,* 230).

Burgess's "own interpretation" of N is more ambiguous, and certainly somewhat less reductive than that of Mme de Staël. At several points the suggestion is clearly enough offered (although not in so many words) that N is a victim of his own Pelagianism. A republican idealist and a basic rationalist (a product of the Enlightenment) at the beginning of his career, N has failed to recognize the real presence of evil and his own vauntingly romantic egocentrism that will so surely lead him into it. Being totally offguard because of his denial of evil and his inability for self-recognition, he is ripe for easy conquest. In fact, he never associates himself with evil and is almost totally unburdened by guilt. At times Burgess presents N as a near-grotesque, and we should remember that in literature the grotesque is frequently both the end result and effective illustration of someone's naïve refusal to recognize the dark, subrational, or evil side of man. In part 4, imprisoned on St. Helena, N is taunted by a pert, fifteen-year-old English girl. She shows N a popular toy of that year: "a gross carven caricature of himself with characterizing military hat but the form else, and even the tail, of a monkey, clinging to a pole which the pulling of a string enabled his simian mock-majesty to climb to the top, whence he tumbled to a flat green-painted bed inscribed with the name *St. Helena*" (*NS,* 296). When the girl's parents shut her up supperless in a room to meditate "on her inexcusable behavior," N, now wiser and more sensitive to others, appears outside the door to speak with her. "I liberated all Europe but you I cannot liberate. I do not wish your incarceration. With all of us there are forces hardly to be controlled. . . . None of us is really free," N says (*NS,* 297). He lets it be known to his jailer, Sir Hudson Lowe, that, like the artist, he has had a rage for order: "a garden is what man must win from the wilderness, it is the order he seeks. . . . Once I sought to turn all Europe into a garden" (*NS,* 306). As if to underline what N has recently learned, a raging storm destroys his small garden on St. Helena. This seems to be "the gods bellowing their ultimate rage at Prometheus"; "chaos seemed to have come again" (*NS,* 338).

Formal and technical elements in *Napoleon Symphony* have strong and obvious precedence, though, over both "ideas" and the clear and accurate representation of history. Several of Burgess's remarks about the absolute primacy of form may cause us to deduce that his is an aesthetic that derives more obviously from music or painting (or perhaps even certain schools of cinema) than from narrative fiction. Other of Burgess's remarks, however, indicate his awareness that he has sometimes veered too sharply in the direction of adherence to pure form. For example, when asked if he could pretend to be a critic of his own work, Burgess replied, in part, that "I think there is, perhaps, an over-concern with form, structure, a tendency to use linguistic tropes for their own sake."[43] *Napoleon Symphony* would, however, scarcely be imaginable if Burgess had adhered to a more conventional form. The aesthetic question remains: Can a novelist expect his reader to take such pleasure and satisfaction from merely the novel's formal elements that he can safely disregard the heavy domination of his "content" by his form? If it is easily possible for a listener of Beethoven's symphony to bathe in the sheer gorgeousness of sound in the first movement—form and content becoming virtually one—can the novelist legitimately expect to achieve something closely analogous to this with his reader? In a review of Styron's *Sophie's Choice,* Burgess described the problem thus: "A novel, like a painting or a symphony, is about itself, but fiction is condemned, which the other arts are not, to deal with the real world, which means, when it is important fiction, history and the philosophical resonances of history."[44] In his "Epistle to the Reader" Burgess modestly explains that his novel is "Dealing in hard particulars but still / Invoking what is always general / In music, the Napoleonic presence / And, *contra punctum,* music's formal essence— / As far as possible—if it can be done— / It can't of course—, and so on, and so on. / The first two movements of the Eroica, / Although (but need I tell you this?) they are / Organized sound, no more, to awe the ear, / Yet do suggest some hero's brief career" (*NS,* 364). Despite Burgess's protestation that he embarked on an effort that "can't be done," many critics and reviewers reasonably found—to their amazement—that Burgess had very nearly pulled it off. Nearly all American commentators, at least, seemed to share Burgess's sentiment that "Muses bless / Failed boldness more than orthodox success" (*NS,* 361).

The reader who begins unaware of just how far the musical analogy implied by the title goes (the "Epistle" not appearing until the end) will still be heavily aware of nontraditional strategies. Points of view shift, melt together, or play off each other to ironic effect; prose suddenly yields to verse; disembodied voices tumble all over each other, sometimes producing the effect of Greek choruses gone crazy; the prose becomes highly rhythmic and sometimes onomatopoeic; clichés, trite proverbs, and popular songs assume a peculiar sort of prominence; an acrostic or two will suddenly call attention to itself; verbal motifs are sounded, developed, and transposed; there are dissolves and cuts suggestive of the filmmaker's art; parodies and pastiches of Henry James, Joyce, Wordsworth, Byron, Dickens, W. S. Gilbert and others slyly intrude; the speech of various characters is occasionally differentiated by typeface; from time to time pronouncedly great alterations of the novel's pace occur; time leaps ahead, and then bends back upon itself, displaying both unrecognized identities and historical continuity. Early in the novel N thinks aloud to his troops about the most efficient means of disposing of a captured enemy: "Consider, for instance, the efficient annihilation of a whole disaffected city. The unventilated room crammed with subjects—we must not think of victims, prisoners, the terms being emotive—and the introduction, by a simple pumping device, of some venomous inhalant" (*NS,* 48). The historical continuum is hinted at in the rise of Nazism that is clearly forecast by the young student, Frederick Stapps, a failed assassin of Bonaparte. His presence in the book reminds us not simply of some common roots of tyranny in the Emperor and the Führer, but certain historical patterns of cause and effect. Insofar as Napoleonic threat and conquest played a part in the unification of the German people and the formation of a national resolve to achieve its own military might, it was a first link in a chain running from Napoleon through the Franco-Prussian War, through World War I, to World War II. Also, the great romantic investment that

Beethoven had initially made in Napoleon is, somewhat ironically, reflected in Stapps's own heavily German romanticism. Stapps tells N that "the *Volk* . . . the German people is becoming aware of its destiny"; that "you don't weep with the joy of the German forest or the German sunrise over the German mountains"; that "we are the only pure race in Europe and must remain so" (*NS,* 134–35). Some other plays with past/present similarities, and of the idea of the pastness of the present, and the presentness of the past, also occur; these often being abetted by literary echoes and allusions. In a "Letter from Europe" Burgess points up one more ironic turn of history that may not have occurred to readers: "He [Napoleon] wanted a united Europe. England, having chopped down her forests and exhausted her iron to defeat him, is now entering the Napoleonic dream (Burgess has in mind Britain's entry into the Common Market, and some real possibility, in the future, of a United States of Europe)."[45]

Burgess has written that it does not really matter very much if his reader discerns the symphonic parallels or not. He seems to have found the discipline of form salutary in itself and the appropriation of musical techniques an effective means "to unify a mass of historical material in the comparatively brief space of about 150,000 words."[46] An excellent device for novelists to employ to unite diffuse materials might well be some intelligent and delicate use of repetition. The symphony, with its sonata form, provides novelists with intriguingly rich suggestions about how they might use highly patterned repetition in analagous ways. The novelists' problem, of course, is that they must seem to advance their action constantly and to not just have it move in circles or elaborate curlicues. Burgess addresses the problem in *This Man and Music*: "only by echoing situations, phrases, preoccupations and structures already encountered, but in a new context of action"[47] will the novelist gain the benefits of repetition without too great a sacrifice. The first section of the novel has its four subsections, which correspond to Beethoven's exposition, development section, recapitulation, and coda. One of the themes employed in this section is N's powerful love for Josephine. The theme is sounded with an early, passionate interior monologue by N (*NS,* 3). The exposition and development sections carry the reader through the next three turbulent years—those of the Italian and Egyptian campaigns. Near the outset of the recapitulation the reader meets with another internal monologue of N (*NS,* 71) and becomes aware that N's love for Josephine remains passionately strong, despite his full knowledge of her infidelities with Lieutenant Charles. N has just been elected First Consul, and as he presides at a Council meeting, he writes repeatedly, "in total automatism" (*NS,* 71) the phrase "God how much I love you" (*NS,* 71)—a detail that has some historic authentication. Josephine (representing a feminine principle) appears in the recapitulation in ways that correspond, fairly exactly, to her appearances in the exposition. N, representing the center of a masculine thematic group, has his themes stirringly sounded (this, in part, representing his constant sexual stirrings), and these are repeated, with variation, in the recapitulation. This, of course, gives only the barest idea of what Burgess has done. He told an interviewer that there was a fairly exact correspondence between Beethoven's score and his novel: "What I have in front of me when I'm working is the score of the *Eroica.* I will make the various sections of the novel correspond to the various sections of the symphony, so that if I take, say, eight bars of Beethoven, it's roughly equivalent to three pages of my own work. I try to be consistent with that correspondence."[48]

Needless to say, Burgess's radical "experiment in form" imposes its own severe limitations. It explains why there is not a much deeper probe into Napoleon, nor a more fully realized and significant presentation of historic events and their backgrounds. It explains why, in his epistle, he refers to it as "comic" (*NS,* 362), telling his reader, in fact, that his working title had been "The Napoleon Comic Symphony." There is every reason to expect that Burgess has an abiding dislike for Napoleon, yet Beethoven, at the time of composition, viewed him as a hero and gave his work epic majesty. Burgess finds himself able to deal with this by shifting the proportions just enough to allow the mock-heroic to prevail. N, a kind of monkey in britches who often wets them in rage, is almost tauntingly demythologized, yet, as other parts of the novel show—particularly the fourth section—he has not been utterly stripped of his accomplishments or his (admittedly very flawed) humanity. "My Ogre, though heroic, is grotesque" (*NS,* 362), writes Burgess. He reminds us that his N "robs and rapes and lies and kills in fun / And does no lasting harm to anyone" (*NS,* 362). Even though its subject is heroic Ogre, *Napoleon Symphony,* needing to follow along with Beethoven, cannot extend itself to a search for the meaning of the human paradox that other Burgess novels embark on so successfully. It does, though, provide a rich panorama of Napoleonic history and a sharply immediate dramatic feel for the eternal drama of men at war. While it does not quite achieve the heights or proportions of the two great Napoleonic novels, Tolstoy's *War and Peace* and Stendhal's *The Charterhouse of Parma,* it is worthy of respectful comparison. Burgess has not forgotten that this novelistic experiment is "really a piece of elephantine fun / Designed to show the thing cannot be done" (*NS,* 363). That is needlessly modest. Perhaps, too, there is a quotient of disingenuity in his disclaimer of the novel's being "a filmscript with no dream of celluloid" (*NS*, 361). In September 1988 he said that "a movie on Napoleon is still in the works. Kubrick is thinking and talking about it. . . . The problem is the budget. It would be impossible in the U.S. But it could be done in the U.S.S.R. with Red Army troops as walk-ons."[49]

Chapter Seven

"History," Imagined Pasts, Illusion/Reality, Strange Futures, and the Mainly Televisual

Earthly Powers

Long before the novel *Earthly Powers* appeared, in 1980, there were reasons to expect that it was going to be Burgess's really major work. Burgess had discussed the idea of it as early as 1966, promising a novel of Tolstoyan proportions. Several times he outlined the basic plan of the novel: the focal character was to be a Pope modeled fairly closely on Pope John XXIII; the narrator, related to this Pope by marriage, was to be a rationalist, homosexual writer of the Somerset Maugham type. From this central irony would radiate smaller ironies that would oddly illuminate some of the darker corners of our troubled and confused twentieth-century civilization. The novel was to have historic sweep, the play of significant ideas, and religious import. Burgess was devoting more time to this novel than any previous work.

One could only anticipate with awe what the rapid-writing Burgess would produce when he actually spent years on a novel. Still, one central element of his outline caused deep misgiving. Strong reason to suspect that the John XXIII–like Pope would be treated with contempt or ridicule seemed to exist. Burgess had not been reticent about expressing his strong distaste for the pontiff called first by Italians, then by much of the world, the "good Pope." To one interviewer, he said: "There's no doubt that the Church is in a mess at the moment. It doesn't know where to turn, has no authority, doesn't know what it believes. I blame this on Pope John. The fact that we've left a noble language and a noble liturgy behind for the sake of the vernacular is a great sin, in my opinion. Pope John was obviously a good priest to have in a Communist town like Milan, but he wasn't for that reason qualified to be a Pope. A Pope should be intellectual."[1] Burgess made clear his dismay with what he considered Pope John's part in causing the Church to shift its emphasis away from sin and guilt, his conflation of Marxism and Christianity, and his general Pelagianism. Burgess is reported to have qualified the following denunciation only when challenged: "I'm inclined to see the Catholic Church now as all Pelagian, and Pope John as the emissary of the Devil."[2]

When the novel finally appeared, it largely—but not entirely—dispelled the uneasiness Burgess's devotees had been harboring. The Pope Gregory XVII of the novel is not quite Pope John XXIII; besides, he is a fictional character in a world of Burgess's creation. Still, this fictive Pope does, as did Pope John, succeed Pius XII in 1958, and must irresistibly remind many readers of Pope John. When Pope Gregory is described, then, as "a waddling banner for the deadly sin of gluttony"[3] and the possessor of a "big complicated nose [that is] a cornucopia of hairs unplucked" (*EP,* 181), and when it is said that "Edward G. Robinson [is] about [his] height though not as ugly" (*EP,* 323), many readers will find Burgess's humor rather maliciously funny. Kenneth Toomey, the homosexual playwright and novelist who is the book's narrator, describes the direction in which Gregory, the brother of his brother-in-law, is taking the Church: "There seemed less emphasis on what was wrong than on what was right, or good, or holy. The big theme was Love or Charity" (*EP,* 317). One might suppose that the Joannine revolution was so repugnant to Burgess that he fired a satiric salvo at it in the form of *Earthly Powers.*

Still, Burgess has made the general observation that he is *not* a satirist. He very plausibly says that "when I say I'm going to write a novel, I immediately see a structure, I see climaxes, I see a *dénouement,* I see a beginning, I see an end—this is what a novel is, it is a structure. I don't know how far the writer of a novel is communicating *himself,* his ideas, his feelings."[4] Burgess's extranovelistic, gadflyish, theatrical statements ought not to be brought to bear too heavily on the novels. *Earthly Powers* is much more than a diatribe, in fiction, against *aggiornamento* (modernization), if it is that at all. It is a wittily intellectual novel that sets up a dialectic between the ideas of Toomey, with a strongly pessimistic view of human nature, and those of Carlo Campanati, the venal glutton who "makes" Pope and believes in man's essential goodness. (And superficial differences *do* exist between Campanati and Angelo Roncalli, the man who became Pope John XXIII; for example, Burgess's character is raised in a wealthy family, while the real Pope was one of thirteen children of a peasant farmer.) Since Toomey (and, to a lesser extent, Carlo) is always in the right place at the right time, a personal eyewitness (much like Herman Wouk's Pug Henry) to some of the most major events that help us trace the confused and malign patterns of twentieth-century history, the novel demands of its reader some grappling with the problems of good and evil, determinism and free will, and the difficulties of artists and religious leaders who seek to provide the order and sustenance that will redeem man from chaos.

Earthly Powers derives its immense readability, however, more from polished wit, verve, rich coloration, and scope than it does from the development of intellectual ideas in depth. In the sweep of its "history" and its play with philosophical ideas, particularly the play of opposites, this novel suggests *The Magic Mountain,* but Burgess does not aim at—nor does he achieve—the sort of concentrated development of philosophical thought that makes Mann's novel very nearly an allegory. Although fastidious and even patrician by nature, Ken Toomey does not spend his time in the rarified mountain air—all too frequently he finds himself involved in the muck of the real world of our century. Burgess "realizes" this real world with savoring, particularizing detail. He is careful to send Toomey to places that he personally knows well: Malta, Monaco, London, New York, Malaya, Tangier, Dublin, Hollywood, and northern Italy. Burgess, however, forgoes naturalistic detail and satiric sideswipes, instead setting his action against selectively represented, and convincing, backgrounds. Although it is rich in all sorts of ways, *Earthly Powers* shows a discipline and restraint unusual for Burgess.

Toomey and Carlo Campanati are immensely interesting and memorable characters apart from what they represent. Toomey is, in many ways, very much like Burgess himself, except for the fact that the fictional creation is a homosexual. That exception, however, is nearly monumental: as he goes about the business of living his life, Toomey's homosexuality more and more begins to define him. Toomey is very much like Somerset Maugham, with something of Noël Coward, and perhaps a small bit of Norman Douglas. Like his creator, though, he has translated *Oedipus,* written a musical play called *The Blooms of Dublin,* another on Shakespeare's life called *Will!,* and authored a drama titled *Gods in the Garden* (much like *The Eve of St. Venus*). As an elderly man, he appears to live in the very house that Burgess lived in on Malta. Much more important, he is a lapsed Catholic with a pessimistic bent, and a polished, but genuinely ingrained, cynicism. Like Maugham, he is self-deprecating about his art, lonely amidst wealth and prestige, and bitter but controlled about the betrayals of younger lovers. His modes of thinking and conversation provide frequent reminders that he shares what many people used to (and perhaps still do) think of as a homosexual character or homosexual sensibility. Although Burgess does not make Toomey the possessor of the kind of mannerisms that are homosexual self-parody, he does represent him as having a deliberately cultivated slight lisp (*EP,* 54). Since a number of Toomey's acquaintances, however, exhibit the mannerisms commonly supposed to be the more usually defining ones, Burgess gives himself a large opportunity for the imaginative reconstruction of campy, homosexual badinage, in-jokes, and bitchiness. This is cleverly done, and is apt to appear to the reader a startlingly accurate representation.

Questioning why Burgess chose to make his narrator and central consciousness a homosexual seems appropriate, but pinning down Burgess's motivation is difficult. This puzzle is a *récit* of the novel, one of the "givens"—there is no reason why Toomey should not be. That a functional irony and tension are added by having a friend and relative-by-marriage of the Pope be a widely known homosexual becomes also apparent. That the strategy provides an obliquely intensified highlighting of the already present conflict of free will/determinism and the sequentially congruent one of the innate/acculturated can also be argued. Toomey's thoughts and narrative make it clear that he has not freely chosen his sexual orientation; thus, he has very largely been predetermined to suffer the stigma of societal and religious disapproval. Burgess does not suggest that homosexuality should be equated with evil, but the idea of a person being psychobiologically predetermined to be a homosexual suggests another that runs on closely parallel lines: are human beings predetermined by their very nature to commit evil? If so, free will by itself has little or no efficacy. This is the very question that torments the basically "Augustinian" Toomey, the one that he argues repeatedly with the pronouncedly "Pelagian" Carlo, who thinks that evil is "external" and can be dealt with. On the other hand, if one does not feel that Toomey was virtually destined by biogenetics to be a homosexual, one would have to argue that the dominantly strong homosexual inclination was psychologically acquired as a result of experience. Toomey, who as anyone else, has an imperfect understanding of himself, feels the latter alternative to be true. Thus say man, not God (in the form of "biology"), caused him life-long difficulty. Toomey recalls a very early experience of his childhood that may have been "the primal scene or something" (*EP,* 144). He had been in his mother's bed, her arms around him, when his father, a dentist, advanced suddenly into the room, his dental forceps squeezing "a monstrous brown and bloody molar" (*EP,* 143), which he thrust toward the boy's "hidden genitals" (*EP,* 144). Toomey thus hypothesized that his sexual inversion may have had its origin in the acute castration anxiety this incident caused him while he was still in the oedipal stage. But the man Toomey holds most responsible for his homosexuality is a real person—the Irish poet George Russell (1867–1935), otherwise known as AE. Toomey recounts that when he was not quite fourteen, he was seduced—on 16 June 1904—in the Dolphin Hotel in Dublin (*EP,* 61).

The presence of real people (under their own names)—Ezra Pound, Jim Joyce, Ford Madox Ford, Ernest Hemingway, Tom Eliot, Heinrich Himmler, and many others—partially caused one reviewer to make the deprecatory comment that Burgess's novel might just as well have been titled *The Ragtime Exorcist.* He alludes to a long, difficult (but very comic in effect) exorcism performed by Carlo that is reminiscent of that in William Peter Blatty's *The Exorcist;* and the meeting of real historic personages and fictional characters might seem to be modeled on E. L. Doctorow's 1975 novel, *Ragtime.* Burgess—astonishingly well read—doubtless knew both of these works, as well as others that are, like *Ragtime,* admixtures of fiction and recorded history: William Styron's *The Confessions of Nat Turner* (1966), Thomas Pynchon's *Gravity's Rainbow* (the 1973 novel that, like *Earthly Powers,* deals with spiritual atrophy and collapse in the modern Western world), and Robert Coover's *The Public Burning* (1977). Burgess is respectful of Styron and has expressed the highest admiration for Pynchon's work. (Liliana Burgess, his wife, has translated Pynchon into Italian.) Still, Burgess did not need the lesson of Doctorow to conceive the idea of putting real people in a novel. Indeed, the same, very real George Russell is a character in *Ulysses,* where, with others at the National Library, he hears Stephen Dedalus's Shakespeare theory. Burgess sets up a real life/fiction hall of mirrors effect by having Toomey report: "I said to Joyce in a bar in Paris in 1924: 'Well, you gave George Russell an eternal and unbreakable alibi for that afternoon. But I know and he knows that he was not in the National Library.' " (*EP,* 61–62). Our perceptions are by now dizzied, and we cannot, at least for the moment, distinguish between the worlds of fiction and reality. Such epistemological and ontological play is much more common in present-day American literature than in British, but among the latter, Fowles's *The French Lieutenant's Woman* (1973), Tom Stoppard's play *Travesties* (1974), and D. M. Thomas's novels *The White Hotel* (1981) and *Ararat* (1983) might be noted.

The portrait of Carlo Campanati that Toomey provides is a complex and somewhat ambiguous one; and this is so even before the reader reflects that Toomey's "facts" may not be unimpeachable, his judgments not objective. That Carlo, full of plump self-assurance of all kinds, does not know a central fact about his own life until well into the book (that he had been adopted as a very young child by the Campanatis) seems designed to underscore the problematic nature of "facts" and "history." The novel seems to pivot on the question of whether Carlo (later Pope Gregory) is a saint or an agent (witting or unwitting) of the devil. The reader begins to become acquainted with this question when, at the very outset, in the "time-present" of the novel, the eighty-one-year-old Toomey is told that the Church is beginning an investigation of possible evidence for Carlo's beatification. Deliberate complexity of various kinds (but much of it stemming from narrative technique) makes a determination extremely difficult. Then, too, Burgess may teasingly have set up a false either/or situation: Carlo may have been neither saint nor demonic agent; or, in slightly relaxed definitions, he may have been both. "You could prove anything in literary scholarship" (*EP,* 529), Toomey says at one point in the novel. It is safe to say, though, that whatever he is, Carlo is not one of Burgess's dreaded "neutrals." Under Carlo's fat there is muscle, and an exorcism, as performed by Carlo, is apt to include the possessed subject's getting a sharp crack in the nose or forehead from a heavy crucifix. "Carlo fought the good fight and I didn't" (*EP,* 424), Toomey admits when reporting on Carlo's heroic defiance of the Nazis. Carlo's detestation of the lukewarm is openly stated to the captured Nazi, Niebeneiner: "I'd be happier if you had real convictions, not just slogans" (*EP,* 422).

Two of the most important critics divide sharply in their interpretations of Carlo. Samuel Coale, while recognizing that Carlo is a Pelagian as well as a gambler and glutton, finds that he is a good man with a simple but genuinely intense religious faith. Coale feels that the reader's view of Carlo is distorted because it is refracted through the eyes of a superficial, jaundiced, and highly secular Toomey: "Carlo's case is lost before it even begins. He's reduced to the cant and rant of a willful priest, whom Toomey can in no way believe in. The Pope becomes a straw man."[5] Conversely, Geoffrey Aggeler, after carefully defining the equivocal nature of Carlo's portrait, definitely suggests that the vainglorious Italian prelate achieved the Papacy as a result of a Faustian bargain that he had made with the Devil.[6] Aggeler's view is supported by a fair amount of internal evidence and, apparently also recommended by Burgess's public animadversion on Pope John as "an emissary of the devil." Two very large ironies (which, with their whiff of contrived sensationalism, fall somewhat short of Sophoclean grandeur) support the Devil's agent theory. First, the miracle that could, presumably, be offered in powerful support of Carlo's candidacy for sainthood, turns out, apparently, to have been a huge, satanic joke. As a young priest, visiting a dying brother in a Chicago hospital in the gangster era, Carlo had healed a child thought by all the physicians to be fatally ill with tubercular meningitis. Some forty years later, and several years after Carlo's death, Toomey happens to learn the result of that suspension of merely earthly principles. The boy who was restored to health, Godfrey ("God," for short) Manning, had grown up to be very much like the real Jim Jones, a darkly charismatic leader of a radical religious sect. Like Jones, Manning, feeling governmental pressure, decides on mass suicide for his group; he employs not Kool-Aid, as did Jones, but "the body of Christ administered as a cyanide tablet" (*EP,* 597) to nearly two thousand followers for a eucharistic feast of death. Among these followers are Toomey's grandniece and her baby. It would thus seem that the Prince of Darkness was able to work through Carlo long before any Faustian compact may have been made.

Another conjunction of Carlo, the eucharist, death, and a Toomey relative, is revealed at about the same point in the novel. As Pope Gregory, Carlo had, like the real Pope John, convened the Vatican Council, one of its purposes being to bring the people closer to the Church. To accomplish this the council would allow the incorporation of national and native custom and ceremony into Church ritual. Toomey's nephew and his wife are killed in Africa as an integral part of a reformed Communion service: they "were used as what are known as the accidents of the Sacrament of the Holy Eucharist" (*EP,* 587).

Satan certainly seems to work through Carlo. Perhaps this is the Diabolic One's revenge on Carlo, the zealous and formidable exorcist who has frequently won hard victories over him in spiritual battles so intense that they have even claimed the physical lives or health of the subject souls. Toomey, though, seems to see it otherwise. He tends to find hubris and shortsightedness in Carlo, a man who is totally vulnerable to the evil within himself because he views Satan, the source of all evil, as a basically external force that can be exorcized from men's souls if it succeeds in gaining brief habitation there. An Italian magazine, in an article unfriendly to Carlo, describes his doctrinal position clearly enough: "He proclaimed many years ago his abhorrence of the most fundamental dogma of the faith—that doctrine of original sin which, long before the Word was made flesh and dwelt among us, presupposed the necessity of divine redemption. Man is God's creation, His Eminence preaches, and hence is good. Evil is wholly external, entirely a diabolic monopoly. Evil is exorcizable" (*EP,* 504).

Pelagians in Burgess's work are almost always fated to meet with disappointment. That, however, is not Carlo's destiny. The point might well be that the quality of his optimistic delusion is so great that he fails to discern that he is both an inheritor of original sin and a personal sinner, guilty, really, of all the deadly sins except lust and sloth. Thus, while he is unaware, the spiritually blind Carlo has long ago been captured by Satan, who still holds him in thrall. Any pact with the Devil is probably more symbolic than actual. Still, Aggeler's suggestion that *Earthly Powers* bears comparison to Thomas Mann's *Doktor Faustus* (1947) is totally convincing. In Mann's work, the personal history of the protagonist, Adrian Leverkuhn, parallels that of Germany from 1870 to 1940, inclining the novel heavily in the direction of political allegory. Mann's protagonist is overtaken by insanity in 1930 and he dies in 1940. Germany's hellish descent into madness, with its enormous spiritual, psychological, and physical losses, is thus symbolically etched on a parallel line. Burgess probably provides no bad end for Carlo because there was none for Pope John XXIII. Yet a strong thematic suggestion is that what Carlo did as Pope will soon result in not quite *Götterdämmerung* (twilight of the gods), but some very bad times for the Catholic Church.

Any attempt to interpret or evaluate *Earthly Powers* on a purely realistic or naturalistic scale is inappropriate. The incidents of the novel, particularly those near the end, will appear contrived and preposterously foolish if one refuses to grant the possibilities of a fairly rich mixture of comedy, irony, satire, allegory, pastiche, and playfulness. When readers look at the scene of the exorcism involving Mahalingham's son, they see immediately that the style, delightfully comic in itself, is a spoof of *The Exorcist* in much the same way that many of the scenes in *Tremor of Intent* are send-ups of Ian Fleming. In ways very much like those of Thomas Pynchon, Burgess mixes the materials of popular culture with elements of serious concern—in this case, a correct theological idea of man's basic nature. The novel gives us the comic outrageousness of the grossly physical Carlo achieving the Papacy, Val Wrigley's sentimental, homosexual reworking of the creation story, and whole, heavy chunks of a theological treatise that is the product of a collaborative effort between Carlo and Toomey. It gives us a comic strip figure in Carlo, a man who cannot really be taken seriously: he is laughable in appearance and a caricature of the sort of man who is completely un-self-conscious about his own frailties. Still like Pynchon, Burgess's novel provides a curiously deliberate blend of sophisticated and sophomoric humor. To a degree it is, from Toomey's talk about writing an arresting opening to his discussion of the difficulty of endings—with speculation, in between, on the "truth" or "confabulation" of his own story that is the novel we are reading—a fiction about fictions. In talking to him and trying to assert their independence (*EP,* 485), Toomey's characters are engaging in the "reflexive" play we find in novels by Barth, Vonnegut, and Fowles.

To maintain that *Earthly Powers* is a novel lacking in sufficient weight and solidity to support the seriousness of its themes is to miss at least part of the point. The comic elements in the novel are enhanced by being played off against the serious; the serious elements are sometimes enhanced by the comic. *Earthly Powers* may not succeed quite as well as *Gravity's Rainbow* in the seriousness of its playfulness, but Burgess's strategies of intermixing the profound and the trivial, the sacred and the thoroughly profane (for example, Sir Dick Bart's seizing the chance to sodomize a sailor temporarily helpless because he is vomiting [*EP*, 131]) are calculated to heighten the reader's awareness of human multiplicity and ambiguity. The strategy and the themes are perfectly congruent, for what the novel both celebrates and laments is the usually hopeless intermixture of opposites in this world. Unlike many other contemporary novelists, Burgess believes that such a thing as truth exists. He would agree, though, that it is nearly impossible to be sure one knows the truth. Toomey may think he does, but we should not implicitly trust our narrator—he is not altogether reliable. History is constantly challenged and rewritten. Burgess may have begun his novel with some intention of challenging the sentimentally idealizing writing on Pope John that was beginning to be seen from would-be hagiographers. *Earthly Powers*, though, is both more and less than a satiric debunking of a Papal architect of change. It is a novel about the mostly sad, but also frequently comic fates that await mankind in a confused but also predictable drama of human recurrence.

Any Old Iron

Any Old Iron (1989) covers very much the same broad range of tumultuous modern history as does *Earthly Powers*. In this case, the events of the novel (although not narrated with strict consecutiveness) begin at the time of the sinking of the *Titanic*, in 1912, and proceed to some slightly vague point that is, however, undeniably close to our own present. At the end, the narrator tells us this about Reg Jones, the main character: "What he wanted, I think, was negative: not to have been reserved for the life of this century."[7] War and other forms of human strife both frame and penetrate the lives of the characters; they are involved in World War I, the Easter Rising of 1916 in Dublin, the Russian Revolution, the Spanish Civil War, World War II, Arab-Jewish conflicts, and the tentative beginnings of some Welsh nationalist terrorism. Again, though, Burgess shows us that twentieth-century horrors are not especially human aberrations by very loosely enclosing his story within a mythic framework. The "old iron" of the title is Excalibur, King Arthur's own sword, in the novel thought by some to have been miraculously preserved. Burgess has said in an interview that the book "is about trying to find some absolute value—what the sword of King Arthur was supposed to symbolize."[8] But the quest for absolutes, although an eternal human need, seems to result in war and carnage, causing the reader to think that the "old iron" is an antiquated piece of junk that might best be discarded. "Any old iron" is the cry of an itinerant junkman in Britain, this suggestion of the title being reinforced by the first epigraph "*Eisen, Lumpen, Papier!* [Iron, Rags, Paper]—Arab Street Cry in Tel Aviv."

The sword, that may or may not be Excalibur, is in the book not because the novel is one of many updated Arthurian romances (it is far from being that), but because Burgess chose to add mystery and mythic resonance to what otherwise might have seemed a mostly naturalistic chronicle of two families. *Any Old Iron,* Burgess's most recent novel, is reminiscent of his first two, *A Vision of Battlements* and *The Worm and the Ring:* in all three minutely realized realistic details are expanded in import by the presence of a mythic frame. Here the mythic basis rests on the sword's being kept first at the Benedictine monastery at Monte Cassino, Italy, to which, legend has it, it was transferred from a Benedictine monastery in Wales. Some of the lore about the sword, such as that passed on by Giraldus Cambrensis, holds that the sword, before it was owned by Arthur, was the sword of Attila the Hun, and that long before that it was the sword of Mars himself, the god of war (*AOI,* 4). (The reader might thus well expect that Burgess has laid down an allegorical basis for all that is to follow.) The Nazis apparently believe most of this lore, since, shortly after the Allied landings at Anzio, they seize the sword, only to lose it shortly thereafter to the Russians. The Russians place it on exhibit in their most famous museum, the Hermitage in Leningrad.

Reg Jones, the novel's chief protagonist, eventually steals the rusty old sword (known as "Caledvwlch" to the Welsh) from the Hermitage and takes it back to Wales. This, though, is toward the end of a long, discursive story that has caused Reg Jones and the other characters to watch, at close range, some of the major bloodlettings—the works of Mars—in our century. Burgess has refrained, though, from providing any easy, interpretive overlays to accompany his mythic framework. The novel is, in fact, teasingly ambiguous to a surprising degree. There is no overt Manichaeanism; no open Pelagian/Augustinian conflicts. A long, winding chain of events begins with David, Reg's father, a young Welshman and crew member of the *Titanic,* surviving the sinking, making his way to New York, and marrying Ludmila, daughter of an émigré who owns a Russian restaurant in Brooklyn. As the sprawling novel moves on, it follows not only David (through World War I) and Ludmila (in Petersburg at the time of the Revolution), but also, fairly soon, the three children born of their union:

Reg[inald], Beatrix, and Dan. It also involves the narrator, Harry Wolfson, a Manchester Jew and Reg's old friend, an engaging raconteur with a manner that is both offhandedly sophisticated and un-self-consciously rambling. Harry loves Beatrix Jones, Reg's sister, and Reg marries Harry's musical sister, Zipporah (usually called "Zip"). Frequently both the characters and the narrator will interpose remarks and speculation about Welsh, Russian, and Jewish racial differences, real or supposed; this, of course, delicately inclines the reader to reflect on one reason why Mars remains forever active.

Readers, compelled by Burgess to do more of the interpretive work themselves than in any of his other novels excepting *MF* and *Napoleon Symphony,* will gradually see patterns emerge. On a surface level, one can easily observe that as in *A Vision of Battlements* and *Napoleon Symphony,* the sympathies lie heavily with the enlisted men. One notices, again and again, soldiers returning home to find clear evidence of wifely infidelity. (There is a sexual referent, too, in the phrase "any old iron.") The oppressed, in fighting their oppressors, will most often descend to the same base level as their persecutors. There is something inevitable and very basically human about this, yet it imposes a sad burden of guilt and ruefulness—also very human. Injustice provokes its own retaliatory injustice. Reg Jones utters a familiar Burgess thought: "The big enemy's always government" (*AOI,* 267). Mostly, though, readers can note the presence of some rather finely tensioned opposites, for example, those of fervent idealism/cool cynicism. If wars are mostly senseless, and if people become embroiled in wars only because of a commitment, sometimes not even examined, to idealized abstractions, why not withhold oneself from a commitment to all abstractions as a significant safeguard against an ultimate insanity? Or, conversely, would banishing ideals—if this, in fact, could ever be done—kill the human spirit? Do people—even those brought up as Christians to turn the other cheek—"die" if they allow past wrongs to go unavenged, even if they know that they will be adding a few links in a long cause and effect chain of death and suffering? Are the thoughts of a George Bernard Shaw or a Bertrand Russell on the subject of war just the spoutings of naïve, canting rationalists blind to the realities of emotion and spirit that make life whole and make it meaningful? But, then again, Burgess seems to cast doubt on whether our asking such questions has any benefit. Perhaps Marx's brute historical necessity rules all, and individuals—whether they choose to recognize it or not (it makes no difference)—are merely the pawns of history. Does Burgess implicitly implant this suggestion only to anger us into affirming the opposite—that we will intelligently chart for ourselves our own intellectually satisfying and spirit-fulfilling destinies?

Reg Jones is awash in great events and feels the pull of conflicting currents. He speaks English, Welsh, and Russian; he lives in Manchester and Wales; he enlists on the Republican side in the Spanish Civil War, serves with the British Army on Gibraltar in World War II, and finally becomes mostly unwillingly involved with Welsh nationalist terrorists. Always, and inevitably, there is a gap between aspirations and actual outcomes, myths and realities. The Spanish Civil War is a disheartening mess; the "just" side in the war, the Republicans, are (as those familiar with George Orwell's experience know) soon given to cutthroatedly deadly internecine conflict. Morality even in World War II does not establish itself on a black/white basis. Wolfson, Reg Jones (and apparently Burgess) agree about the story of the return of Russian POWs who had volunteered, or who had been impressed, to serve with the German army as civilian laborers. Over a thousand such prisoners (including some women, and even children) were captured by the British at Normandy, and subsequently interned at a minimum security camp in Suffolk. Many of these Russians, however, did not wish to return to Russia, fearing (correctly, as it turns out) that they would be executed. Nonetheless, at Yalta Churchill yields to Stalin's demand for their return, knowing full well that he has virtually signed their death sentence. Reg, now an army interpreter, accompanies these Russians to Odessa where, indeed, he personally sees them efficiently slaughtered almost as soon as they have disembarked (*AOI,* 223). Among those killed is Marya Ivanovna Sokolova, a medical officer with the Russian group, who had been having an adulterous affair with Reg. Reg had truly loved her, and he cannot choke back his rage. "Churchill and Stalin had licked their podgy fingers at a feast of roast suckingpig and chortled over the bloody division of Europe" (*AOI,* 213), he says. Mythologizing/demythologizing forces are always at work, and Burgess himself, throughout his career, has encouraged the demythologizing of Churchill (although not so strongly as that of Pope John). The novel suggests that certain realities are stretched into myth because they can be made to fit certain psychological needs, but, eventually, becoming febrile, break into curious shards sometimes seen as ugly, sometimes puzzling. Although it may not be widely known, historians have generally indeed come to believe that Churchill complied with Stalin's demand for the return to the Soviet Union of even non-Soviet citizens born in prerevolutionary Russia.

After the slaughter of the forcibly repatriated Russians, Reg keeps alive a sense of melancholic beauty and a faith that individual humans will do good somewhat more than ill. He is profoundly distrustful, however, of people in groups, of movements, of governments. He arrives at a position very near the one his father held at the end of World War I. David Jones had asked his wife, "What is history but slashing the innocent with a sword? . . . Food's what matters. . . . Melt the sword down and make knives and forks out of it" (*AOI*, 59). Reg's position seems to be one of mature pessimism: "It has been a negative war, defending the bad against the worse, as the poet put it" (*AOI*, 168), Reg says, even before he witnesses the machine-gunning of the Russian civilian group containing his beloved Marya. At times, though, this slides off into a more jaundiced cynicism: "To hell with His Majesty; to a deeper hell with His Majesty's myrmidons and functionaries, who had learned lies and hypocrisy from the Russians and ruthlessness and efficiency from the Germans" (*AOI*, 193). These are his sentiments after learning that the Russian group will be forcibly repatriated. None of the themes of the novel is quite so anti-British as this, but the only slightly modified pessimism seems to be Burgess's. In being interviewed about the novel, Burgess offered that "I don't think there's any optimism in the book, except the scent of oranges and tangerines in the end."[9] Readers of most of Burgess's oeuvre will note too that various decided opinions in this novel have also come from the mouths of other characters in earlier novels. When, for example, the Welsh-Jewish Dr. Lewis says to Reg that "America and Russia are the same man with two different hats on" (*AOI*, 321), we can recall the same thought in *Honey for the Bears*.

The characters all learn, perhaps simply in the process of growing older, a kind of wisdom of the heart. Part of that wisdom is that history repeats itself, and the young repeat the mistakes of their elders. Apart from this, the characters do not, very understandably, achieve any intellectual illuminations. David Jones (Reg's father) tells Harry Wolfson that he always wanted just one thing from his children's education: "an explanation . . . of the kind of world we are living in" (*AOI*, 110). Harry replies, "Look . . . I studied philosophy, and that's supposed to give you all the answers to the big questions, but it doesn't. It doesn't even begin to. What you learn is that there's no answer" (*AOI*, 111). Wolfson's conclusion seems fair and honest, but it should be noted carefully that Wolfson is merely saying (and the fact of his being the narrator gives it added weight) that there is much irreducible mystery at the core of human experience, not that existence is without meaning. Wolfson is both clear-eyed and committed—a terrorist with expert skills who employs them on behalf of the new state of Israel. He is a man who has examined the seeming self-contradiction of being both a terrorist and a humane teacher of philosophy, and found that he can, without deceiving himself, reconcile the two. Burgess gives every indication of approving, having remarked outside the novel that what the Israelis have done, and are doing, involves "the only absolute struggle in our age."[10]

Reg is very much contemporary man with his emotional need for commitment, but his intellectual doubts about the efficacy of any cause. He feels some sympathy with the Sons of Arthur, a Welsh nationalist group that most people are inclined to regard as a group of barmy playactors, because, as he says, "there have to be romantics" (*AOI,* 320). He also, however, feels the full weight of the argument offered by Dr. Lewis: "romanticism is always frustrated and always turns to violence. Terrorism for the sake of terrorism" (*AOI,* 320). Thus it is that Reg hurls the sword into the Welsh lake associated with it in much Arthurian lore (*AOI,* 359). He concludes, "I had to grasp a chunk of the romantic past and find it rusty. I had to fit myself for the modern age" (*AOI,* 360).

Beard's Roman Women

Beard's Roman Women (1976) is a novel that is, in several ways, a successful hybrid. It combines realism, surrealism, swatches of barely disguised autobiography, and photographs of Rome. Burgess is remarkably ingenuous about its origin:

> That novel was written on commission. I didn't want to write it, but a young Bostonian had some very good photographs of Rome and came to me and said to me, would I write some text to go with his photos? I said yes. I couldn't write a text of the kind he wanted, and said: "Let's see if we can combine fiction and photographs."
>
> I must have been lacking in inventiveness at the time, so I fell back more than ever I would normally on the facts of my own life. I had been greatly disturbed in 1968, when my first wife died, with certain psychic phenomena, or psychological phenomena—I don't know what one really calls them—in which I was aware that this wife of mine had not really died and was still there.[11]

Although Burgess seems almost embarrassedly dismissive of his own finished product, the novel is a fictional meditation—sometimes eerie—on the blurry boundaries of life and death, art and life. *Beard's Roman Women* is decidedly not a major Burgess effort, but it is lively, memorable, and possessed of a kind of resonating depth that is curious only because it is seemingly effortlessly achieved. The British critic Christopher Ricks judged that "it would be gravely wrong to treat this humorous and moving book as if it were slight; it seems to me one of Anthony Burgess's best novels."[12] Some other critics were inclined to agree; others, very decidedly, were not.

Burgess's theme and style were obviously chosen to provide a firm complement to the photographs of David Robinson. These photographs of Rome are all odd-angled, moist-looking, shimmering, surreal; his images ones that are reflected in glass or pools. Burgess matches this with the spectral effects that intrude upon his protagonist, the writer Ronald Beard, a man haunted by the memory of his recently deceased wife. Burgess's narrative firmly provides still another basis for the Robinson photographs by involving Beard in a love relationship with Paola Lucrezia Belli, a photographer who is photographing Rome in exactly the same way as Robinson. All of this ties in closely, of course, with implicit questions about the ways in which art reflects life.

The novel is, in fact, as well as being a thinly disguised patch of near-autobiography, an oblique means for Burgess to deal with some questions of art and craft that were obviously on his own mind at the time. Like his creator, the English Ron Beard has served as an education officer in the sultanate of Brunei, been to Hollywood as a scriptwriter, and suffered the death of his Welsh wife, from cirrhosis of the liver, on the first day of spring. Paola Belli, his Italian lover, is a direct descendant of the Roman dialect poet, Giuseppi Belli, and Beard begins to translate some of his erotic poetry. Burgess was himself more than just mildly interested in Belli's poetry, since he was at the time translating into English at least the seventy-one sonnets that appear in his novel of the next year (1977), *Abba Abba*. Ron Beard, though, is only a partial, not a whole, Burgess. He is a film script writer, not a novelist. Ironically, the other part of Burgess—the "serious" novelist—is represented by a minor character, P. R. Pathan, a famous West Indian novelist who writes in English. Pathan's skin color is different ("brown"), but he assumes a virtual identity with another Burgess incarnation, F. X. Enderby. Like Enderby of *The Clockwork Testament,* Pathan had been a visiting professor in New York, but quit because he could not tolerate "black poems about tearing the white man's balls off."[13] Pathan (Paola's ex-husband) and Beard—both Burgess other-selves—have a heated verbal exchange. Pathan drips with scorn at what the screenwriter provides: "Crisp nervous dialogue. Don't use many words, but repeat the ones you do use" (*BRW,* 61). It seems probable that this reflects part of a real internal dialogue Burgess, moving more heavily into scriptwriting at the time, was likely to be having with himself.

Life/art reflections and parallels appear in the novel in other ways as well. The novel invites us to see what transpires as a modern version of the

Orpheus-Eurydice myth. Beard is the modern Orpheus mourning his Eurydice, and although he does not descend to the underworld to recover her, he seems to unnervingly find her when he hears her voice repeatedly on the telephone. Four tough bisexual young women who (skilled in the arts of stimulation) each rape Beard in his apartment, should be interpreted, it seems, as contemporary bacchantes, members "of the new international sorority of unchained youth, female chapter" (*BRW,* 108), as Beard, not yet violated, thinks of them. Before this quartet (reminiscent of the visit of Alex and his three "droogs" to Alexander's house) attack Beard, they notice his film script on Byron, Shelley, and Mary. With this script for a musical film that involves the events leading up to Mary Shelley's creation of *Frankenstein* (most especially, Byron's proposal that he, Polidori [his physician], Shelley and Mary embark on a contest to see who could write the best "ghost" story), Burgess seems to intend a thematic and tonal echo of sorts. Mary Shelley was haunted by death, and this comes out in *Frankenstein*; Beard is haunted by irrational guilt associated with the death of his wife, if not by her actual ghost. Beard is also haunted by an intensified awareness of his own mortality, and, toward the end of the novel, comes under the sentence of death of an incurable disease. He begins to feel that he is in some intermediate world between life and death. Burgess mines the ready ore of his own psyche—the intense feelings caused by the death of his wife as well as those caused by his own medical death-sentence and "miraculous" survival. Burgess's private psychological "material" lies closer to the surface than Mary Shelley's and was obviously far more consciously recognized by its creator. Still, it gives this novel authentically deep and intriguing contours that allow it to be more than the rather facile contrivance it would otherwise remain.

Abba Abba

Several connecting links exist between *Beard's Roman Women* and *Abba Abba* (1977). Both are set in Rome, and both involve the sonnets of Giuseppi Belli (1791–1863), the Roman dialect poet. Close surrogates of Burgess are present in each work.

At the center of *Abba Abba* is a bit of imagined literary history. In Rome, in 1820, the dying John Keats meets Belli, the blasphemous sonneteer. Burgess indulges in blasphemy of a sort in the very title of the book. Abba is not only the rhyme scheme of the octave in a Petrarchan sonnet, it is also Burgess's initials, once repeated. Moreover, the Aramaic word means "father," the word Jesus used on the cross in his "Father, father, why hast thou forsaken me?" The oblique allusion to Christ crucified is probably intended in part to point readers toward the first Belli poem they hear about, one in which they learn that Belli's slang term for the male organ is *dumpennente* and that a pun can be made about two ways in which a man can be said to be "hung." We are directed (*AA,* 15) to this line in the "Stabat mater": "Dum pendebat filius" (while the son was hanging). When this is communicated to Keats, he is very nearly represented as hugging himself with the delight of it. This might be hard for most readers to believe, or, if they believe, to share Keats's delight. Only when the sacred is taken very seriously can the blasphemous purely shock or cause an explosive shock of laughter. Seventy-one Belli sonnets, as translated by Burgess, appear in the novel; and many American and British readers will probably react with bored distaste at what they consider to be bad-boy sophomoric humor.

Part 1 of the novel, both exuberant and poignant in its presentation of the decline and death of Keats (the verifiable elements apparently taken from Robert Gitting's biography), is, in itself, a slightly quirky but fascinating, often brilliant, novella. Part 2 gives the reader four sonnets purportedly written by a J. J. Wilson, graduate of the University of Manchester, followed by Wilson's translation of the seventy-one Belli sonnets. A narrative voice informs the reader that Wilson's "sonnets are juvenile and tasteless, as one might expect from a Manchester schoolboy, but the same charges have been made against the work of Belli himself" (*AA,* 89). The actual translator of the Belli sonnets is, of course, Burgess himself, who is (despite the difference of middle initial and absence of Italian lineage) largely the very same Wilson. An estimation of the merits of Burgess's translations of Belli's Roman dialect is difficult. Some have found his versions tighter and more ingeniously rhymed than those of the American Harold Norse. A sharply deprecatory view of Burgess's translations has been taken by a Roman, Guido Almansi, who represents himself as expressing a view general among a coterie of Belli devotees. Almansi animadverts that of Burgess's translations "not a single one of them manages to catch the spirit of the original."[15] He charges that Burgess isolates and emphasizes smutty elements that can induce sniggering, but that Belli's "glorious and resonant blasphemousness" goes uncaptured.

An appreciation of Belli's sonnets, whether in the original, Burgess, or any other translation, is of course, a matter of taste. In fact, Belli's own internal contradictions caused him to constantly oscillate between positions of rebellion and conformity—an almost Manichaean division that Burgess would find strongly appealing. The man who wrote 2,279 coarse, ribald, and (frequently) blasphemous sonnets, was simultaneously employed, for several years, as a censor. What the reader of *Abba Abba* will appreciate more, however, is the less sensational, quite unsentimental, but very moving and very human divisions in the dying Keats that Burgess provides here.

The End of the World News

The End of the World News (1983) is subtitled, in the former manner of Graham Greene, "An Entertainment." Burgess seems thereby to warn reader and critic off any attempt to find serious depths or artistry in this fairly long novel. The author's caution is justified since the novel is three separate stories pressed together beneath the same covers. To be sure, Burgess skillfully, albeit sometimes playfully, works in various kinds of connective links among the three. Some evidence supports the suspicion, though, that many readers probably will have harbored: that Burgess took from his desk three already completed manuscripts and lightly revised each so as to produce some necessary interlinkages. The end product is short on genuine artistry, but it is, indeed, for at least two-thirds of its length, very good entertainment.

As with *Abba Abba*, Burgess employs the Nabokovian device of creating a commentator who stands wholly outside the "story"; in this case, there is a foreword by John B. Wilson, B.A., literary executor of the late author. Wilson is, of course, Burgess himself (not yet dead), and his remarks in the foreword are very much on target. He describes what he found when he looked at the manuscript of the book: "There appeared to be here arbitrarily assembled a fantastic tale of the end of the world, a brief biography of Sigmund Freud clearly intended, on the evidence of a preponderance of simple dialogue and a minimum of *récit*, as the raw material of a television series, and the libretto of a musical play on the theme of the visit of Leon Trotsky to the city of New York in 1917. . . . The three works, if they may so be called, were so to speak, shuffled casually together, but very occasionally there appeared to be tentative verbal devices, roughly pencilled, in the nature of loose subliterary stitching, clearly designed as points of cross-reference between them."[16] So nearly naked an admission is apt to come across as a form of postmodernist play, and this admission partially succeeds in denying the very thing that it is admitting.

Stylistic evidence strongly suggests that all three stories were indeed originally written for television, the movies, and the musical stage. "Wilson" remarks, correctly, on "the subliterary nature of the style" in all three stories, "the only internal indication that this was intended as a single work" (*EOWN*, viii). In 1977 Burgess wrote to Geoffrey Aggeler that he had completed the writing of a new musical called *Trotsky's in New York*, "which may or may not come to something off-Broadway."[17] In nineteen-seventy-five, in Iowa, Burgess told an interviewer that, at the behest of Messrs. Brown and Zanuck of Universal, he was working on a script for "the ultimate disaster film about the end of the world."[18] What he proceeds to describe highly corresponds to the science fiction story of the novel. Burgess may or may not have written a television script of his Freud story, but he has spoken about completing part of a projected opera about Freud. This is not to suggest that this novel is so meretricious in its origins that any possible merits are wholly vitiated. The Freud story, unfolded mostly in dialogue, is fully absorbing, presenting a desanctified father of psychoanalysis, both likable and believable in his flaws, as he is betrayed by his "sons," Jung, Adler, and Rank. And while the Trotsky in New York story could perhaps only be appreciated if given a strong musical score, and expertly mounted on the Broadway stage, the science fiction story is entirely likable because we can enjoy a familiar plot if it is pushed forward with robustly interesting characters and stylistic flair. The designation of the novel as "an entertainment" provides both a serious caveat and a justified self-recommendation.

Man of Nazareth

Lord Lew Grade, the titled British film mogul, successfully moved the idea for a six-hour television film on the life of Jesus. Burgess was soon aboard the project as chief scriptwriter, and Franco Zeffirelli as director. The program, called *Jesus of Nazareth*, was first telecast in the United States on Palm Sunday and Easter evenings, 1977. There was a luminous cast that included Laurence Olivier, Ralph Richardson, Peter Ustinov, Donald Pleasence, Anne Bancroft, James Earl Jones, and many others. This film was generally accounted, at least in relation to the usual standards of television, an artistic success, and Burgess seemed to have felt that his intensive, studious laboring had been worthwhile. (He read the New Testament in Greek, and Josephus's *History of the Jews*; he wrote enough versions of the script to "fill a whole long shelf."[19]) He later signed on to do still another miniseries, *A.D.*, which roughly picks up the lives of the early Christians after *Jesus of Nazareth* leaves off. This "tale of corruption and faith" was first aired in America on 30 March 1985.

The book jacket of the novel *Man of Nazareth* (1979) states that it is the novel on which the television series, *Jesus of Nazareth,* was based. Some Burgess remarks, however, seem to indicate that the creation of the novel and the miniseries were nearly simultaneous—that he was writing the novel during intervals when he was not being pressed for script revision. Burgess knew well that fictionalized biographies of Jesus win the praise of both the average reader and the literary intellectual establishment only very seldom, if at all. Pleasing both the pious and the less pious (those simply in it for a good read) is next to impossible. Burgess's self-imposed mediation is prudent and disciplined. He allows his natural inventiveness and stylistic flair to have some play, yet he remains mostly faithful to the synoptic gospels. (He uses the more romantic gospel of St. John as his basis very infrequently.) His departure from Scripture is intended mostly to provoke thought about, and to dramatize, the humanity of Jesus. Thus, there is the surprise of the bridegroom of the wedding at Cana being none other than Jesus himself. Burgess individualizes the apostles by assigning them each some characterizing trait. Jesus is memorable for his powerful plain speaking and rugged athleticism. He comes across as a muscular, indiscreet intellectual.

Reviews of *Man of Nazareth* in the religious press (Catholic and Protestant) in America and Britain were not highly prominent, but were, in general, more favorable than not. In France, the novel, in translation, found favor with clerics and reading public alike, and, in fact, became a best-seller. Still, this novel, the product of a skilled and clever craftsman, seems at times quite hollow. Something important (real artistic vision or commitment, perhaps) seems missing; something seems compromised. As scene after scene flows by in the novel, we can almost see that the author has coolly framed each scene and decided, with an economical, no-nonsense approach, on a ready point of attack. In its method, the novel never wanders too far away from its sibling, the television script. In the way that it combines a basic faithfulness to Scripture with a few audacious departures, lessons in historical background with fictional imaginings about the everyday lives of Jesus and his disciples, the book displays a cool, perhaps overly calculated professionalism. It is only the here quite controlled unleashing of Burgess's verbal gifts and zest that convince us that the novel is slightly more than the product of one of the most talented literary hacks.

The Kingdom of the Wicked

Burgess is listed as the cowriter (with Vincenzo Labella) of the twelve-hour miniseries *A.D.* The "international cast of superstars" for this "motion picture of epic grandeur" includes Ava Gardner, John Houseman, Colleen Dewhurst, James Mason, Anthony Andrews, Richard Kiley, and Ian McShane. In the same year (1985) *A.D.* was originally telecast, Burgess turned out his *The Kingdom of the Wicked,* a novel that uses the fruits of some assiduous research he did for the television movie. (A novelized version of the film also appeared in 1985; it was titled *A.D.* and authored by a certain Kirk Mitchell, with copyright held by the film company.)

Despite the dogged labor that obviously went into it, *The Kingdom of the Wicked* does not really provide a reconciliation of opposites, nor a satisfying artistic tension between the two. Burgess mostly yields to the nearly irresistible impulse of taking the low, popular road by displaying the corrupt Rome of Caligula, Claudius, Nero, and Domitian in lavishly gory detail. In an "Author's Note," however, Burgess eagerly or defensively informs the reader that, in doing his research, he took a high road, indeed: he read Tacitus, Suetonius, Josephus, and the Acts of the Apostles "in the original tongues."[20] The novel is virtually required by its scheme to provide both the interweaving and contrast of saints and sinners, the ascetic and the decadent, the small concerns of the provincial Christian communities and the annals of imperial Rome. As a chief narrative and tonal effect, Burgess even tries to bounce the comic off the solemn; he is quoted, in fact, as saying that "it is a comic novel."[21] This is puzzlingly hyperbolic, but it does go a small way toward explaining some dialogue of deliberately banal, awkward, or incongruous manufacture. For example, Matthew says this to John shortly after Pentecost: "You're right in a way, John. Things have got a bit complicated. God has a son now, and they've sent down a sort of bird" (*KOW,* 40–41). Although Burgess's point seems to be that times of rapid change (such as those described in the novel) are apt to be productive of the incongruities that can provide the basis of comedy, he does not achieve any consistent effect of comedy in the book. Incongruities will not be the stuff of comedy here, but merely an annoying source of puzzlement or confusion for the reader. In fact, it remains unclear just what any of the aimed-for effects are, just as it remains unclear whether the novel has any animating purpose or genuine point of view. The novel, artistically the weakest of all of Burgess's novels, is unable to transcend the entirely predictable difficulties that beset it.

Conclusion

Burgess has almost—but not quite—secured himself a place as a major contemporary novelist. To suggest, with confidence, how he will be ultimately "placed" is to ignore the vagaries of changing literary tastes and politics. His permanent assignment to the ranks of major writers is undoubtedly still threatened by the absence of a single great, fully realized, and representative novel. *Earthly Powers* falls somewhat short of filling that void, and *Napoleon Symphony* is more an extendedly daring and admirable experiment than an artistically whole and satisfying achievement. If appearing on the syllabi of college literature courses becomes an even more important criterion for a lasting reputation, one can note that even now the only Burgess novel that appears to receive large representation is *A Clockwork Orange,* although *Nothing Like the Sun, The Wanting Seed,* and *Tremor of Intent* sometimes show up. Burgess's first (and he says last[1]) volume of short stories, *The Devil's Mode,*[2] appeared in late 1989. If one of these stories is selected for inclusion in one of the few surviving and, as a result, increasingly influential college anthologies of English literature, it might give a lasting boost to Burgess's reputation. These stories are very entertaining, cleverly contrived, and, in their own way, thought provoking, but some readers will judge that Burgess's wit and craft do not make up for a lack of thematic depth.

Any prediction about Burgess's reputation in the future is difficult, because, to many casual readers, there seem to be several Burgesses. (The difficulty of categorizing Burgess according to type might also tend to work against him.) One might think of the brilliant Dickensian comedy of character and caricature in *Enderby,* or of the satiric and dystopian visions of *The Wanting Seed, The Right to an Answer, A Clockwork Orange,* or *1985* that stand so firmly next to the work of the great English satirists of this century—Huxley, Waugh, and Orwell. Or one might immediately think of the clear discipleship to Joyce, in both his linguistic exploration and his modernist ironies, both evidenced in so many of the novels. Some think of Burgess as a literary mandarin, much like Vladimir Nabokov, whom he resembles in several ways. In this same vein, although considerably more negatively, a few see Burgess as a bundle of mere "clevernesses"; as a writer largely devoid of genuine vision or sure aesthetic instinct. Many see Burgess as a nontraditional and "un-English" sort of novelist: he is interested in mythic overlays and elaborate wordplay rather than soul-searching explorations of the self, or sensitive accounts of the conflict of self and society. Others see him as a totally unsolemn experimenter, unself-consciously running along the modernist/postmodernist frontiers until he encounters some boundary at a farther edge, against which he can playfully throw his robust explorer's weight. Occasionally, there is in Burgess some detectable evidence of facile contrivance or slapdash construction, but mostly there are well-thought-out elements of content and technique that catch readers up and carry them along in ways that can only be described as seriously entertaining.

Apparently, Burgess continues to be read and enjoyed. As of this writing, a rather remarkable twenty-two of his books are still in print in the United States. The second volume of the autobiography will soon appear. He has announced that he is now working on a massive study of language to be called *A Mouthful of Air.* Although some may say it is envy, there are literary people and ordinary readers who are suspicious of the possibility of high quality in the midst of all this fecundity. One always wonders: if Burgess ceased all activities save those of novel writing and ordinary living, what might he achieve? If he waited for his best vision and slowly allowed it to grow, if he wonderfully concentrated his attention and used intelligence, instinct, and patience in employing his resources, would he produce the great English novel of the last fifty years? We have no right to demand this test of Burgess, since the man has proved himself more than abundantly capable time and again. But we do wonder. In the meantime, we are extraordinarily thankful.

Notes and References

Chapter One

1. *Little Wilson and Big God* (New York: Weidenfeld & Nicolson, 1986), 17. Page references to this work are hereafter cited in the text as *LWBG.*
2. Anthony Lewis, "I Love England, but I Will No Longer Live There," *New York Times Magazine,* 3 November 1968, 64.
3. C. Robert Jennings, "*Playboy* Interview: Anthony Burgess. A Candid Conversation with the Visionary Author of *A Clockwork Orange,*" *Playboy* 21 (September 1974):84.
4. "Biographia Musicalis," in *This Man and Music* (New York: McGraw-Hill, 1983), 26.
5. "Letter from Europe," *American Scholar* 38 (Autumn 1969): 685.
6. "Dr. Rowse Meets Dr. Faustus," *Nation* 200 (1 February 1965):117.
7. Interview with Burgess, Robert Robinson, "Anthony Burgess—on Being a Lancashire Catholic," *Listener* 96 (30 September 1976):397.
8. *The Pianoplayers* (New York: Arbor House, 1986), 16; hereafter cited in the text as *P.*
9. Samuel Coale, "An Interview with Anthony Burgess," *Modern Fiction Studies* 27 (Autumn 1981):431.
10. *Mad River Review* 1 (Winter 1964–65):33–39.

Chapter Two

1. "The Great Vowel Shift and All That," *Encounter* 26 (May 1966):70.
2. "Joyce Can't Really Be Imitated," *Books and Bookmen* 15 (July 1970):9.
3. "Bless Thee, Bottom . . . ," *Times Literary Supplement,* 18 September 1970, 1025.
4. "Epilogue: Conflict and Confluence," in *Urgent Copy* (New York: Norton, 1969), 269.
5. *This Man and Music,* 103.
6. *Re Joyce* (New York: Norton, 1966), 9; hereafter cited in the text as *RJ.*
7. "Dickens Loud and Clear," in *Urgent Copy,* 41.
8. "Letter from England," *Hudson Review* 20 (1967):458.
9. Lewis, "I Love England But I Will No Longer Live There," 63.
10. *1985* (Boston: Little, Brown, 1978), 53.
11. John Mowat, "Joyce's Contemporary: A Study of Anthony Burgess' *Napoleon Symphony,*" *Contemporary Literature* 19 (1978):180–95.
12. A. A. DeVitis, *Anthony Burgess* (New York: Twayne, 1972), 65.

13. *The Long Day Wanes: A Malayan Trilogy* (New York: Norton, 1977), 351; hereafter cited as *LDW* in the text.

14. "The Writer and Music," *Listener* 67 (May 1962):761–62.

15. "The Writer and Music," 762.

Chapter Three

1. *Urgent Copy,* 270.

2. For a strong discussion of historical forces at work in *The Long Day Wanes,* see Robert K. Morris, "Anthony Burgess: *The Malayan Trilogy*—the Futility of History," in his *Continuance and Change* (Carbondale: Southern Illinois University Press, 1972), 71–91.

3. "Up with the Here-and-Now," *Books and Bookmen* 10 (December 1965):80.

4. *Honey for the Bears* (New York: Norton, 1978), 116; hereafter cited in the text as *HB.*

5. *Tremor of Intent* (New York: Norton, n.d.), 70–72; hereafter cited as *TI* in the text.

6. *Ninety-nine Novels: The Best in English since 1939* (New York: Summit Books, 1984), 74.

7. April 1987, 116.

8. Ronald J. Palumbo, "Names and Games in *Tremor of Intent,*" *English Language Notes* 18 (September 1980):48–51.

9. James I. Bly, "Sonata Form in *Tremor of Intent,*" *Modern Fiction Studies* 27 (Autumn 1981):489–504.

10. DeVitis, *Anthony Burgess,* 155–56.

11. Lawrence Graver, "House of Burgesses," *New Republic* 155 (15 October 1966):25.

12. Gertrude Jobes, *Dictionary of Mythology, Folklore, and Symbols* (New York: Scarecrow Press, 1961), 435.

13. "The Ludic Loves of Anthony Burgess," *Modern Fiction Studies* 27 (Autumn 1981):455.

Chapter Four

1. *The Novel Now: A Guide to Contemporary Fiction* (New York: Norton, 1967), 39.

2. In his *But Do Blondes Prefer Gentlemen? Homage to Qwert Yuiop and Other Writings* (New York: McGraw-Hill, 1986), 113.

3. *The Wanting Seed* (New York: Norton, 1976), 18–19; hereafter cited as *WS* in the text.

4. Matthew Hodgart, *Satire* (New York: McGraw-Hill, 1969), 13.

5. Brian Wilkie, review of *The Wanting Seed,* "Satiric Ramble," *Commonweal* 79 (17 January 1964):465.

6. Walter Allen, "The Novels of Graham Greene," *Penguin New Writing* 18 (1943):150.

7. "Utopia and Science Fiction," in *Essays from Oceania and Eurasia,* ed. Benoit J. Suykerbuyk (Antwerp: Universitaire Instellung, 1984), 17.

8. Thomas Churchill, "An Interview with Anthony Burgess," *Malahat Review* 17 (January 1971):110.

9. *A Clockwork Orange,* First Revised Edition (New York: Ballantine Books, 1988), 42; hereafter cited as *CO* in the text.

10. "On the Hopelessness of Turning Good Books into Films," *New York Times,* 20 April 1975, Arts and Leisure section, 14–15.

11. Geoffrey Aggeler, *Anthony Burgess: The Artist as Novelist* (University: University of Alabama Press, 1979), 171.

12. Quoted by Christopher Ricks, "Horror Show," *New York Review of Books* 18 (6 April 1972):28.

13. "A Very Tragic Business," in *Urgent Copy,* 192.

Chapter Five

1. Dante Alighieri, "The Inferno," 3. 32–39, *Divine Comedy,* trans. John Ciardi (New York: Norton, 1977), 14.

2. *The Right to an Answer* (New York: Ballantine Books, 1966), 9; hereafter cited as *RTA* in the text.

3. Quoted in "Speaking of Writing—VIII: Anthony Burgess," *London Times,* 16 January 1964, 13.

4. *The Doctor Is Sick* (New York: Norton, 1979), 6; hereafter cited as *DIS* in the text.

5. John Cullinan, "The Art of Fiction XLVIII: Anthony Burgess," *Paris Review* 14 (1973):151.

6. *One Hand Clapping* (New York: Knopf, 1972), 4; hereafter cited as *OHC* in the text.

7. *TV Guide,* 18 September 1982, 12–13.

8. John Osborne, *Look Back in Anger* (Harmondsworth, England: Penguin Books, 1982), 17.

9. Cullinan, "The Art of Fiction," 135.

10. *The Eve of St. Venus* (New York: Norton, 1979), 8; hereafter cited as *ESV* in the text.

11. "The Novel," in *New Encyclopaedia Britannica in 30 Volumes,* 15th ed., Macropaedia (Chicago: Encyclopedia, 1974), vol. 13, 297.

12. *The Worm and the Ring* (London: Heinemann, 1970), 117; hereafter cited in the text as *W&R.*

13. Jim Hicks, "Eclectic Author of His Own Five-Foot Shelf," *Life* 65 (25 October 1968):93.

14. Letter to the author, dated 31 May 1989.

15. "Wagner's *The Ring:* Anthony Burgess on a Number of Interpretations," *Listener* 72 (17 September 1964):419.

16. Christopher Derrick, "This Our Exile: The Novels of Anthony Burgess," *Triumph* 2 (February 1967):30.

17. Derrick, "This Our Exile," 32.

18. "Wagner's *The Ring,*" 419.

19. Bruce Cook, "Here's Mr. Burgess, Full of Swagger and Guilt," *National Observer,* 27 April 1970, 19.

20. *The Eve of St. Venus* (New York: Norton, 1970), 1–2; hereafter cited in the text as *ESV.*

Chapter Six

1. *A Vision of Battlements* (New York: Ballantine Books, 1965), 44; hereafter cited as *VOB* in the text.

2. D. J. Enright, "Mr. W. S.," *New Statesman* 65 (5 April 1963):496.

3. Christopher Ricks, "The Epicene," *New Statesman* 65 (5 April 1963):496.

4. *Nothing Like the Sun,* (New York: Norton, 1964); hereafter cited in the text as *NLTS.*

5. "Genesis and Headache," in *Afterwords: Novelists on Their Novels,* ed. Thomas McCormack (New York: Harper, 1969), 39.

6. Harold Bloom, in the introduction to his edited volume, *Anthony Burgess: Modern Critical Views* (New York: Chelsea House, 1987), 3.

7. For further elaboration, see my article "*Nothing Like the Sun:* The Faces in Bella Cohen's Mirror," *Journal of Modern Literature* 5 (1976):131–47.

8. Paul Theroux, "Shades of Enderby," *Washington Post Book World,* 9 March 1975, 1.

9. *Enderby* (New York: Ballantine Books, 1969), 21; hereafter cited in the text as *E.*

10. Kingsley Amis, "What We Need Now Is Savage Laughter," in *Opinions and Perspectives from the "New York Times Book Review,"* ed. Francis Brown (Boston: Little, Brown, 1964), 280.

11. "A. W. E." "PW Interviews: Anthony Burgess," *Publisher's Weekly* 201 (31 January 1972):182.

12. "My Dear Students; a Letter," *New York Times Magazine,* 19 November 1972:22.

13. "Viewpoint," *Times Literary Supplement* 72 (11 May 1973):526.

14. George W. Shea, *Times Literary Supplement,* 20 July 1973:834.

15. Peter Prince, "Intramural," *New Statesman* 87 (21 June 1974):894.

16. *The Clockwork Testament; or, Enderby's End* (New York: Knopf, 1975), 117; hereafter cited in the text as *CT.*

17. *Enderby's Dark Lady; or, No End to Enderby* (New York: McGraw-Hill, 1984), 8; hereafter cited in the text as *EDL.*

18. James Joyce, *Ulysses* (New York: Vintage Books, 1961), 682.

19. "The Muse: A sort of SF Story," *Hudson Review* 21 (Spring 1968):109–26.

20. *Shakespeare* (New York: Knopf, 1970).

21. Joyce, *Ulysses,* 209.

22. "Genesis and Headache," in McCormack, *Afterwords,* 43.

23. Samuel Schoenbaum, "Burgess and Gibson," in his *Shakespeare's Lives* (Oxford: Clarendon Press, 1970), 766. Schoenbaum's comments on *Nothing Like the Sun* are by no means entirely negative, however.

24. *The Novel Now,* 138.

25. Hicks, "Eclectic Author," 97.

26. "Speaking of Writing—VIII," [London] *Times,* 16 January 1964, 13.

27. Samuel Coale, "An Interview with Anthony Burgess," *Modern Fiction Studies* 27 (Autumn 1981):444.

28. Charles T. Bunting, "An Interview in New York with Anthony Burgess," *Studies in the Novel* 5 (1973):513.

29. Cullinan, "The Art of Fiction," 142.

30. *MF* (New York: Knopf, 1971), 206; hereafter cited in the text.

31. "The Novel in 2000 A.D.," *New York Times Book Review,* 29 March 1970, 19.

32. "The Seventeenth Novel," *New York Times Book Review,* 12 April 1970, 2.

33. Thomas Churchill, "An Interview with Anthony Burgess," *Malahat Review* 17 (1971):126.

34. "If Oedipus Had Read His Lévi-Strauss," *Washington Post Book World,* 26 November 1967, 6.

35. "Oedipus Wrecks," in *This Man and Music,* 165.

36. Claude Lévi-Strauss, *The Scope of Anthropology* (London: Jonathan Cape, 1967), 35–37.

37. Lévi-Strauss, *The Scope of Anthropology,* 37.

38. "Oedipus Wrecks," 171–72.

39. Ibid., 167.

40. Ibid., 179.

41. *Napoleon Symphony* (New York: Knopf, 1974), 362; hereafter cited in the text as *NS.*

42. Bunting, "An Interview in New York," 505.

43. Robinson, "On Being a Lancashire Catholic," 399.

44. "The Mystery of Evil: *Sophie's Choice* by William Styron," in *But Do Blondes Prefer Gentlemen?,* 507.

45. "Letter from Europe," *American Scholar* 41 (1972):428.

46. "Letter from Europe," 428.

47. "Bonaparte in E Flat," in *This Man and Music,* 182.

48. Bunting, "An Interview in New York," 505.

49. Pierre Assouline, "Burgess: Writer and Whirlwind," *World Press Review* 35 (September 1988):59.

Chapter Seven

1. Jennings, "*Playboy* Interview," 86.

2. Malcolm Page, "Anthony Burgess: The Artist as Performer," *West Coast Review* 4 (January 1970):22.

3. *Earthly Powers* (New York: Simon & Schuster, 1980), 164; hereafter cited in the text as *EP.*

4. Pierre Joanon, "Entretien: Anthony Burgess," *Fabula* 3 (March 1984):161.

5. Samuel Coale, *Anthony Burgess* (New York: Frederick Ungar, 1981), 193.

6. Geoffrey Aggeler, "Faust in the Labyrinth: Burgess's *Earthly Powers,*" *Modern Fiction Studies* 27 (Autumn 1981):517–31.

7. *Any Old Iron* (New York: Random House, 1989), 360; hereafter cited in the text as *AOI.*

8. Amy Edith Johnson, telephone interview with Burgess, "King Arthur's Sword," *New York Times Book Review,* 26 February 1989, 12.

9. Johnson, "King Arthur's Sword," 12.

10. Ibid. 12.

11. Robinson, "On Being a Lancashire Catholic," 399.

12. Christopher Ricks, "Faces in the Mirror," (London) *Sunday Times,* 6 February 1971, 41.

13. *Beard's Roman Women* (New York: McGraw-Hill, 1976), 63; hereafter cited in the text as *BRW.*

14. *Abba Abba* (Boston: Little, Brown, 1977), 15; hereafter cited in the text as *AA.*

15. Guido Almansi, "Burgess and Belli," *London Magazine* 357 (April 1978):61.

16. *The End of the World News* (New York: McGraw-Hill, 1983), viii; hereafter cited in the text.

17. Aggeler, *The Artist as Novelist,* 17.

18. William M. Murray, "Anthony Burgess on Apocalypse," *Iowa Review* 8 (1977):37.

19. "Telejesus (or Mediachrist)," in *But Do Blondes Prefer Gentlemen?,* 36.

20. Author's Note, *The Kingdom of the Wicked* (New York: Washington Square Press, 1986), 469.

21. Joanon, "Entretien," 166.

Conclusion

1. Letter to the author dated 31 May 1989.
2. *The Devil's Mode* (New York: Random House, 1989).

Selected Bibliography

PRIMARY WORKS

I have listed here the editions likely to be more accessible to American readers. Many of Burgess's novels are available in both Norton and Ballantine paperback editions. Heinemann was the original British publisher of many of Burgess's books, but others have been published by Peter Davies, Sidgwick and Jackson, Penguin, Cape, Hart-Davis & MacGibbon, and Hutchinson.

Novels

Abba Abba. Boston: Little, Brown, 1977.

Any Old Iron. New York: Random House, 1989.

Beard's Roman Women. New York: McGraw-Hill, 1976.

Beds in the East. London: Heinemann, 1959. Part of *The Malayan Trilogy* (published in America as *The Long Day Wanes*).

A Clockwork Orange. New York: Ballantine Books, 1988.

The Clockwork Testament. New York: Knopf, 1975.

Devil of a State. New York: Norton, 1962.

The Doctor Is Sick. New York: Norton, 1960.

Earthly Powers. New York: Simon & Schuster, 1980.

The End of the World News: An Entertainment. New York: McGraw-Hill, 1983.

Enderby. New York: Norton, 1968. Originally published in Britain as *Inside Mr. Enderby,* 1963 (as Joseph Kell); and *Enderby Outside,* 1968.

Enderby's Dark Lady; or, No End to Enderby. New York: McGraw-Hill, 1984.

The Enemy in the Blanket. London: Heinemann, 1958. Part of *The Malayan Trilogy (The Long Day Wanes).*

The Eve of Saint Venus. New York: Norton, 1970.

Honey for the Bears. New York: Norton, 1964.

The Kingdom of the Wicked. New York: Arbor House, 1985.

The Long Day Wanes. New York: Norton, 1965. (Published in Britain as *The Malayan Trilogy.*)

Man of Nazareth. New York: McGraw-Hill, 1979.

MF. New York: Knopf, 1971.

Napoleon Symphony. New York: Knopf, 1974.

1985. Boston: Little, Brown, 1978.

Nothing Like the Sun. New York: Norton, 1964.
One Hand Clapping. New York: Knopf, 1972.
The Pianoplayers. New York: Arbor House, 1986.
The Right to an Answer. New York: Norton, 1961.
Time for a Tiger. London: Heinemann, 1956. Part of *The Malayan Trilogy (The Long Day Wanes).*
Tremor of Intent. New York: Norton, 1966.
A Vision of Battlements. New York: Norton, 1966.
The Wanting Seed. New York: Norton, 1963.
The Worm and the Ring. London: Heinemann, 1970. Revised edition of the suppressed edition of 1961.

Other Book-length Fiction, Drama, Poetry, and Translation

Blooms of Dublin. London: Hutchinson, 1986. A musical play for radio based on Joyce's *Ulysses.*
Cyrano de Bergerac. New York: Knopf, 1971. Translation and adaptation of the Edmond Rostand play for the modern stage.
The Devil's Mode. New York: Random House, 1989. A novella and eight stories.
The Land Where the Ice Cream Grows. New York: Doubleday, 1979. A fantasy for children. Story by Fulvio Testa; "told" by Burgess.
A Long Trip to Teatime. New York: Stonehill, 1976. Fantasy for children.
Moses: A Narrative. New York: Stonehill, 1976. Verse.
Oedipus the King. Minneapolis: University of Minnesota Press in association with the Guthrie Theater. A translation and adaptation from Sophocles.
A Shorter Finnegans Wake. New York: Viking, 1967. A condensation, with synopses, of Joyce's novel to about one-third its original length.

Nonfiction Books

The Age of the Grand Tour. New York: Crown, 1967.
But Do Blondes Prefer Gentlemen? Homage to Qwert Yuiop and Other Writings. New York: McGraw-Hill, 1986.
Coaching Days of England. New York: Time-Life Books, 1966.
English Literature: A Survey for Students. London: Longman, Green, 1958; new ed., 1974.
Ernest Hemingway and His World. New York: Scribner, 1978.
Flame into Being: The Life and Work of D. H. Lawrence. New York: Arbor House, 1985.
Joysprick: An Introduction to the Language of James Joyce. New York: Harcourt Brace Jovanovich, 1975.
Language Made Plain. New York: Crowell, 1965.
Little Wilson and Big God. New York: Weidenfeld & Nicolson, 1987.
New York: Amsterdam: Time-Life International (Nederland), 1976.

Ninety-nine Novels: The Best in English since 1939. New York: Summit Books, 1984.

The Novel Now. New York: Norton, 1967.

Obscenity and the Arts. La Valletta: Malta Library Association, 1973.

On Going to Bed. New York: Abbeville Press, 1982.

Re Joyce. New York: Norton, 1965. (Published in Britain as *Here Comes Everybody.*)

Shakespeare. New York: Knopf, 1970.

This Man and Music. New York: McGraw-Hill, 1983.

Urgent Copy: Literary Studies. New York: Norton, 1969.

Essays, Reviews, Introductions, and Occasional Pieces

Burgess's output in these areas has been so prolific, and, generally, of such high quality, that any attempt at a selective compilation is neither practicable nor useful. Burgess's selection, in *Urgent Copy* and *But Do Blondes Prefer Gentlemen?,* is careful and judicious. The former reprints fifty-five earlier pieces; the latter, 191. Boytinck's 1985 bibliography lists about 605 such pieces.

SECONDARY WORKS

Bibliographies

An indispensable bibliographical guide to the study of Anthony Burgess is Paul Boytinck's *Anthony Burgess: An Annotated Bibliography and Reference Guide* (New York: Garland Publishing, 1985). This is a virtually exhaustive list of writings by and about Burgess—in newspapers, magazines, journals, books, and sections of books. The annotations are full and very useful. A very lively biographical sketch of Burgess appears also at the beginning.

A selected checklist of criticism of Burgess's writing was compiled by Samuel Coale for the "Anthony Burgess Number" of *Modern Fiction Studies* 27 (Autumn 1981):533–36.

Earlier bibliographic checklists have been almost entirely superseded by Boytinck's exemplarily thorough 385-page reference guide. Readers not having access to it, however, might still wish to consult one of the following.

Brewer, Jeutonne. *Anthony Burgess: A Bibliography.* Metuchen, N.J.: Scarecrow Press, 1980.

David, Beverly R. "Anthony Burgess: A Checklist (1956–1971)." *Twentieth Century Literature* 19 (July 1973):181–88.

Holte, Carlton. "Additions to 'Anthony Burgess: A Checklist (1956–1971).' " *Twentieth Century Literature* 20 (January 1974):44–52.

Books and Parts of Books

Aggeler, Geoffrey. *Anthony Burgess: The Artist as Novelist.* University: University of Alabama Press, 1979. Still the best book on Burgess. Admirably clear and thorough thematic discussion of the novels; provides an expert and highly sympathetic representation of Burgess's views on art and life in the contemporary world. Burgess read and commented on each section of the book as it was completed.

———, ed. *Critical Essays on Anthony Burgess.* Boston: G. K. Hall, 1986. This intelligently compiled critical anthology reprints fourteen previously published essays and publishes two new ones, along with an excellent introduction by the editor.

Bloom, Harold, ed. *Anthony Burgess: Modern Critical Views.* New York: Chelsea House, 1987. This critical anthology reprints twelve previously published pieces, chronologically arranged. Also contains an original, somewhat odd-angled introduction by Bloom, which focuses on Burgess's relation to Joyce.

Coale, Samuel. *Anthony Burgess.* New York: Frederick Ungar, 1981. Contains quite full plot summaries of the novels, followed by necessarily brief, but well-balanced and astute critical comment. A very useful companion for the Burgess reader.

DeVitis, A. A. *Anthony Burgess.* New York: Twayne, 1972. The first book-length assessment of Burgess's work; especially good on influences on Burgess, Catholic backgrounds, and Burgess's presentation of antiheroes.

Dix, Carol M. *Anthony Burgess.* London: Longmans, for the British Council, 1971. This British Council pamphlet in the Writers & Their Work series provides sensible and gracefully compressed commentary.

Ghosh-Schellhorn, Martina. *Anthony Burgess: A Study in Character.* Frankfurt am Main: Lang, 1986. A published dissertation somewhat given to ponderousness and wooden theorizing. Still, it makes some good points as it seeks to establish a "typology of Burgess's characters." Extended examination of *The Malayan Trilogy, The Doctor Is Sick* and *Earthly Powers* as representative works.

Kennard, Jean. "Anthony Burgess: Double Vision," in *Number and Nightmare: Forms of Fantasy in Contemporary Fiction,* 131–54. New York: Archon Books, 1975. An interesting discussion of dualisms and paradoxes in *A Clockwork Orange, The Wanting Seed, Tremor of Intent, Enderby,* and *MF.*

Matthews, Richard. *The Clockwork Universe of Anthony Burgess.* San Bernardino, Calif.: Borgo Press, 1978. This monograph-length study focuses on *The Malayan Trilogy* and other novels that appeared before the mid-sixties. Makes some good points, but also contains some factual error.

Morris, Robert K. *The Consolations of Ambiguity: An Essay on the Novels of Anthony Burgess.* Columbia: University of Missouri Press, 1971. Although only of monograph length, this is an important, sophisticated, and powerfully articulated study of the early novels.

———. "*The Malayan Trilogy:* The Futility of History," in *Continuance and Change: The Contemporary British Novel Sequence,* 71–91. Carbondale: Southern Illinois University Press, 1972. Excellent comment on the inexorable, cyclical forces of history in *The Long Day Wanes.*

Interviews and Biographical Accounts Based on Interviews

Assouline, Pierre. "Burgess: Writer and Whirlwind." *World Press Review* 35 (September 1988):58–59. A very brief interview. Burgess talks of jealousy among writers, his relation to Joyce, and current plans and aspirations. He gives a short reply to the question, "How much of you is an act?"

A. W. E. "PW Interviews: Anthony Burgess." *Publishers Weekly* 201 (31 January 1972):182–83. Discusses the two versions of *A Clockwork Orange*; English reviewers' hostility toward *MF;* plans for future novels.

Bunting, Charles T. "An Interview in New York with Anthony Burgess." *Studies in the Novel* 5 (1973):504–29. A wide-ranging interview in which Burgess discusses his research for *Napoleon Symphony* and experimentation in the contemporary novel.

Churchill, Thomas. "An Interview with Anthony Burgess." *Malahat Review* 17 (1971):103–27. Covers a broad array of subjects. Burgess says some interesting things about *A Clockwork Orange, Enderby,* and *Nothing Like the Sun.*

Coale, Samuel. "An Interview with Anthony Burgess." *Modern Fiction Studies* 27 (1981):429–52. Burgess talks about his life, religion, modernism, language, free will, and his novels. A good interview.

Cullinan, John. "The Art of Fiction XLVIII: Anthony Burgess." *Paris Review* 14 (1973):118–63. Reprinted as "An Interview with Anthony Burgess." *Writers at Work: The Paris Review Interviews,* edited by George Plimpton and introduced by Wilfrid Sheed, 323–59. New York: Viking, 1976. Also reprinted in *Critical Essays on Anthony Burgess,* edited by Aggeler, 23–55. A highly informative interview that never goes off the track and arrives at many interesting points. Excellent.

Dix, Carol. "Anthony Burgess: Interviewed by Carol Dix." *Transatlantic Review* 42/43 (1972):183–91. Comments on the film version of *A Clockwork Orange;* English philistinism; the composition of *MF;* plans for future novels.

Hicks, Jim. "Eclectic Author of His Own Five-Foot Shelf." *Life,* 25 October 1968, 89–98. Accounts of how he came to teach in Malaya, his "terminal year;" and some film scripts for *Enderby* and Shakespeare.

Jennings, C. Robert. "*Playboy* Interview: Anthony Burgess." *Playboy* 21 (September 1974):69–86. Wide-ranging; a compendium of Burgess's usual views, interestingly expressed. Discusses his sale of the film rights for *A Clockwork Orange,* his views on many modern authors, Pope John XXIII; B. F. Skinner, British entry into the Common Market.

Joanon, Pierre. "Entretien: Anthony Burgess." *Fabula* 3 (1984):159–68. Questions in French, Burgess's responses in English. Burgess refers to *The Kingdom of the Wicked* as a "comic novel."

Lewis, Anthony. " 'I Love England, But I Will No Longer Live There.' " *New York Times Magazine,* 3 November 1968, 39+. Broadly ranges over many subjects, but Burgess returns, several times, to his reasons for leaving England.

Malko, George. "*Penthouse* Interview: Anthony Burgess." *Penthouse* 3 (June 1972):82–84, 116, 118. Interesting for Burgess's extended comments on the charges that *A Clockwork Orange* has incited violence.

Murray, William M. "Anthony Burgess on 'Apocalypse.' " *Iowa Review* 8 (1977): 37–45. Burgess had been hired as a scriptwriter for a big Hollywood "disaster film"; although the film was never made, it can clearly be deduced that this gave rise to the science fiction portion of *The End of the World News.*

Page, Malcolm. "Anthony Burgess: The Author as Performer." *West Coast Review* 4 (1970):21–24. Account of Burgess's visit to Simon Fraser University on March 5, 1969. Shows how Burgess handles himself before student audiences. Burgess refers to Pope John XXIII as "the emissary of the Devil."

Reilly, Lemuel. "An Interview with Anthony Burgess." *Delaware Literary Review* 2 (1973):48–55. Burgess says, "I try to make each novel as different as I can"; he remarks on a resurgent interest in myth.

Riemer, George. "An Interview with Anthony Burgess." *National Elementary Principal* 50 (May 1971):8–21. Burgess on the education of the young, particularly on differences between the British and American systems.

Robinson, Robert. "On Being a Lancashire Catholic" An interview with Burgess. *Listener* 96 (30 September 1976):397, 399. An interesting source of biographical information.

Articles and Essays

Aggeler, Geoffrey. "Faust in the Labyrinth: Burgess' *Earthly Powers.*" *Modern Fiction Studies* 27 (Autumn 1981):517–31. A rounded and critically rich article in which Aggeler identifies Carlo Campanati not only as a Pelagian heretic, but as a man who has struck a bargain with the Devil. So far, the definitive piece on what is perhaps Burgess's greatest novel.

________. "Incest and the Artist: Anthony Burgess's *MF* as Summation." *Modern Fiction Studies* 18 (Winter 1972–73):529–43. Sees Burgess's fusion of the Algonquin Indian and Greek myths as Burgess's way of providing a "devastating satiric indictment of contemporary Western cultural values."

Bly, James I. "Sonata Form in *Tremor of Intent.*" *Modern Fiction Studies* 27 (Autumn 1981):489–504. Given several Burgess statements on how his novels are frequently structured on musical analogues, this is a thorough and convincing demonstration.

Coale, Samuel. "The Ludic Loves of Anthony Burgess." *Modern Fiction Studies* 27 (Autumn 1981):453–63. Sensible comment on playful and game-playing elements in Burgess's plots.

Fitzpatrick, William P. "Black Marketeers and Manichees: Anthony Burgess' Cold War Novels." *West Virginia University Philological Papers* 21 (December 1974):78–91. An excellent essay on *Honey for the Bears* and *Tremor of Intent,* showing how the themes of each embody Burgess's Manichaean worldview.

Kennard, Jean. "MF: A Separable Meaning." *Riverside Quarterly* 6 (1975):200–206. Although brief, this provides a fine elucidation of the themes and techniques of *MF.*

LeClair, Thomas. "Essential Opposition: The Novels of Anthony Burgess." *Critique: Studies in Modern Fiction* 12 (1971):77–94. Points out that "in Burgess's novels dialectic is itself a central theme as well as a method."

McNeil, David. "The Musicalization of Fiction: The 'Virtuosity' of Burgess's *Napoleon Symphony.*" *Mosaic* 16 (1983):101–115. Reprinted in Aggeler, ed., *Critical Essays on Anthony Burgess,* 198–212. An illuminating discussion of how Burgess's novel parallels the *Eroica* not only in its four-part structure, "but also in its use of such unconventional techniques as verse sections, fluidity of point of view and rhythmic language" (198).

Mowat, John. "Joyce's Contemporary: A Study of Anthony Burgess' *Napoleon Symphony.*" *Contemporary Literature* 19 (1978):180–95. A very successful effort to show that *Napoleon Symphony* is "Burgess's attempt to make his own fiction a practical demonstration of what he has learned from Joyce about the possibilities of language, myth, and comedy" (180).

Palumbo, Ronald J. "Names and Games in *Tremor of Intent.*" *English Language Notes* 18 (September 1980):48–51. Explains some of the word play and the codes; briefly comments on these in relation to the theme of the novel.

Ricks, Christopher. "Faces in the Mirror." (London) *Sunday Times,* 6 February 1971, 41. Finds much more merit in *Beard's Roman Women* than most other commentators. Maintains that there is "an autobiographical graphicness which is not self-absorption but is a brave self-interrogation" (41).

Stinson, John J. "*Nothing Like the Sun:* The Faces in Bella Cohen's Mirror." *Journal of Modern Literature* 5 (1976):131–47. Attempts to show that a highly deliberate quality of artifice characterizes the novel; most specifically, that the story is constructed on the Shakespeare theory Stephen Dedalus puts forth in *Ulysses.*

Theroux, Paul. "Shades of Enderby." *Washington Post Book World,* 9 March 1975, 1, 3. A review of *The Clockwork Testament,* but also a strongly appreciative comment on the first three Enderby books by the American novelist. Maintains that he has read *Inside Mr. Enderby* twelve times.

Index

The Author

John Stinson is professor of English at the State University of New York College at Fredonia, where he joined the faculty in 1965. He has taught a wide variety of courses, but his specialty is modern British literature. He received his Ph.D. in English from New York University in 1971.

In addition to several articles on Anthony Burgess, Stinson has published essays in various academic journals on William Golding, Graham Greene, David Storey, William Trevor, and Arthur Miller. Three of these have been reprinted in critical anthologies. He was also a contributor to the Twayne volume *The English Short Story, 1945–1980*, and he is presently at work on a book-length study of V. S. Pritchett's short stories for Twayne's Studies in Short Fiction.